Ordo ab Chao

The Original and Complete Rituals of the first Supreme Council, 33°

*Transcribed from newly discovered
manuscript rituals in a private collection*

VOLUME ONE

Poemandres Press
Boston & New York
1995

Kessinger Publishing's Rare Reprints
Thousands of Scarce and Hard-to-Find Books!

- • • •
- • • •
- • • •
- • • •
- • • •
- • • •
- • • •
- • • •
- • • •
- • • •
- • • •
- • • •
- • • •
- • • •
- • • •
- • • •
- • • •
- • • •
- • • •
- • • •

TABLE OF CONTENTS
VOLUME 1

Table of Contents

INTRODUCTION

In Liber 1, Number 2 of our Hermetic and Masonic Journal, A∴R∴A∴R∴I∴T∴A∴, we invited readers to offer publication suggestions and apprise of us any interesting manuscripts or out-of-print books they might know of. The response was overwhelming. As a result of that invitation, we soon printed five new books, including two interesting rituals; but we *never* anticipated the reception of the material which is now printed here for the first time ever.

A reader from upstate New York informed us that his family owned a set of Masonic manuscript rituals which had been its possession since the 1830's. What makes this more remarkable is that neither the corespondent nor any member of the immediate family belongs to the Masonic fraternity. Intrigued, we traveled upstate to meet with our corespondent and examine the documents first hand.

The manuscript collection consists of five leather-bound books (of various sizes), numerous loose pages of "detached degrees" and several letters. Each of the leather-bound books is signed by the original transcriber. Inside the first volume, the ancestor of our corespondent penned the following:

> These M.S.S. was Purchas'd of Mr. [*name withheld*], a renouncing & Seceeding Free Mason for $45— & one new Pack & Shoval—this 22^d Day of December 1835. There is nothing Hid but what shall be Seen & known.

At the request of the present owners we have withheld both the name of the original transcriber and their ancestor, as the owners have no desire to part with their heirloom. They wish to make it emphatically clear that they do not wish to be bothered in any way as a result of this publication. Poemandres Press has been requested by the family to protect their privacy, and cannot respond to any requests for information regarding the present owners, or the ritual collection itself.

Be that as it may, the manuscripts are a veritable gold-mine of Masonic information, for they constitute, as far as we are aware, the most complete set of early Scottish Rite rituals in the United States.

The reader will note that each of the five books was transcribed from rituals belonging to Giles F. Yates, 33°. Mr. Yates was a member of both the Northern and Southern Supreme Councils, and by 1827 was in possession of most, if not all, of the manuscript rituals of Mr. Frederick Dalcho, one of the founders of the first Supreme Council.[1] At one point the *original* Dalcho manuscripts ("a strange farrago of bad English")[2] were lost or sold. When the collection was rediscovered in 1938, it had several rituals missing.[3] Our collection includes *all* the rituals from the 4° SECRET MASTER, up to and including the 33° SOVEREIGN GRAND INSPECTOR GENERAL.[4]

Each of the rituals is preceded by a header which frequently gives the dates 1801 and 1802. We believe this indicates the rituals are copies of the Dalcho versions, although we have not had the opportunity to compare them with the originals in the archives of the Northern Jurisdiction, at Boston. It should be noted that for some unknown reason the rituals are divided into two groups, i.e., "first series" and "second series." The "second series" rituals are all dated after 1804, which may indicate that some type of reconstruction took place. Further, some of the rituals have apparently been switched around in numerical order.

Among the more curious instances of revision is the 29° GRAND MASTER ECOSÉ, OR SCOTTISH ELDER MASTER, AND KNIGHT OF ST. ANDREW. Following the degree (which closely follows the Pike's version)[5] is the outline

---

[1] R. Baker Harris, *History of the Supreme Council, 33°...1801-1861* (Washington, D.C., 1964), pp. 177, 196.

[2] Ibid., p. 172.

[3] Ibid., p. 92.

[4] In 1829 J.J.J. Gourgas, of the Northern Supreme Council, wrote to Moses Holbrook, of the Southern Council, requesting a copy of the "Charleston 33rd" (Ibid. p. 195). If Yates had a copy, why didn't he share it?

[5] "Grand Maitre Ecossais, or Scottish Elder Master and Knight of St. Andrew" in *Albert Pike's "Reprints of rituals of Old Degrees"* (Boston & New York: Poemandres Press, 1995), pp. 116-139.

of an apparent 1806 revision which is a radical departure from the earlier form, yet similar to that found in Albert Pike's *Magnum Opus* (1857). Did Pike have this 1806 ritual?

Consider the 30TH, 31ST AND 32ND DEGREE, SOVEREIGN, OR SUBLIME PRINCE OF THE ROYAL SECRET, which seems to have become the 32° only after a 31° TRIBUNAL OF GRAND INQUISITORS appears in 1804. And then, twenty-three years later, the latter is itself drastically revised.

One of the most interesting rituals is the 33° SOVEREIGN GRAND INSPECTOR GENERAL. Not only is it the earliest form of this degree, but it includes a copy of a "Letter of Credence" (Patent) and an early version of the *Constitutions, Statutes and Regulations.*

In editing the manuscripts, we have corrected the spelling in many instances (e.g. *sholdhers* to *shoulders*, etc.), but tried to retain as much of the original format as possible. Interlineations have been introduced at the points indicated without indication, and several marginal notations have been eliminated, as they are not in the original writer's hand. Finally, all hand-drawn illustrations in this book, including the Masonic alphabets, were scanned from photocopies of the original manuscripts.[6] We have enhanced and cleaned these up as best we could, and are satisfied with the results. We regret that all of the original illustrations could not be used, but the manuscripts had apparently sustained some water damage many years ago and are barely legible on several pages. In these instances we have reconstructed the original drawings using a computer graphics program.

---

[6]By agreement with the owners, we were not permitted to retain photocopies of any document, once scanned and edited.

BOOK 1st

*Copied from that of Ill^{trs} Brother
Giles F. Yates, R ✠, K—H, S.P.R.S. &
Sov. G^d Ins. Genl of 33:rd. A.L. 5833*

4th Degree of the First Series (1801) of the Southern
Jurisdiction of the United States of America,
at Charleston, South Carolina, called

🙿 🙿 🙿

Secret Master

⸸

his Lodge must be hung with black, and strewed with tears.
The Master represents Solomon, and is styled Most Powerful,
who comes to the Temple to replace the loss of Hiram Abiff by
seven experts.

There is only one Warden, who is called Adoniram; it was he who had the
inspection of the workmanship at Mount Lebanon. He was the Secret Master.[1]

§. *Form of the Lodge.*

Solomon holds a scepter in his hand, is clothed in mourning robes, lined with
Ermine, and sits in the East before a triangular altar, on which is a Crown of
Laurel and Olive leaves.

Adoniram, the Inspector, is placed in the West. No iron tools are used,
because the work is suspended in consequence of the death of Hiram Abiff.

Order and Jewel. Solomon is decorated with a large blue, watered, ribbon
from the right shoulder to the left hip, to which is suspended a triangle.

Adoniram is decorated with a broad which ribbon, bordered with black, round
his neck in a triangular form; having an Ivory Key hanging thereto, with the letter
Z cut on it. All the Brethren should wear the same, with white

Aprons & Gloves, the strings, of the Aprons, black, the flap blue with an Eye
painted thereon in gold.

---

[1] Brother Yates changes this to "He was the first Secret Master."

The white signifies the innocence of the Master and his black the mourning for their Chief.

This Lodge should be Illuminated by 81 candles, distributed by 9 times 9, but may be done by 9, 3 times 3.—

§. *To Open.*

S. Brother Adoniram, are you a Secret Master?

A. Most Powerful I have passed from the square to the Compass; I have seen the Tomb of our respectable Master Hiram Abiff and have, in company with my Brethren, shed my tears thereon.

S. What's the Clock my Brother?

A. The dawn of the day has drove away darkness; and the Great Light begins to shine over this Lodge.

S. If the Great Light has drove away darkness, and we are all Secret Master, it is time to begin our work; give notice that I am going to open this Lodge of Secret Masters.

The Inspector gives notice, after which the Most Powerful strikes 7 times with his hand, then the Inspector, and afterwards, all the Brethren.

The Most Powerful then makes the Sign of Silence, with his right hand, which the Brethren answer with their left.

He then says, "Illustrious Brethren, This Lodge is Open, as it is "devoted to God."

LET US PRAY

He then repeats the usual prayer.

§. *Form of Reception.*

The Blue Past Master or Candidate, must be examined in the Ante-chamber (by the Master of Ceremonies) in his three first Degrees, and in the secrets of the Chair. The Master of Ceremonies having finished, he knocks 7 times on the door, when he is let in and gives an account of the examination to Adoniram, the Inspector, who reports it to the Most Powerful in the following words.

"Most Powerful, there is in the Antechamber a Past-Master who solicits the honor of being initiated into the mysteries of the Sublime Grand Lodge of Perfect Masons."

The Most Powerful desires the Candidate to be introduced in the ancient form, if the Inspector will answer for his capacity, zeal and constancy.

If the Inspector consents to do so, the Candidate is introduced having his head bound, as if blinded, as square upon his forehead and a Great Light in his hand, and conducted to Adoniram, to whom he must give an account of himself — Conducted by Adoniram, he advances, then, near the altar, falls on his right knee, and while in this position, the Most Powerful delivers the usual address, and concludes thus,

"My Dear Brother, you have seen until now, the thick veil, only, which covers the Sanctum Sanctorum your fidelity, zeal and constancy have gained you the favor which I now grant you. It is to show you the great treasure, and introduce you, in due time, into the holy and secret place. Come and contract your obligation."

Adoniram raises him and leads him to the foot of the altar, where he kneels and takes the obligation of a blue Master with this addition—

"And I do furthermore promise and swear, that I will not reveal to any person below me this Degree; that I will be an exact observer of all such laws as shall be prescribed to me, and will fulfill and obey all orders and decrees from the Grand Council of princes of Jerusalem and the laws and regulations of this Sublime Grand Lodge; under the penalty of all my former obligations—So help me God, and keep me steadfast in the same. Amen."

He kisses the Bible.

Adoniram now raises him, and the Most Powerful invests him with the ribbon, key and apron; places on his head a crown (or wreathe) of laurel and olive leaves, and says to him,

"My Dear Brother, I receive you Secret Master, and give you rank among the Levites. This Laurel, which I have invested you with, alludes to the victory which you are to gain over your passions. The Olive is the symbol of that peace and Union which should reign among us. It rests with you to desire the fervor that God may, one day, enable you to arrive at the Secret place; and there to contemplate the pillar of Beauty.

The Ivory Key, suspended by a white and black ribbon is the symbol of your fidelity, innocence and discretion. The Apron and Gloves are emblematical of the candor of all the Secret Masters; among whom, at your own solicitation, you are introduced. My dear Brother, in quality of Secret Master, I give you rank among the Levites, to be a faithful guardian of the Sanctum Sanctorum; and have placed you among the number 7 to supply the place of our dear Master Hiram Abiff and have, also, appointed you one of the Conductors of the works, which are to be raised to the Divinity. The eye on your apron is to remind you to be ever vigilant and to watch, closely, the conduct of the workmen!"

The Master of Ceremonies then gives to the Candidate, the following Sign, Word and Token.

§. *Sign, Token & Words.*

Sign.—The Sign is that of Silence which is made by placing the two first fingers of the right hand upon the lips, which is answered by the two first fingers of the left hand.

The Pass Word—is ZIZO, a Chaldean word, which signifies Gallery.

The Token.—first give the Masters gripe, and creep up, reciprocally, to the Elbows, then balance seven times and during balancing, cross your legs.

Secret Words.—The Words are

JOHA,   יה

ADONAI   אדוני

JUA.

These are the first names which God gave himself when he manifested himself unto Moses on the mountain; of which you see the three initials traced on the plane of the triangle.

Go Brother, pass the Brethren, and listen to our doctrine.

§. *Lecture.*

S. Are you a Secret Master?

A. I have the honor of being received and acknowledged as such.

S. In what manner were you received a Secret Master?

A. I passed from the Square to the Compass.

S. Where were you made a Secret Master?

A. Under the laurel and olive tree.

S. In what place were you received?

A. In the Sanctum Sanctorum.

S. Who made you?

A. Solomon, with Adoniram the Inspector of the works.

S. What did you perceive on entering the Sanctum Sanctorum?

A. A brilliant Delta, enclosing certain Hebraic characters, from which emanated nine beams of the Sheckinai, bearing, each, an initial of a Divine Name as derived from an attribute; and the whole surrounded by a Great Circle.

S. Pray what is the meaning of those Hebraic Characters in the Delta?

A. They describe the Ineffable and real name of the Grand Architect of the Universe, which was forbidden to be pronounced by a law of Moses, in consequence of which, we lost the true pronunciation.

S. It is true, my Brother, the just pronunciation of those characters was lost to all but Grand Elect Perfect and Sublime Masons, a knowledge, of which I hope, you will one acquire by virtue of your attachment to our Order, and your zeal in discharging the duties of your obligation—But pray can you tell me what those names are, the initials of which you saw in the nine beams of the Sheckinai?

A. Those which God gave himself when he spoke to Moses on Mount Sinai, intimating to him, at the same time, that his future issue should, one day, know his real name.

S. Give them to me with their explanation.

A. אדוני (ADONAI) Supreme Lord.

    יהוה (JEHOVAH)

    אלהים (ELOHIM) Supreme Judge.

    אל (AIL) Powerful.

    שדי (SHADAY) Omnipotent.

    צבאות (TSEBOUT) Lord of Hosts.

    עיזוז (GNIZUS) Mightiness.

    גיבור (GIBOUR) Strength.

    אחד (ECHAD) Only One.

which compose altogether 888 letters and 72 names, which are, like the Ineffable name, to be found in the mysteries of the Cabala, and the Angels Alphabet.

S. I presume, my Brother, that you are unacquainted with these mysteries, but they will be fully explained to you in the Degree of Perfection and having now done with the Delta and its awful characters, can you tell me the meaning of the great circle which surrounded them?

A. It represents, Masonically, as all circles do, the immensity of the power and glory of God which hath neither beginning or end.

S. What else did you perceive in the Sanctum Sanctorum?

A. A luminous circle enclosing a brilliant star of five points with the letter G in its center.

S. What is the meaning of that Letter?

A. GLORY, GRANDEUR and GOMEL.

S. What do you understand by those words?

A. By GLORY—God, by GRANDEUR, the man who may be great by Perfection. GOMEL, is an Hebrew word, which signifies, thanks to God for his supreme power, it was the first word which Adam spoke on discovering his adorable Eve.

S. What is represented by the five beams of the brilliant Star?

A. The five orders of Architecture which adorned the Temple; and the senses of Nature without which man cannot be perfect.

S. What else did you perceive in the Sanctum Sanctorum?

A. The Ark of Alliance, The Golden Candlestick with 7 branches, having a lamp in each, and a table.[2]

S. Where was the Ark of Alliance placed?

A. In the middle of the Sanctum Sanctorum. under the brilliant star and the shadow of the wings of the Cherubim.

S. What does the Ark represent?

A. The Alliance which God made with his people.

S. What figure was the Ark?

A. A Parallelogram.

S. What were its dimensions?

A. It was two cubits and an half in length. One cubit and an half in breadth and the same in height.

S. Of what was it made?

---

[2]Exod. 25.10-23-31.

9

A. Of shittim wood, covered within and without with gold, decorated with a golden crown, and borne by two Cherubims of Gold.

S. Had the cover of the ark a name?

A. It had; it was called propitiary, or place that served to appease God's anger.

S. What did it contain?

A. The testimony which God gave to Moses, the tables of the laws.[3]

S. What did these tables contain and of what were they made?

A. Of white marble, and contained the decalogue written in Hebraic characters.

S. What did these commandments teach and how were they disposed of on the tables?

A. The four first pointed out the obligations of Man to his God and were engraved on the first table, the remaining six pointed out the obligations of man to man and were engraved on the 2nd table.

S. How were the commandments of the different tables distinguished?

A. Those of the first, collectively taken, were termed the divine law, those of the second the Moral Law.

S. Of what use was the table?

A. To place thereon, the 12 loaves of unleavened bread, which must always be in the presence of the Divinity agreeably to his commandment to Moses.[4]

S. Of what were these loaves made?

A. Of the purest flour.

S. How were they placed?

A. Six on the right and six on the left hand, forming two heaps.

S. What was placed above?

A. A bright ewer filled with Incense.

S. For what reason?

---

[3]Exod. 20.1 — Exod. 31 Ch. 18. — Exod. 25 Ch, 21.
[4]Exod. 25 Ch., 30.

A. To be a memento of the obligation made to God.

S. What was the name of the Sanctum Sanctorum in Hebrew?

A. DABIR.

S. What is the meaning of that word?

A. Speech.

S. Why so?

A. Because it was there the Divinity resided, and where he delivered his commands to Moses.[5]

S. Who constructed the Ark?

A. Moses, by the command of god, for that purpose, made choice of BEZALEEL, of the tribe of Judah, son of URI and MIRIAM, sister to Moses; and of AHOLIAB, son of AHISAMACH of the tribe of Dan, the most learned of the people.[6] The Israelites testified so much ardor for the works, and with so much zeal to carry on the same, that Moses proclaimed, by sound of trumpet, that he wanted no more.[7] They worked after the model which God had given to Moses who also instructed him, in the number and form, of the sacred vessels, which were to be made and, placed in the Tabernacle to serve in the sacrifices.

S. To what do the 7 lamps, on the branches of the golden candlesticks, allude?

A. To the seven planets.

S. Of how many parts was it composed?

A. Of Seventy.

S. For what reason?

A. In allusion to the decani, or seventy divisions of the planets.

S. What does the eye over the door of this Lodge represent?

A. The eye of God, to whose name our works are dedicated, and from whose inspection our actions can never be concealed.

S. How did they go up to the galleries of the Temple?

---

[5]Exod: 25 Ch: 22.
[6]Exod: 31 Ch. 1.
[7]Exod: 36 Ch. 6.

A. By a staircase in the form of a screw, which went up by 3, 5 and 7 steps fixed on the wall, on the North side.

S. What was the name of the staircase?

A. Cockles, which is to say in the form of a screw.

S. How many doors were in the Sanctum Sanctorum?

A. Only one on the East side, which was called ZIZO and was covered with Gold, Purple, Hyacinth and Azure.

S. What do these colors represent?

A. The four Elements?

S. How old are you?

A. Three times 27 accomplished 81.

S. What is the Pass Word?

A. ZIZO, or Gallery.

S. Thank you, my Brother, It has afforded me much satisfaction to find by the correctness of your answers, that you have attended to the duties of your Lodge, and have treasured up in your mind; the rich fruits of our sublime mysteries. I flatter myself, from your merit and perseverance, that you will soon be capacitated to deserve the summit of our knowledge, in receiving the Degree of Perfection, wherein you will be presented with the splendid reward of all your labors.

§. *To Close.*

S. Brother Inspector, pray what's the clock?

A. The end of day.

S. What doth there remain to do?

A. To practice Virtue, shun vice, and remain in Silence.

The Most Powerful says—"Since there remains no more to do than to practice virtue and shun vice, let us again enter into silence, that the will of God may be done and accomplished. It is time to rest. Brother Inspector give notice by the mysterious number, that the Lodge is going to be closed."

The Inspector strikes 7 times with his hands, which is answered by all the Brethren, and then by the Most Powerful, after which, he gives the Sign of Silence, which they answer, and the

LODGE IS CLOSED

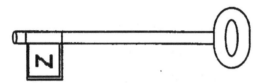

5th Degree of the First Series of the Southern Jurisdiction of the United States of America, called

✿ ✿ ✿
Perfect Master

he Lodge must be hung with Green. Four white columns on each side, placed at equal distances. Before the canopy a table covered with black, strewed with tears.

Illuminated by 16 Lights, four in each Cardinal point.

On the floor must be placed the following painting.[8]

§. *Form of the Lodge.*

The Right Worshipful and Respectable Master, represents the Noble Adoniram, who was the first that was made Perfect Master. He commanded the workmen of the Temple, before Hiram Abiff arrived at Jerusalem; after which, he had the inspection of the workmen at Mount Lebanon.

He must be decorated with the ornaments of a Prince of Jerusalem. He sits, in the seat of Solomon, under the canopy in the East.

There is but one warden, who represents Stokin in the function of Inspector. He sits in the West, decorated with the ornaments of his highest Degrees.

The Master of the Ceremonies, represents ZERBAL, the Captain of the Guards; he must be decorated with the ornaments of Perfect Master, and have a drawn sword in his hand.

Apron—White leather, the flap green, in the middle of the apron, must be painted, within three circles, a square stone, in the center of which, must be the letter J. The strings green.

---

[8]No painting appears in the original.

14

Jewel—A compass extended to 60 Degrees suspended by a green ribbon round the neck.

§. *To Open the Lodge.*

A. Brother Inspector, is the Lodge tiled, and are we all Perfect Masters?

S. Right Worshipful, we are well tiled, and are all Perfect Masters.

A. Give notice I am going to open a Lodge of Perfect Master.

S. Brethren, take notice that the Right Worshipful Master is going to open a Lodge of Perfect Master.

The R.W.M. then strikes   4 with an iron

The Inspector————————4

The Secretary——————4

The Treasurer——————4

The Brethren then make the Sign of Admiration together.

A. Brother Stokin, pray what's the Clock?

S. Right Worshipful, it is four.

A. Since it is four, it is high time to set the workmen to labor, give notice that the Lodge of Perfect Master is open.

The Inspector repeats the same and the

LODGE IS OPEN

§. *Form of Reception.*

The Candidate must be decorated in the Antechamber with the Order of Secret Master. The Master of Ceremonies enters the Lodge and strikes 4 on the Inspector's shoulder, and says:—

"There is in the Antechamber a Secret Master who solicits the honor of being received and admitted a Perfect Master."

The Inspector reports the same to the Right Worshipful Adoniram, who says:—

A. Is he well qualified and worthy of receiving that distinguished favor? Will you answer for his zeal, fervor and constancy?

S. I answer for him.

A. Let him be introduced agreeably to ancient form.

The Inspector orders the Master of Ceremonies to instruct the Candidate, who goes to him, examines him in his former Degrees, and takes from him all offensive arms, puts round his neck a green silk cord, which he holds in his left hand, and a naked sword in his right, and conducts him to the door, on which he knocks 4 times, which is repeated by the Inspector within, who informs the Right Worshipful Master that somebody knocks.

The Right Worshipful orders him to see who its is.

The Inspector orders the Captain of the Guard to open the door half way, that he may see who knocks. After the Captain of the Guard has asked, he reports it to the Inspector and shuts the door.

The Inspector reports it to the Right Worshipful who orders the Candidate to be introduced.

The Candidate is introduced to the South side of the tomb, which is placed on the floor of the Lodge.

When the Right Worshipful sees the Candidate with the Sign of Secret Master on him, he demands

A. What do you solicit my Brother?

S. The honor of being received Perfect Master.

A. Brother Inspector teach the Candidate to travel.

The Inspector leads him, by the silk string, from the South, and carries him four times round the Lodge. Every time he passes the East, he gives one of the signs of his preceding Degrees, beginning with the Entered Apprentice. He then orders him to kneel, after which he passes through the tomb, on each side of the column Soltair, and the Candidate having the Sign of Secret Master on him. He is then placed opposite to the altar with his right knee a little bent. Having waited a little in this position, he is ordered to kneel and place his right hand on the Holy Bible, and take the following

§. *Obligation.*

I —— do most solemnly and sincerely swear and promise on the Holy Bible, in the presence of the Grand Architect of the Universe, and this Illustrious Lodge, erected and dedicated to his most Holy Name, that I never will reveal or communicate to any person whomsoever, to whom the same doth not belong, the secrets of this Degree, under any pretense whatsoever; and not to converse, on this subject, with any but true Brothers who have been lawfully received; that I will pay due obedience to all the commands and decrees of the Grand Council of Princes of Jerusalem, under the penalty of being, for ever, dishonored among men, and to suffer all the penalties of my former obligations. So God keep me in right and equity. Amen. Amen. Amen.

He kisses the Bible.

The Right Worshipful Adoniram then takes the string from around his neck, and says,

A. My Dear Brother, I draw you from your vicious life, and by the power which I have received from the most powerful King of Kings, I raise you to the Degree of Perfect Master, on condition that you faithfully observe, what shall be presented to you by our Laws.

The Right Worshipful then invests him with the Apron and Jewel.
The Grand Master of Ceremonies then gives the following

§. *Signs, Token and Word.*

1:ˢᵗ Sign—Is that of admiration, by extending the arms and hands, open, looking up to Heaven, then letting them fall on your belly and cross them, fixing your eyes on the ground.

2:ⁿᵈ Sign—Advance, reciprocally, the points of your right shoes to each other, then touch the right knees, mutually, and bring the right hand on the heart, then draw it to the right side in a square, both do the same.

Token—The token is that of the Blue Masters grip, placing your left hand on the back of the other, and pressing them hard, 4 times, when the other answers MAHABON.

Then grip one another's right hand, the fingers clinched, the thumbs upwards forming a triangle.

Pass Word—ACASIA.

Secret Word—JEVA. One of the Initials of the Ineffable name.

§. *History.*

Mahabon, one of Solomon's Intendants was highly esteemed by him, he was an upright, virtuous man, and a great friend of our deceased Master Hiram Abiff. This man, King Solomon employed, with others, to search for the body of his friend, who was supposed to have been murdered, from the blood which was seen in the Temple. He was also desired to discover the assassins, and the Masters Jewel which Hiram Abiff used to wear.

The blood was traced to a well on the North side of the Temple, which induced Mahabon to believe that the body had been thrown into it.

The immediately discharged the water from the well and he descended, but found not the body as he expected, however, they were richly rewarded for their labor by finding the Master's Jewel, which in all probability, when Hiram Abiff was attacked by the assassins, he tore from his neck and threw there, to prevent it from falling into their hands. Mahabon, with his companions, offered a prayer of thanksgiving to the Almighty, for the discovery of this treasure. They then went in search of the body, which was at length discovered by Stokin, by means of a sprig of Acasia, as is mentioned in the symbolic Degrees.

When the body was brought to the temple, Solomon was highly gratified to be able to pay to the memory of that great Man, those high, Masonic, honors, which his talents and virtue so justly entitled him to. He accordingly gave orders to the Noble Adoniram, his Grand Inspector, to make the funeral as magnificent as possible. He also gave orders that the blood which was spilled in the Temple should not be effaced, until revenge should be obtained.

The Noble Adoniram, Grand Master Architect and Chief of the Works, immediately gave the plan for a superb monument, which was to be raised to his mourning, and which, was to be composed of black Marble. Through the exertions of the workmen, the monument was finished in nine days. On the top thereof, was a triangular stone, on which was engraved M.B. in Hebraic characters, and a sprig of Acacia ornamented the top.

It was erected in the middle of a great hall, in an apartment, separate from the Temple, where Solomon kept his chapter, and conferred with Hiram, King of Tyre, and Hiram Abiff on the sacred mysteries. The body of our respectable Master was interred under this monument, with the highest Masonic honors, attended by all the Brethren in white aprons and gloves. His heart was enclosed in an Urn pierced through with a sword, which was placed on the top of a superb obelisk, erected near the West part of the Temple, a little to the North side.

The Jewel of Hiram Abiff was carefully deposited among the treasures of the Temple.

Three days after the ceremony, Solomon, with his whole court, went to the Temple, where the workmen were arranged in the same order, as they were at the funeral. He examined the tomb, obelisk, the triangular stone with the letters which were engraved on it, when he raised his eyes and hands towards heaven and offered up a prayer to the Lord of Hosts, and said with joy in his heart, it is complete, and by a Sign of Admiration the Brethren raised their eyes and hands towards heaven, leaned their heads on their right shoulders, and then crossed their hands over their bellies, said

Amen. Amen. Amen.

§. *Lecture.*

A. Are you a Perfect Master?

S. I have seen the Circle and square placed on the two crossed columns.

A. Where are they situated?

S. In the place where the body of our respectable Master Hiram Abiff was deposited.

A. What do those columns represent?

S. The Pillars of Jachin and Boaz which I have passed, to attain the Degree of Perfect Master.

A. In what part of the Temple were those pillars erected?

S. In the Porch.[9]

A. Have those words any meaning?

S. Right Worshipful they have. The first is, cemented, the second is strength. Besides the beauty which they added to the building, they conveyed to the minds of those, who entered, a knowledge of the Divine attributes of that Being, to whom the Temple was dedicated. During the building of the Temple, the Entered Apprentices were called by the name of the first pillar, at which they met and received their wages. The Fellow Crafts bore the name of the second pillar for the same reason.

A. What was Solomon's intention in creating this Degree?

S. To excite the Brethren to an active inquiry after those bloody ruffians, who had assassinated our dear Master Hiram Abiff the names of whom they were ignorant of. But suspecting that they were among the workmen, Solomon ordered a strict and general search, to be made among them, when they found, that three of the number were missing, whom they supposed to be guilty. He desired Adoniram to raise a superb tomb at the West end of the Temple, and place on the top thereof, in an urn, the heart of Hiram Abiff well embalmed, of which none had any knowledge, but the perfect Masters. Agreeably to these orders the heart of our respectable and much lamented Chief, was enclosed in an Urn, and placed on the top of the obelisk, until vengeance should be

---

[9] 1 Kings—7 Ch: 21.

accomplished. Through the urn was a drawn sword, an emblem of the anxious desire of all the Brethren, to assist in discovering the assassins, and obtaining Vengeance. The body was buried in a separate apartment from the Temple, where Solomon kept his Chapter.

A. What have you learned, from the Degrees you have already passed through?

S. To rule my Actions, purify my heart, in order to merit the Degree of Perfection.

A. What signifies the square stone in the center of the Circles?

S. It teaches us that our edifice should have for its foundation, a perfect stone, that is, that our conduct should be raised upon a permanent and imperishable basis, that it may stand the test of times and seasons.

A. What is the meaning of the three Circles?

S. They are emblematical of the Divinity, who hath neither beginning or end.

A. What is the meaning of the letter J which is in the Center of the square stone?

S. It is an initial of the Ineffable name of the Grand Architect of the Universe, and of the Sacred Word of the Perfect Master.

A. Pronounce it.

S. JEVA.

A. How were you received a Perfect Master?

S. With the point of a spear to my heart, and an halter round my neck.

A. Why the point to your heart?

S. To cause me to recollect that I have given my consent to have it torn from out of my breast, if I should infringe my obligations and reveal the secrets of Masonry.

A. Why the halter round your neck?

S. To teach me that my humiliation should increase as I proceed in Masonry and Virtue.

A. How many signs have you?

S. One by five.

A. Why one by five?

S. In remembrance of the five points at my reception.

A. What do they signify?

S. The four turns which I made when traveling and the fifth of Admiration.

A. What is the meaning of the tomb you passed, when you entered this Lodge?

S. It is the representation of the burial of Hiram Abiff.

A. What signifies the rope which comes from the Coffin, and is extended as far as the Temple?

S. The rope of green with which the Brethren made use of to raise the body of Hiram Abiff to place in his Coffin.

A. What was you taught at entering?

S. To alter my steps from Apprentice to Fellow Craft and Master, and to cross the two columns.

A. Why so?

S. To call to my recollection that it has been by passing the first Degrees, that I have attained the Degree of Perfect Master.

A. Is there any mystery his under this signification?

S. Yes, Right Worshipful. It teaches us that we cannot arrive at the Sanctum Sanctorum but by purity of manners, righteousness of heart, and the secrets of the first Degrees, of which they are the school.

A. Why did you enter at the side of the Sanctuary?

S. To teach me to abandon the common road.

A. What is the color of your Lodge?

S. Green.

A. Why green?

S. To remind me that, being dead in vice, I must hope to revive in virtue, and by that attain the last Degree in order to make some progress in the sublime sciences, a knowledge which I hope one day to possess.

A. Who can communicate it to you?

S. God alone, whose knowledge is beyond human comprehension.

A. What is the meaning of the two Pyramids in your draft?

S. Egypt, where the sciences first took their rise.

A. What signifies your Jewel?

S. That a Perfect Master should act within measure and always be attentive to Justice and Equity.

A. What is the Pass Word?

S. ACACIA.

A. What is the meaning of that word?

S. It is the name of a plant which was placed on the grave of Hiram Abiff and was common about Jerusalem. It is the MIMOSA NICOLITA of Linnæus, and belongs to his 23rd Class and first order, called POLYGAMIA MONÆCIA.

§. *To Close.*

A. Brother Stokin, pray, what's the clock?

S. Right Worshipful Adoniram it is five.

S. Since it is five, and the work finished, it is time to refresh ourselves. Give notice I am going to close this Lodge.

S. Take notice Brethren. The Right Worshipful Adoniram is going to close this Lodge.

Adoniram strikes ————4

The Inspector ————4

The Secretary————4

The Treasurer————4

Adoniram then makes the Sign of Admiration, which the Brethren answer, and admire the tomb, when the

LODGE IS CLOSED

6th Degree of the First Series of the Southern Jurisdiction of the United States, called

Intimate Secretary

here are only two Wardens in this Lodge at a reception, who represent, Solomon King of Israel, and Hiram, King of Tyre. They are covered with blue cloaks lined with Ermine, with crowns on their heads and scepters in their hands, a roll of Parchment, and two naked swords, crossed, on the Table.

The place where the Lodge is kept, represents the Hall of Audience of Masons, furnished with Black hangings, strewed with tears, and should be enlightened by 27 Lights in 3 candlesticks of 9 each, arranged in the same order, as in the Symbolic Lodge.

This Lodge is opened and closed, by 27 Knocks, 9 at a time, with a little interval between the 9th and 10th.

§. *To Open.*

Solomon knocks 27 which is answered by Hiram, when all the Brethren in the Lodge bend their right knees, with their hands crossed in such manner, that the 2 thumbs touch the forehead, when they all repeat in a low voice JOVA, JOVA, JOVA, then rise and draw their swords.

Solomon appoints a Captain and Lieutenant of the Guards, and the rest of the Brethren go by the name of the Guards. Solomon charges them to behave themselves well and with decency, to take particular care of the security of the Lodge and keep off all Brethren, or others, that would come near. The Guards then withdraw into the Anti-chamber.

The Guards and Brethren of the Lodge are looked upon as Perfect Masters and should wear Aprons lined and bordered with a fiery colored ribbon, and a triangle painted on the flap.

Jewel—A triple triangle hanging on the breast, by a fiery red ribbon, round the neck, the gloves bordered with red.

After the Guards withdraw, there remain only Solomon of Israel and Hiram of Tyre.

§. *Form of Reception.*

The Candidate being in the Anti-Chamber the captain of the Guards, takes from him his hat, sword, Apron and gloves, and the string of Perfect Master; and all offensive weapons. He then places him at the door of the Lodge, which is purposely left a little open. The Candidate places his hands across the door, and peeps and listens, to what passes within, so that Hiram may perceive him, when the Guards make a little noise at the door, which obliges the King of Tyre to turn his head that way. When he perceives the Cowan, he raises his eyes towards heaven and exclaims—"Heavens, there's a listner."

Solomon says—"That cannot be since the Guards are on the outside."

On which Hiram rises without speaking, and runs to the door, seizes the curious Brother by the hand and drags him into the Lodge and says to Solomon—"Here he is."

Solomon says—"What shall we do with him?"

Hiram answers (putting his hand to his sword)—"We must kill him"*—on which Solomon quits his place, and puts his hand on the guard of Hiram's sword and says—* "Stop my Brother," *then gives a loud knock on the table, on which the Captain of the Guards, with 5 or 6 more, enter, and salute the Kings respectfully.*

*Solomon then says to them—*Let that guilty man come forth when wanting you shall answer for him.

When the guards have departed with their prisoner, Solomon and Hiram remain by themselves some time, speaking very low. Solomon strikes a loud blow on the table, on which the guards enter, conducting the Candidate in the middle of them and by a Sign given by Solomon to the guard, they advance him to the foot of the Throne and when the Brethren are seated Solomon addresses the Candidate as follows—

I have interceded, by my intreaties with the King of Tyre, my Ally, whom your curiosity had offended, for which he had pronounced sentence of death on you. I have not only obtained you pardon, but also his consent, to receive you as an Intimate Secretary to our new Alliance. Do you find yourself capable of keeping inviolably secret, the matter which we are willing to discover to you, and are you willing to take an obligation in the most solemn and sacred manner?

The Candidate answers—I consent.
He then kneels and takes the following

§. *Obligation.*

I —— do most solemnly and sincerely promise and swear in the presence of the Grand Architect of the Universe, and this right worshipful assembly, never to reveal, either directly or indirectly, to any person under the canopy of Heaven, any matter or thing, which has been, is now or shall be hereafter be communicated to me in this Degree of Intimate Secretary, nor to any Brother of a lower Degree. And I do furthermore promise and swear, that I will attend all summons's sent to me from this Lodge, and strictly observe and keep, as faithfully as possible, all the laws and Constitutions of this Lodge, and that I will pay due Obedience to all mandates decrees and commands, of the Grand Council of the Princes of Jerusalem, under no less penalty, than to have my body dissected, my heart cut into pieces and the whole to be thrown to the wild beasts of the Forest, so help me God, and preserve me steadfastly in the same.

Solomon then shews him the draft and explains it as follows (vizt.)—The window in the cloud, represents the vault in the Temple, and in the glazing therein, there is an I, which is the initial of the name of the Grand Architect of the Universe. The edifice at the end, represents the Palace of Solomon, and the door of the great gate by which they enter. The tears and Mausoleum refer to the chamber of audience of Masons in the palace, lined with black cloth, where Solomon used to retire and grieve, for the loss of Hiram Abiff and where Hiram, King of, found Solomon when he came to visit him.

The letter A in the Mausoleum signifies ALLIANCE. The P at the right of the mausoleum, is PROMISE and the P on the left signifies PERFECTION.

My dear Brother, I receive you an Intimate Secretary, promise me to be faithful and diligent in the discharge of the duties of your new office as was that great man whose place you now supply.

The color of the ribbon, with which you are invested, should bring to your remembrance, the blows which the cruel assassin gave him, and his blood, of which he rather chose to spill the last drop, than reveal the mysteries of Masonry. We hope, my dear Brother, your fidelity will be steady and equal to every proof, and this sword, with which I now arm you, will defend you against those, who may dare to surprise you, in what we are going to entrust you with.

§. Sign, Token & Words.

The first Sign—is made by carrying your right hand to your left shoulder, and drawing it from thence to your right hip, in token of your obligation.

The second Sign—Cross your arms on your breast, raising up your thumbs to your temples (as if resting on them) then let them fall on your sword, at the same time raising your eyes to Heaven.

Token—Take each other's Right hand, when one says BERITH turning the other's hand with the back part downwards, then the other turns and says NEDER, the first turns again and says SELEMOTH which signifies Alliance, promise and Perfection.

1st Pass Word—Is JOABERT, the name of the curious Brother.

2nd Pass Word—Is ZERBAL, the name of the Captain of the Guards.

Grand Word—The Grand Word is JOHA (יה) an initial of the Ineffable name.

§. *The History*

Solomon, in consequence of the Treaty which his ambassador made with the King of, was obliged to give him in return for the materials which had been taken from Mount Libanus, and the Quarry of (besides the measure of oil, honey and wheat, with which he had already furnished him) a province of 20 cities in Galilea, which was to be given to Hiram of, when the Temple was completely finished. Solomon, having neglected this for a year, King Hiram visited the Cities, and finding the lands barren, the people rude and uncultivated, and their morals bad, he was convinced they would be more expense than profit to him, he therefore determined to go in person to Solomon and complain of his breach of the promise and agreement which he had made. Being arrived at Jerusalem, he passed through the Guards who were in the court, and proceeded directly to the kings Apartment, where he found Solomon, giving himself up to grief for the loss of Hiram Abiff.

King Hiram went in, in so hasty a manner, that one of Solomon's favorites named Joabert, who perceived it, fearing he had gone ion with an intention of executing some evil design against Solomon, followed him to the door and listened. Hiram perceiving it, exclaimed, Oh Heavens they hear us! and ran immediately to the door and dragged him into the chamber and said, here he is. Solomon seeing him, could not doubt and said, what shall we do with him? to which Hiram replied, we must kill him, and seized his sword for that purpose, when Solomon ran from his throne and said, stop your hand my Brother. He then gave a loud knock on the table, on which the guards entered, to whom he said, seize this guilty man, withdraw with him, you will answer for his appearance. When Solomon was alone with Hiram he said, Sire, Joabert is the greatest favorite I have, and of all the Lords in my Court, he is the most attached to me. I am well convinced of his design and what he has done, was to preserve me from your displeasure. The alteration he saw in your face, when you passed through the Court, induced him to listen. I pray you to revoke your sentence, and I will answer for his zeal and discretion. The King of, perceiving by the intercession which Solomon made for his favorite, how dear he was to him, freely gave his consent to every thing which Solomon desired. Before they separated, they signed a treaty, renewing their former alliance, with engagements, that they were allied for Offensive and Defensive operations. This treaty was kept unalterable, with other matters, to which was the Intimate Secretary.

It is this, my Dear Brother, which was represented to you, in your reception of Intimate Secretary.

END OF THE HISTORY

§. **Lecture.**

Q. Are you an Intimate Secretary?

A. I am (and raises his eyes towards Heaven)

Q. How were you received?

A. By curiosity.

Q. What danger did you risque?

A. The losing of my life.

Q. What did they do to you after you was surprised?

A. They put me into the hands of the Guards and I received sentence of death.

Q. Where they Intimate Secretary's or Perfect Masters?

A. Of that I was ignorant, but my resolution, firmness and zeal, proved to me, that I have been the first initiated in that Degree.

Q. What are the Pass Words?

A. JOABERT and ZERBAL.

Q. What do you mean by Joabert and Zerbal?

A. Joabert is the name of Solomon's favorite who listened at the door, and Zerbal is the name of the Captain of the Guards.

Q. What is the Grand Word?

A. Joha and initial of the Ineffable name.

Q. What was you before you was received Intimate Secretary?

A. A favorite of Solomon.

Q. Of what province?

A. Of Capula.

Q. Your sir name?

A. Capulist.

Q. How many cities did Solomon give to the King of, to recompense him for the materials he had furnished for the construction of the Temple?

A. Twenty.

Q. Where was you received?

A. In Solomon's apartment, lighted by 27 lights and hung with black cloth.

Q. What doth the letter J signify which you saw in the window?

A. It is the initial of the third name of the Grand Architect of the Universe, which in this Degree signifies—Give thanks to God, the work is done.

Q. What signifies the A's and two P's in the Triangle?

A. The A is ALLIANCE, the first P is PROMISE and the 2nd P signifies PERFECTION.

Q. Why is the Lodge lighted by 27 Lights?

A. To represent the 2700 Candlesticks which Solomon made use of for the Temple.

Q. What was the grand door represent?

A. The door of Solomon's palace.

Q. What signifies the Triple triangle which hangs at the lower end of your ribbon?

A. The three Theological virtues of faith, Hope and Charity. You may give it another interpretation—Solomon, Hiram of Tyre and Hiram Abiff.

§. *To Close.*

Q. What's the clock?

A. It is nine.

The Lodge is closed as at the opening by 27 knocks, 3 times 9, a little interval between the 9th and 10th.

THE END

7th Degree of the First Series (1801) of the Southern Jurisdiction of the United States of America, called

Provost and Judge

this Lodge must be adorned with red, and lighted by 5 great lights, one in each corner, in the center.

The Master is called Thrice Illustrious, who is placed in the East, under a Blue canopy with a number of stars round him. He represent TITO, Prince of Herodim, the eldest of the Provost and Judges; first Grand Warden and Inspector of 300 Architects, who used to draw plans for the workmen.

There are two Wardens in this Lodge.

§. *To Open.*

Q. Illustrious Brother Warden, are we well tyled?

A. Thrice Illustrious we are well tyled.

Q. Where is your Master's place?

A. Every where.

Q. Why so my Brother?

A. To superintend the conduct of the workmen and preside over the works, rendering Justice to every one.

Q. What's the clock?

A. Break of day, 8 o'clock 2 and 7.

The Thrice Illustrious then knocks 4 times quick, and 1 separate, which is repeated by the two Wardens.

36

The Master then says—As it is 8 o'clock 2 and 7 it is time to proceed to work, *which is repeated by the 2 Wardens.*

All the Brethren then clap with their hands 4 and 1 separate. The Master says, "The Lodge is Open."

§. *Reception.*

The Master of Ceremonies proceeds to the antechamber, and when the Candidate is prepared, he knocks on the door 4 and 1, which is repeated by the Master, and 2 Wardens, when the Thrice Illustrious orders the Captain of the guard to see who knocks. When the Tyler informs him that Brother N.N. desires to pass to the Degree of Provost and Judge, which he repeats to the Master, who gives orders that the Master of Ceremonies must examine the Candidate, and then introduce him in the ancient form.

The Master of Ceremonies introduces him, and places him between the 2 Wardens. The Senior Warden takes him by the hand and orders him to kneel and say CIVI, at the same time lays a naked sword on his left shoulder. After a minutes, the Thrice Illustrious says CUM, on which the Senior Warden raises him and leads him 7 times round the Lodge, and at every turn, when opposite to the Master, he pays his obedience by making the signs of his preceding Degrees, beginning with that of the Entered Apprentice, he is then led to the altar, when the Thrice Illustrious speaks to him as follows, vizt—

Respectable Master, with great joy, I am going to recompense your zeal and attachment for the Master of Masters and to appoint you Provost and Judge over all the workmen of this Lodge. As we are convinced of your discretion, we will confide in you the most important secret. Do your duty in the Degree in which you will be elevated, as you have done in your preceding Degrees. I trust you with the key of the place where is kept the body and heart of our respectable Master Hiram Abiff and assure us you will never discover the place where those are interred, kneel and pronounce the

§. *Obligation.*

I —— do most solemnly and sincerely promise and swear, before the Grand Architect of the Universe and these Illustrious Brethren here present, never to reveal any matter or thing which concerns the Provost and Judge, either directly or indirectly to any person whomsoever, below this Degree, and

38

that I will regulate justly and impartially all matters or differences between Brethren, that I will be just and equitable to all the world, as I am constituted by this Lodge to render Justice, and that I will pay just and due obedience to all decrees, mandates and commands of the Grand Council of Princes of Jerusalem, and regulate myself by their recommendation. All this I solemnly swear and promise under the penalties of all my preceding obligations. So God maintain me in Equity and Justice. Amen Amen Amen.

The Thrice Illustrious then orders the Candidate to rise and come to him, and giving him a stroke with a naked sword upon each shoulder, says,

Jewel—By the power given me, and with which I am invested, I constitute you Provost and Judge over all the workmen of the Temple, I therefore decorate you in this quality with a golden key, suspended to this red ribbon, which you are to wear in the form of a collar.

Apron—The Apron is lined with the same color; the red signifies the ardor of the Master, and the pocket on the center of the Apron, is to keep the keep of the plans.

§. *Sign, Token & Words.*

Sign—The Sign is to bring the 2 first fingers of the right hand to the nose; the answer is to put the first finger of the left hand to the nose, the thumb under the chin, forming a square and vice versa.

Token—The Token is, interlacing the fingers of the right hand, and then striking 7 times in the palm of each others hand.

Words—The Words are sevenfold; CIVICUM, JUA, HIRAM, STOKIN, GEOMETRAS, ARCHITECT and XINXE.

Grand Word—The Grand Word is SHEKINAI.

N.B.—There must be a key painted on the flap of the Apron.

§. *Lecture.*

Q. Are you a Provost and Judge?

A. I render justice to all the workmen without exception.

Q. How were you introduced into this Lodge?

A. By 4 and 1 distinct knocks.

Q. What signifies the 4 and 1 separate numbers?

A. The 4 signifies the 4 sides of the Temple and the 1 the inside, in which we should pay our adoration and devotion to God.

Q. Who did you meet at the entrance of the Lodge?

A. A Warden who conducted me to the West.

Q. What was done afterwards?

A. The Senior Warden made me kneel on my right knee and pronounce the word CIVI.

Q. What did the thrice Illustrious answer?

A. After a little pause he said CUM.

Q. What is the meaning of those words?

A. CIVI is command and CUM is to rise.

Q. What did the Thrice Illustrious do after that?

A. From his opinion of my zeal, he constituted me Provost and Judge.

Q. What did he deliver to you?

A. A Golden key to distinguish this Degree: he then gave me the Sign, token and words.

Q. What is the use of this key?

A. To open a small ebony box, wherein are kept all the plans, necessary for the instruction of the Temple.

Q. And what does all this signify?

A. It signifies that, only the Provost and Judges know, where the heart of out much lamented and respectable Hiram Abiff is deposited.

Q. What is the word?

A. TITO.

Q. What is the meaning of that word?

A. It is the name of the first Grand Master, Prince Herodim, the Eldest of the Provost and Judges, who had the inspection over 300 Master Architects of the Temple.

Q. What did you perceive in this Lodge?

A. A curtain, within which was suspended a small ebony box enriched with jewels.

Q. What was in the box?

A. All the designs which were necessary for the construction of the Temple.

Q. Did you see anything else?

A. A saw a Triangle in the center of the Lodge, in which was **GA**

Q. What is the meaning of those two letters?

A. That God, who was the Grand Architect of the Temple, had inspired David and Solomon with the design thereof.

Q. What was there more?

A. A Balance.

Q. What was the meaning of the Balance?

A. To put us in mind of the exact equilibrium which we aught invariably to observe in our conduct, as we are particularly named to decide all matters and differences which may arise among the workmen.

Q. Where is deposited the heart of the most respectable Hiram Abiff?

A. In and urn of Gold, on the top of the obelisk.

Q. What signify the letters X and S?

A. XINXE and SHECKINAI, the seat of the soul, which is the pass.

Q. What signifies the letters IHS with the with the sprig of Acasia over them?

A. The I signifies JUA, the H, HIRAM and the S signifies STOKIN. The last is the name of him who found the body of Hiram Abiff under the sprig of Acasia, which had been put on the grave, and by which means it was discovered.

Q. In what place were you received?

A. In the Middle Chamber.

Q. Have you ever worked anything remarkable in quality of Provost and Judge?

A. I was put to perfect the tomb of Hiram Abiff.

Q. What did the Thrice Illustrious invest you with, when he constituted you Provost and Judge?

A. With a white Apron lined with red, of a fiery color, in which was a pocket; and a red and white rose — and a golden key on the flap.

Q. What is the use of the pocket?

A. To keep the plans secure for the eldest Provost and Judge when carrying them to the Temple, to communicate them to the Masters.

Q. What is the meaning of the red and white rose, and the Golden key?

A. The red signifies the blood of Hiram Abiff and the white, the candor of the Masters, the Golden key, has been before explained.

Q. What was Solomon's intention in creating this Degree?

A. As it was necessary to establish order among such a number of Brethren, JOABERT was honoured with the intimate confidence of his monarch, and received a new mark of his favor and distinction; Solomon first created TITO, Prince Herodim, ADONIRAM, and his father Provosts and Judges, and gave orders to them to initiate Joabert, his favorite, into the most secret mysteries, and to give him the key of all the planes of the buildings, which were enclosed in a small ebony box, suspended in the Sanctum Sanctorum under a rich canopy. When Joabert was admitted into that sacred place, he was seized with the greatest admiration, and falling upon his knees he pronounced CIVI. Solomon seeing him prostrate, said to him CUM, and gave him a balance as a badge of office, and his knowledge was greatly augmented thereby.

§. *To Close.*

Q. What age are you?

A. Four times sixteen.

Q. From whence came you?

A. I came from and am going every where.

Q. What's the clock?

A. Break of day 8, 2 and 7.

Q. How so?

A. Because a Provost and Judge must be ready at any hour to do Justice.

Then close by 4 and 1 as at opening.

FINIS

Heiroglyphics of this Degree

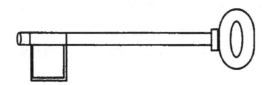

8th Degree of the First Series of the Southern Jurisdiction of the United States of America, called
✿ ✿ ✿
Intendant of the Building, or Master in Israel
(Many French Lodges call it, J.J.J.)
✤

his Lodge must be decorated with red hangings, lighted with 27 lights, distributed by 3 times 9 round the Lodge, and 5 other great lights in the altar, before the Thrice Puissant, who represents Solomon.

The first Warden, called Inspector, represents the Illustrious Brother Tito, Prince Herodim.

The second Warden represents Adoniram, the son of Abda. The rest of the Brethren are ranged regularly.

Order and Jewel—The Thrice Puissant and all the Brethren are decorated with a broad red ribbon from the right shoulder to the left hip, to which, is suspended a triangle hanging by a Green ribbon, on one side of the Triangle must be three Hebraic words BENCHORIM, ACHAD and SHECKINAI, which signifies FREE MASON — ONE GOD, OH! YOU ETERNAL. And on the other side JUDEA, KY, JEA— GOD, PUISSANT GOD.

Apron—A white Apron lined with red, bordered with green, a star with 9 points in the center, above it a balance, on the flap, must be painted a Triangle, with these three letters B.A.S. one at each angle.

The Thrice Puissant is placed in the East.

44

The Right Worshipful Tito in the West, and Adoniram the conductor in the other angle, ready to receive the orders from the Right Worshipful Tito, the Inspector.

§. *To Open.*

Q. Brother Tito, are we tyled?

A. Thrice Puissant, we are well tyled.

Q. What's the clock?

A. The break of day.

The Thrice Puissant then knocks 5 times with his scepter on the altar, which is repeated by Tito and Adoniram.

The Master then says

"Since it is break of day my dear Brethren, it is time to begin our work.

The Lodge is open."

The Brethren then knock 5 times together and make the signs of surprise and admiration.

1st Sign.—That of surprise is, The right hand to the forehead, extended from the thumb, as if to prevent a glaring Light.

2nd Sign.—That of Admiration is, to extend both arms and hands, looking up, the head reclining on the right shoulder.

§. *Reception.*

The Thrice Puissant speaks to Brother Tito and says—"Brother Tito, shall we repair the misfortune of the loss of our dear chief Hiram Abiff you know he had in charge the ornaments of the secret chamber, which contained the Holy Ark, to assure the Israelite, of the presence and protection of the Most High God. He is now taken away from us, by a most horrible crime, and we are by this means, deprived of this Respectable Chief. Can you, my Illustrious Brother give me any advice on this great and momentous question?"

Tito answers—"I feel conscious, Most Illustrious sir, of the extreme difficulty we shall find, in repairing the loss which we have sustained, by the death of our Grand Master Architect., and the best advice which I can give is, to create one Chief, from each of the Orders of Architecture, to recruit all our capacities, and endeavor to finish the work of the Secret Chamber in the third story."

The Master then says—"Your council my Brother, is too good not to be observed, and to prove that I am willing to follow it, I will establish Brother Tito, Brother Adoniram and Brother Abda, Inspectors and Conductors of this work, and see, if in the Middle chamber, you can find 5 Chiefs of the 5 Orders of Architecture, excellent Brother Adoniram, go into the Middle Chamber."

Adoniram the Conductor goes into the Middle Chamber, where he finds Joabert, and says to him—"Brother, are here any Chiefs of the 5 orders of Architecture?"

Joabert answers—"I regard it, as the greatest happiness and advantage of my life, cheerfully to comply with every Order and duty, which the Thrice Puissant may require of me, in raising the Edifice to his honor and glory."

Then Adoniram demands the Signs, Tokens and Words of the three first Degrees, which are given. After which the Introducer knocks 3, 5 and 7 on the door. They demand from within , What he wants? Who replies—"There is one who is to be employed in the works of the middle Chamber," *when the door is opened.*

Then the Conductor gripes him by the Masters grip, and introduces him before the altar, and lays him down. Tito stands behind him, and gives him a branch of acasia in his right hand, and in this position he takes the following

§. *Obligation.*

I —— do most solemnly and sincerely promise and swear in the presence of the Grand Architect of the Universe, and before the Thrice Illustrious Brethren here present, to keep eternally secret, all the mysteries of this Degree, that are at this time, or at any time hereafter, may be revealed to me; and that I will pay due deference and submission to all the Laws, Rules and regulations of this Lodge, that I will pay due obedience to all the orders and decrees of the Grand Council of Princes of Jerusalem, under all the penalties of my former obligations, with this addition, to have my body severed in two, and my bowels torn from thence. So God maintain me in Equity and Justice. Amen.

He kisses the Bible.

The moment the Candidate finishes the obligation, Brother Tito covers his body with a red veil, and relieves him by the Masters gripe, with the left hand to the Elbow, he raises him and places him on a stool. When the Thrice Puissant speaks to him as follows—

My Dear Worshipful Brother, Solomon being desirous of carrying on the work, which was already begun, to the highest Degree of perfection, he was obliged to employ the 5 Chiefs of the 5 orders of Architecture and gave the command of them to Tito, Adoniram and Abda his father, as Solomon was convinced of their Capacities in perfecting such a magnificent and glorious work:— We flatter ourselves, my dear Brother, that you will contribute all in your power to the same end, and the situation of death in which you have been represented, points out to you, that you can replace our respectable Hiram Abiff in his work, only by the same firmness in despising and suffering death, rather than deliver up the mysteries of our order. We flatter ourselves it will be the same with you. I am going to relieve you in the same manner, as he was raised under the sprig of Acasia. On which he is raised properly.

§. *Signs, Token & Words.*

Then the Thrice Excellent Brother Tito gives him the following Signs, Token and words—

1st Sign.—The first Sign is that of surprise, put the thumbs of both hands to the Temples, the fingers extended, forming a square, going 2 steps backwards and then 2 steps forwards, then bring the hands over the eyebrows and say BENCHORIN, which signifies a Free Mason.—

2nd Sign.—The second Sign is, interlacing the fingers of both hands, the palms turned downwards, as low as the waist, looking up to heaven, saying ACHAD, signifying an only God.

3rd Sign.—The third Sign is of grief, figurative of the Fellow-Crafts Sign, with the left hand on the hip, and balancing with the knees 3 times. One says KUM, the other answers JEA, which is "Raise in the name of God."

The Token.—The token is, to clap each others heart with the right hand, after which, pass each others right hand to the middle of each others arm, and with the left hand, take hold of the Elbow, pass it 3 times, the one says SHEKINAI, that is the Glory of God; and the other answers JUDEA, signifying THE GLORY OF GOD IS IN JUDEA.

§. *Lecture.*

Q. Are you an Intendant of the Building?

A. I have made the 5 steps of exactitude; I have penetrated into the innermost parts of the Temple; I have seen a great light, in the middle of which I saw 3 mysterious letters I.S.I. in Hebraic characters, without knowing what they were.

Q. How were you received?

A. By acknowledging my ignorance.

Q. Why was you received?

A. To dissipate darkness, and procure me the true light; to rule my heart, and to enlighten my understanding.

Q. Where was you introduced?

A. In a marvelous place full of charms where Truth and Wisdom reside.

Q. What is your duty?

A. To encourage the Brethren by my example to the practice of Virtue, and to correct the works.—

Q. How came they to desire of you a proof of your being an Ancient Fellow craft and Master, before you was received?

A. To shew that it is by gradual promotion I am able to arrive at perfection.

Q. What do the 3 first Degrees teach you?

A. The Apprentice,—Moral Virtue,

The Fellow Craft,—Political Virtue, and

The Master,—Heroic Virtue.

Q. How came they to make you advance in the steps of this Degree, backwards and forwards.

A. To demonstrate that, as men and as Masons, we ought to set in opposition humility to pride, which is natural to us, and that we are to advance in virtue, and make it a rule for our actions, never to do any thing, but what is decent and praise worthy.

Q. Do you know how to explain the mysteries of your Lodge?

A. I will endeavor to do so, as much as possible.

Q. What signifies the 3 mysterious letters in the angles of your Jewel?

A. SHECKINAI, JUA, and JEVA — these words signify Divine Beauty, Divine Wisdom, and the Initial of the Sublime, Inexpressible word.

Q. What signifies the circles in the third triangle?

A. To mark the immensity of God, who hath neither beginning nor End.

Q. What signifies the 4 letters in the circles I.A.I.N.?

A. Oh! you Eternal possessing all divine attributes. —

Q. What are the principle attributes of the Divinity?

A. Beauty --6

Wisdom ------------------------------------7

Boundless Mercy -------------------- 14

Omniscience ---------------------------- 11

Eternity --------------------------------------8

Perfection ---------------------------- 10

Justice --7

Tenderness--------------------------- 10

Creation --------------------------------------8

———— in all 81.

Q. Explain to me the square which you saw in the Triple Triangle?

A. It alludes to the 9 Virtuous Attributes.

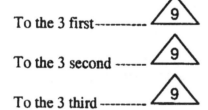

To the 3 first---------- 9

To the 3 second ------ 9

To the 3 third -------- 9

9	9	9
9	9	9
9	9	9

Q. How came Solomon placed in the temple?

A. Because he was the first, who consecrated a Temple, to the only true and living God.

Q. Why was a Brazen Sea placed on the outside of the Temple?

A. As the Temple of the Most High God, was pure and Holy, none should enter therein, but those who have been purified from all uncleanliness.

Q. What signifies the Left side of the Temple?

A. A Masonic Order, under the laws of types and ceremonies.

Q. What signifies the right side of the Temple?

A. True Masonry, under the law of Grace and Truth.

Q. What signifies the tomb, which is on the pavement neat the door of the Sanctuary, in the Degree of Provost and Judge.

A. It teaches us that after being purified by death, we can be introduced into the presence of the Divinity.

Q. What signifies the Candlestick with seven branches?

A. The presence of the Holy Spirit, in the breast of every true observer of the law of god, whereby we are enlightened.

Q. What was the reason of your being barefooted at your reception?

A. Because I entered on Holy things following the example of Moses, who did the same when he drew near the Burning Bush.

Q. What did you hear, before you entered?

A. Five loud knocks.

Q. What do they allude to?

A. The five points of fellowship.

Q. What did they produce?

A. A Warden.

Q. What did he do with you?

A. He led me 5 times round the Temple and sustained me.

Q. For what purpose?

A. To admire the beauty of it.

Q. In what manner did those 5 steps impress your mind?

A. With great surprise, admiration and grief. —

Q. Why so?

A. On account of what I saw enclosed in the Blazing Star.

Q. What was enclosed therein?

A. The Holy Name of the Grand Architect of the Universe.

Q. What is the reason the Star has only five points?

A. There are several reasons for it (vizt.) The five orders of Architecture, which was made use of in the Construction of the Temple. The five points of felicity. The five senses of Nature, without which, man cannot be perfect. The five Lights of Masonry and the five zones of the world, inhabited by Masons.

Q. What are the five points of felicity?

A. To go, To intercede, To pray, Love and help your Brother.

Q. How came you to be seized with grief and admiration?

A. On seeing the beauty of the Temple and its ornaments.

Q. Did you see all its ornaments?

A. I saw only a part.

Q. What was the reason of your not seeing the whole?

A. A thick veil covers the rest preventing me, but my zeal to arrive at perfection in the Royal Art, will one day remove from my eyes the present obstacles.

Q. How came you to grieve?

A. Because these ornaments brought to my mind, our dear Brother and respectable Grand Master Hiram Abiff who was inhumanely sacrificed.

Q. Was you overpowered with grief?

A. No; I should have been so, if I had not been sustained, and held by some, whom I afterwards knew to be Brothers.

Q. How did you know them to be Brothers?

A. By the Grand and Awful word which they invoked, after they had pronounced SHECKINAI, which is the sacred name I saw in the Center of the Blazing Star.

Q. Have you promised to keep inviolably secret, all those things?

A. Yes I have, Illustrious Master.

Q. What did you impose on yourself in case of failure?

A. To have my body severed in two, and my bowels torn from thence.

Q. How have you marched?

A. By five grave steps, which I made in advancing to the Illustrious, when I went to pronounce my Obligation.

Q. For what reason was you made to appear as a dead man, covered with a red veil?

A. To understand that the Brethren must be dead to the world, and all its vices.

Q. What signifies the balance which was given to you?

A. The balance is an attribute and emblem of Justice, which was given me to exercise impartially, among Masons, and to regulate my own conduct, if I am willing to deserve the title and name which was given me, when I received the Degree of Provost and Judge of the Buildings. —

Q. Have you seen your Illustrious Master today?

A. Yes, I have seen him.

Q. Where was he placed?

A. In the East, under a canopy spread with brilliant stars.

Q. How was he closed?

A. In Blue and Gold.

Q. Why in this dress?

A. Because God appeared in blue and gold unto Moses on Mount Sinai, when he gave him the tables of the Laws.

Q. Did you continue in darkness?

A. I enjoyed the effulgence of the morning and had the mysterious star for my guide.

Q. Where have you been conducted?

A. I cannot tell.

Q. What age are you?

A. Twenty seven.

Q. What numbers have you marked?

A. Five, Seven and fifteen.

Q. How have you attained those numbers?

A. From the manner they place the lights.

Q. What do they signify?

A. I have already explained the two first, the last represents the Fifteen Masters who found the body of our Respectable Master Hiram Abiff under the sprig of Acasia.

Q. Why is your Apron bound with Green?

A. To put me in mind, that I can only arrive at the most sublime knowledge, by my virtue, zeal and study of Masonry.

Q. What signifies your Jewel?

A. The Triple Essence of the divinity.

Q. What is the hour?

A. Seven at night.

§. *To Close.*

The Master says—My Dear Brethren, as you practice the five points of felicity, it is high time to refresh and repose ourselves.

Then the Thrice Illustrious knocks 5, which is repeated by the Wardens, and then by all the Brethren by 5, 7 and 15.

The Master then says—This Lodge is Closed.

FINIS

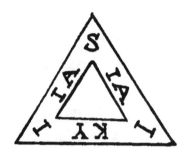

Form of the Jewel of the Intendant of the Building, to hang on the left side from a broad red order, by a green ribbon, engraved with these letters.

The Apron lined with red and bordered with green, in the center a star with 9 points, above, a balance, and on the flap a triangle with these 3 letters A^BS one in each angle.

The Jewel is a triangle, on one side these letters B.N. A.D. S.I. two on each angle, and on the other side these letters I.A. I.A. K.Y. two on each angle, and in the corners an I in each, an S in the upper one—suspended to a red order, from the right shoulder to the left hip, by a green ribbon.

BOOK 2nd

Copied from the M.S.S. of Ill^{trs} Brother
Giles F. Yates, R ⚒ K—H, S.P.R.S. &
Sov. Gr^d Ins. Genl of 33:rd. A.L. 5833

9th Degree of the First Series of the Southern Jurisdiction of the United States of America, at Charleston, South Carolina, called

♠ ♠ ♠
Chapter of Elected Knights
🜊

he Thrice Puissant is placed in the East, a table before him covered with black. In this Chapter there is only one Grand Warden, who is called Stokin, he is placed in the West, with seven other Brethren round him. There must be one Light in the East, and Eight in the West. A bloody head on a pole.

§. *To Open.*

Q. Are you an Elected Knight?

A. One Cavern received me, one lamp lighted me, and a spring refreshed me.

Q. What's the hour?

A. Break of day.

The Thrice Puissant knocks 8 quick and 1 slow, which is repeated by Stokin. Then by all the Brethren with their hands.

The Thrice Puissant says, This Chapter is open.

§. *Reception.*

There must be a small place very dark, the representation of a Cavern, in which must be a Lamp, a fountain of running water, a little table, on which must be a poniard, and a bloody head, with hair upon it, A large stone to sit on by the table, and under the Lamp must be wrote in large letters VENGEANCE.

The Candidate, who represents Joabert, must be in another room, not close to the cavern, where he waits till sent for.

N.B—This Chapter must be hung in Black, and all the Brethren, must be in black, their hats flapped, and sitting with their right leg over their left knee. Their Aprons bordered with black, a broad black order from the left shoulder to the right hip, a poniard hanging thereto, nine pink roses on the Order, 4 on each side, and one at the bottom.

The Master of Ceremonies goes out to the Candidate and knocks 9 times. When the Thrice powerful gives orders to let him in. All the Brethren in their proper attitudes.

On his entering with the Candidate behind Stokin the Master demands
Q. What do you want?
A. To be admitted a Knight Elected.
Q. Have you courage enough to revenge the death of your Master?
A. I have.

If you have, I will acquaint you with the place where one of the murderers is hid, which I learned of a stranger, and if you have resolution enough as you say, to revenge the death of your Master, follow the stranger.

On which his eyes are bound, he is carried to the Cavern and placed on the Stone near the head of the Traitor.

The Master of Ceremonies tells him—After I am gone, you may take off the bandage from your eyes, don't be afraid but take courage, I will not be absent from you long, but will return and succor you, you must drink some of the water which you will find in a cup near you.

N.B. A little Elixir of Vitriol must be put into the water to make it taste sour. He is left alone and the door shut upon him for 2 or 3 minutes, after which the Master of Ceremonies goes to him, and desires him to take the head in his left hand, and the poniard in his right, and leads him to the door of the Chapter; on which he knocks 8 and 1, very hard with his foot.

When the Master of Ceremonies (who has given him his Lesson and is come into the Chapter) opens the door and demands

Q. What do you want?

A. An Intendant of the Building demands to enter the Chapter.

Q. Have you finished your time, and satisfied your Master?

A. I have rendered an honor and service to the Craft, by an action, which I have done, and which, makes me deserving of the Degree I now desire.

Stokin makes the report to the Thrice Powerful, who orders the Candidate to be introduced, who is directed to take 8 steps quick and one slow (holding the head in his left hand, and with his right, the poniard as if ready to strike) which brings him to the altar, where he falls upon his knees.

The Thrice Powerful seeing him in this situation, says—Oh! dismal, what have you done? Do you know that you have deprived me of the opportunity of punishing the Villain myself? Therefore, Stokin, put him to death immediately.

On which all the Brethren fall on their knees, who with Stokin, assure the Thrice Powerful, that he did it through zeal and not with an intention of wresting the power out of his hands.—

The Thrice Powerful, then orders Stokin to stop, and tells Joabert, he forgives him this second time, but to take care for the third.

After which Stokin takes the head from him and lays it at the foot of the altar, and the poniard on the top.

The Candidate remains on his knees and takes the following

§. *Obligation.*

(N.B.—While he is taking the obligation, all the Brethren stand ready to plunge their swords into him.)

I — — do most solemnly and sincerely swear, in the presence of the Grand Architect of the Universe, and this Illustrious Chapter, never to reveal either directly or indirectly, the secrets of Knights Elected, to any person on earth, but to a true and lawful Brother, known to be such, on the penalty of this, and my former obligations. And I furthermore do promise and swear, to revenge the Most execrable murder, which has been committed, and to follow with vengeance all Villains, who shall betray or discover the secrets of this Degree. And to help protect the Order with all my might, and my Brethren with all my credit and power when occasion shall require it; that I will observe and obey all lawful commands, sent me from the Grand Council of Princes of Jerusalem, duly and lawfully established. And if I fail in this, my obligation, I consent to be struck with the terrible vindictive hand of vengeance, which is now presented to me, [*here the Brethren make a faint thrust at the Candidate's body*] my head severed from my body and stuck on the highest pinnacle of the World, as a token of my Villainy, so God maintain me, and recompense me for my zeal, fervor and constancy. Amen—Amen—Amen.

He kisses the Bible.

Then the Most powerful raises him and the Grand Orator delivers the following

§. *History.*

Sometime after the death of Hiram Abiff (whose murderers, Solomon was unable to discover) there was an assembly of a great number of Masters, who sat in consultation, on the means of discovering the Assassins of Hiram Abiff whose loss is the constant object of Grief, of all the Knights and Princes of Masons. The Captain of the Guards interrupted their deliberations by announcing that, there was a stranger who demanded to speak with the King in private, and who declared that he knew where the traitor JUBULUM AKIROP, one of the Assassins, had secreted himself, and offered to conduct those whom the King would appoint to go with him. On which all the Brethren desired permission to take ample vengeance for the death of the beloved Chief.

Solomon put a stop to their zeal by saying, there should be only 9 to undertake the task, and their names to be wrote and put in an urn, and the first nine that should be drawn from thence, should be the persons elected to proceed in company with the stranger, to seize the Traitor, and when taken, to bring him to his presence, in order to make a memorable example of him. In short, Joabert and Stokin with seven others, departed at night fall with the stranger, and traveled through many difficult and dangerous roads, when the stranger acquainted Joabert that the Cavern which held this detestable wretch was situated by the sea side, on the coast of Joppa, on which Joabert increased his pace with the most ardent zeal and being before his companions, he entered the cavern alone, and by light of a Lamp, discovered the Traitor a sleep, with a poniard at his feet, which, Joabert immediately seized, and stabbed the Traitor with on the head and the heart, who had only time to pronounce NECUM or NECAH, signifying VENGEANCE IS DONE, when he died.

Immediately after Joabert had done this, he perceived a spring of which he drank, and being fatigued, he slept until the other Brethren came and awake him, and when they perceived the head of the Traitor daubed with blood, they all exclaimed NECUM, Vengeance is done.

When Joabert acquainted them with what had happened, they all envied him the Glory, of having alone, revenged the death of their venerable Chief Hiram

Abiff and having refreshed themselves at the fountain Joabert cut off the head, and divided the body into four parts, which were burnt and the ashes thrown into the air.

After this, Joabert took the head in his left hand and the poniard in his right, and exclaimed VENGEANCE.

They proceeded to Jerusalem where they arrived at day break, and when Solomon saw Joabert, with the head of the Traitor in his hands, he was exceeding wrathful, that he should be deprived of inflicting an exemplary punishment himself, and that the power of acting, should be thus taken from him, immediately gave orders to Stokin to put him to death for his presumption; but the Brethren being convinced that it was the zeal of Joabert and not an intention of offending, fell on their knees, and begged his life, which at their intercession was granted him a second time.

Solomon ordered the head of the Traitor to be fixed on the East pinnacle, until the other two accomplices should be found. Solomon honored with his most Intimate confidence, and gave him, with the eight other Brethren, the title of Elected Knights, and also gave them the following signs, token and words.

§. *Signs, Token & Words.*

Sign—The Sign is double, first, one raises the poniard and strikes the other on the forehead and then on the heart, when the other answers, by clapping his hand first on his forehead and then on his heart.

Token—The token is, you take the thumb of a Brother's right hand, in the bottom of your right hand, clinch all your fingers, and put your thumb up, which signifies the 9 Elected—eight close together and one by himself.

Pass Words—The pass words are—One says NECUM, the other answers. Then the first says ABIRAIM (Traitor) the other answers AKIROP (Assassin).

Grand Word—The Grand Word is BOUGULKOL, signifying by him or through him is discovered everything, in allusion to, who first discovered the Assassin Abiram.

63

§. *Lecture.*

Q. Are you an Elected Knight?

A. One cavern I know, and have entered it.

Q. What have you seen in that Cavern?

A. A Light, a spring, a poniard, and the traitor Akirop.

Q. Of what use were they to you?

A. The light to enlighten me, the poniard to revenge the death of our respectable Master and the spring to refresh me.

Q. Where was you received an Elected Knight?

A. In Solomon's Audience Chamber.

Q. How many intendants were chosen to be elected Knights?

A. Nine, including myself.

Q. From what number were the nine, elected?

A. The number, exclusive of those, were ninety.

Q. What was your reason and intention in being received?

A. To revenge the death of Hiram Abiff and exterminate the traitor and assassin, Jubulum Akirop.

Q. Where did you find the Assassin?

A. In the bottom of a cavern, situated near a burning bush, or rainbow, on a cleft near the sea, on the Coast of Joppa.

Q. Who conducted you there?

A. A Stranger.

Q. Where did you travel to come at the cavern?

A. A dark and intricate road.

Q. What did you do when you came to the Cavern?

A. I seized a poniard which I found at the entrance, and stuck so violent a blow on the head and heart of the traitor, Jubulum Akirop, that he expired immediately.

Q. Did he say anything before he died?

A. He said one word.

Q. What was that word?

A. N-E-C-U-M- (*he letters it.*)

Q. What signifies those letters?

A. NECUM—Vengeance.

Q. In what manner was your election consummated?

A. By Vengeance, Disobedience, Mercy, and Eight by one.

Q. Explain this.

A. By Vengeance, I destroyed the Villain; by Disobedience, in neglecting the Kings orders; by Mercy, in obtaining pardon, through the solicitations of my Brethren, and 8 and 1, because the number of the Elected were nine.

Q. What did you do after killing the Traitor?

A. I cut off his head, and refreshed myself at the spring that was at the bottom of the cavern, and being much fatigued, I fell asleep, until my fellow Travelers arrived and awoke me, who, on seeing the bloody head of the traitor, exclaimed, VENGEANCE.

Q. How did Solomon receive you after presenting him with the head of the traitor?

A. With marked indignation, because he had reserved to himself the punishment of the Villain for an example but he forgave me in consequence of my zeal.

Q. What signifies the mourning Chamber into which you were conducted before your admission?

A. The Cavern of the Traitor.

Q. What was the reason of your being left and blindfolded?

A. To put me in mind of the sleep of the traitor, and to intimate how often we think ourselves secure, after committing a crime, when we are most in danger.

Q. Why do the Brethren, in this Chapter lean their heads on their right shoulders, and sit with their legs crossed?

A. Darkness obliged them to put their hands before their heads to prevent being hurt, for the same reason of the difficulty of the roads obliging them to cross their legs one over the other, is the reason why the Exalted Knights in a Chapter, have their legs crossed.

Q. What does the Dog in the road, represent, which you see in the draft?

A. The Stranger who conducted the Elected.

Q. What does the naked arm with a poniard represent?

A. That vengeance is always ready to strike the guilty.

Q. What signifies the black ribbon with a poniard suspended therefrom, which you wear?

A. To express our grief for the irreparable loss which we have sustained by the death of our death master Hiram Abiff who was horribly murdered by some of the Craft.

Q. What allusions have you to the nine elected and can you explain them?

A. First by the nine roses, at the bottom of which hangs the poniard; Secondly, by the nine lights; Thirdly, by the 9 knocks; all these represent the 9 Elected, and the blood which was spilled, is represented by the red color of the roses.

Q. How do you wear your ribbon?

A. From the left shoulder to the right hip.

Q. Of what color is your Apron?

A. A white skin, lined and bordered with black, specked with blood, on the flap an arm bloody, holding a bloody head by the hair.

Q. What color is this Chapter clothed with?

A. Red and White; the red with white flames, the white with red flames. The red is the blood which was spilt, and the white the purity of the Elected.

Q. Why is there but one Warden?

A. Because the Chapter was kept by Solomon, and he had only his favorite with him.

Q. What remains now to be done?

A. Nothing, because everything is accomplished and our Worshipful Hiram Abiff is avenged.

Q. Give me the pass word?

A. NECUM or NECAH.

Q. What is the word?

A. BOUGULKOL; signifying, by him or through him, is discovered every thing, in allusion to who first discovered the Assassin Akirop.

Q. Have you any more?

A. I have two others.

Q. What are they?

A. and STOKIN.

Q. What time went the Elected to search for the traitor?

A. Evening.

Q. When did they return?

A. At break of day.

Q. What age are you?

A. Eight by one, accomplished.

END OF THE LECTURE

§. *To Close.*

Q. What's the time of day?

A. It is Evening.

After which the Thrice powerful knocks 8 by 1 which is answered by Stokin, and then by all the Brethren, by clasping their hands on heads and hearts.

The Master says—NECUM.

They all answer—VENGEANCE.

When the Chapter is Closed.

FINIS

10ᵗʰ 𝔇egree of the 𝔣irst 𝔖eries (1801) of the 𝔖outhern
𝔍urisdiction of the 𝔘nited 𝔖tates of 𝔄merica, called

🙛 🙛 🙛
𝔄llustrious 𝔈lected of 15

𝔶

his Chapter must be hung in Black, with red and white Tears. In the East is a Skeleton, representing *JUBELLUM AKIROP*, by some called *ABIRAM*, and by others *HOBEN*. In the West a Skeleton representing *JUBELLA GRAVELOT*, of whose blood the flies have sucked. Each of them are armed with the tool, with which they assassinated Hiram Abiff and stand as if ready to strike with them.

This Chapter represents Solomon's Apartment. There are two Wardens, the first of whom is called Inspector. All the Brethren must wear Black clothes and a sword.

§. To Open.

The Most Illustrious Master strikes 5, when 5 Candles are lighted and placed at his left side. Then the Inspector strikes 15, when 5 more candles are lighted, and placed before him. Then the Junior Warden strikes 5 and 5 other candles are lighted, and placed before him.

Then the Most Illustrious says, Brother Inspector what's the clock?

A. Most Illustrious Master, it is five.

Then the Most Illustrious Master says, If it is 5, it is time my dear Brethren to begin the work. Give notice that the Chapter of Masters Elected of 15 is Open.

The Inspector repeats the same and the Chapter is open.

§. *Form of Reception.*

There can be no more than 15 Masters Elected in a Chapter, when a reception is made. If there are more than 15 present, the Eldest to the number of 15 continue and the others withdraw into the Anti-Chamber.

The Junior Warden conducts the Candidate, from the Antichamber to the door of the Chapter, and knocks 3 times 5, when the Inspector orders a Brother to go and see, the cause of the knocking—he opens the door a little, and asks, "Who is there?" the Brother on the outside answers, a Brother Elect of 9, who wants to know the other two Assassins of our respectable Master Hiram Abiff and to arrive at the Degree of Most Illustrious Elect of 15. The door is then shut, and he reports the same to the inspector, who acquaints the Most Illustrious of it. Who orders the Candidate to be admitted. When he enters, the Senior Warden makes him take 15 steps in a triangular manner, and advance to the altar. He must have a bloody head in each hand, the Brethren standing with their swords ready to strike. The stand about a minute, when they drop their swords, interlace their hands on their foreheads, with the palms upwards, and in this posture beg pardon for the Candidate.

Then the most Illustrious says

Q. Why do you beg pardon for him?

A. Because he is not guilty.

Q. If he is not guilty, why solicit forgiveness, how comes this?

A. The grace we ask for him is, to admit him into the Degree of Master Elected of 15.

Q. Is he qualified for that sublime Degree?

A. All the Brethren answer yes.

Then the Most Illustrious says, If so, let him kneel—*and then addresses him as follows—*

The Grand Masters here present, beg me to admit you to the Degree of Master Elect of 15, in order that you may enjoy the same advantages with themselves. Do you feel yourself able to keep this Degree secret and conformable there to take a solemn obligation?

The Candidate answers Yes— when the Wardens divest him of the heads, and placing both his hands on the Bible he takes the following

§. *Obligation.*

I —— do most solemnly and sincerely swear and promise, on the Holy Bible never to reveal, either directly or indirectly, the secrets of this Degree, nor receive any person into it, without full permission, first had and obtained, for that purpose, from my superiors. Nor to assist at any such reception, unless in a regular Chapter of this Degree, and in failure of this my obligation, I consent to have my body opened perpendicularly, and be exposed for 8 hours in the open air, that the Venomous flies, may feed on my entrails, my head to be cut off, and stuck on the highest pinnacle of the World, and always inflict the same punishment in those, who should disclose this Degree, and break their obligation. So God maintain me. Amen.

He kisses the book.

§. *Sign, Token & Word.*

Sign.—The Sign is double, one takes the poinard and touches his chin with his fingers, and draws it downwards, as if he would cut open his belly. The other answers with the Sign of an Entered Apprentice, with his fingers clinched.

Token.—Put your hand with the fingers clinched to each others body, the thumb upwards, as if you would cut each others body open.

Word.—One says ZERBAL, and the other answers ELOHIM.

The fist is the name of the Captain of the guards, who apprehended the 2 Assassins in the Quarry, and the last signifies Supreme Judge.

§. *History.*

My Dear Brother, you have learnt in the Degree of Elected of 9, which you have already received, that Jubellum Akirop, one of the Assassins, was killed in the Cave near Joppa. That Skeleton which you see in the East, was him— You see him armed with a setting maul, with which tool, he destroyed the life of Hiram Abiff— Solomon had his head embalmed, that it might keep and be exposed, until the other two assassins were discovered.

Six months after the Akirop was killed, Bangebee, one of Solomon's Intendants made inquiry in the Country of Gath, which was tributary to Solomon, whether any persons had lately taken refuge there, for Crimes which they had committed in Jerusalem, and caused a description of their persons to be published. Soon after this, Solomon was informed, that two person had lately retired there, and supposing themselves protected they had proceeded to work. He immediately wrote to MAACHAH, King of Gath, to deliver these two Villains, to the people he should send, that they might receive at Jerusalem, the punishment due to their crimes. In consequence of which, Solomon elected 15 of the most worthy Brethren and zealous Masters, in which number were included those who went to the cave of Akirop. They began their march on the 15th of the month SIVAN, which answers to the month of June, and arrived on the 28th of the same month in the country of Gath, when they delivered Solomon's letter to Maacha, who trembled at the news, and ordered immediately, as strict search to be made for the two Ruffians, and when found, to be delivered to the Israelites, at the same time declaring that he should be happy in having his country rid of such monsters.

They made a strict search for five days, when ZERBAL and were the first who discovered them in a Quarry of Bendaca, when they chained them together, and loaded them with irons, on which was engraved the crimes they had been guilty of.

They arrived at Jerusalem, on the 15th of the following month, and were conducted to Solomon, before whom they confessed their crimes. They were their confined in the Tower of ACHIZAS, until the day of execution, when they were to repeat their guilt, by a most excruciating death. At ten o'clock in the morning of the day, when they were to be publicly executed—they were brought forth, and tied to two stakes by the neck and feet, with their arms behind them, when the Executioner opened them, from heart to the ass pubis, and cross ways, when they were left in this situation for 8 hours, that the flies and other insects, might suck their blood, and glut on their entrails. At six o'clock in the evening their heads were cut off, and fixed with that of Akirop on the East, South and West gates of Jerusalem, and their bodies thrown over the walls, as food for the crows and wild beasts of the forest.

END OF THE HISTORY

§. *Lecture.*

Q. Are you a Grand Master Elected?

A. My zeal and my works, have procured me this Degree.

Q. By whom and where have you been received?

A. By Solomon himself, in his Audience Chamber.

Q. When did he receive you, and on what occasion?

A. When he sent me with my Companions to find the 2 other Assassins of Hiram Abiff.

Q. Was you inquiring after them yourself?

A. Yes, Most Illustrious Sovereign, and if I had not been named by Solomon, I should have gone at my own expense, to shew my zeal in revenging the death of our much respected Master.

Q. You felt then great joy when you saw the Villains executed?

A. The Three heads which I wear on my ribbon is a proof of it.

Q. What did you mean by the 3 heads?

A. The heads of the 3 Assassins of Hiram Abiff

Q. You told me just now, that you went in search of 2 Villains—how can there be three heads?

A. Because one of the 3 had already been taken, and had suffered death.

Q. What was the name of the 2 you brought to Jerusalem?

A. One was called JUBELLA GIB, and the other JUBELLO GRAVELOT.

Q. How were they discovered?

A. By the diligence of Bengabee, Solomon's Intendant in the country of Cheth.

Q. What method did Solomon take to get them?

A. He wrote a letter to MAACHAH King of Cheth, desiring him to make a strict inquiry for them.

Q. Who carried and delivered Solomon's letter to Maacha?

A. Zerbal, Captain of the Guards.

Q. Did King Maacha hesitate to grant Solomon's request?

A. No, on the contrary, he gave us guides and a guard.

Q. Where were they found?

A. In a Quarry belonging to BENDACA.

Q. Who was this Bendaca?

A. On of Solomon's Intendants, who had married one of his daughters.

Q. How came these 2 Ruffians to be discovered?

A. By means of a Shepherd, who shewed us their retreat.

Q. Who perceived them first?

A. Zerbal and, after five days inquiry.

Q. How were their chains made?

A. In the form of a rule, square and mallet, on which was engraved Crimes, and the punishment they were to suffer, according to Solomon's order.

Q. On what day did you return with them to Jerusalem?

A. The 15th of the month THAMUZ which answers to our July.

Q. how many Masters were elected by Solomon to go on this Expedition?

A. 15 in all, of which number I was one.

Q. Was there nobody else with you?

A. Yes, King Solomon sent troops to escort us.

Q. What did you do with the ruffians after your arrival at Jerusalem?

A. We carried them directly into the presence of Solomon.

Q. What orders did Solomon give?

A. After reproaching them with the enormity of their Crimes, he ordered Achizas, Grand Master of his household, to confine them in the Tower, which bore his name—that they should be executed the next morning at 10 o'clock.

Q. What kind of death did they suffer?

A. They were tied, naked, by the neck and heels to posts, and their bellies cut open, lengthwise and across.

Q. Did they continue any time in that situation?

A. They were exposed in this manner for 8 hours in the hot sun, that the venomous flies and other insects, might suck their blood, which made them suffer, even more than death itself. They made such lamentable cries and complains, that they even moved their executioners.

Q. What did they do afterwards with them?

A. The Executioner moved by their cries, cut off their heads, and threw their bodies over the walls of Jerusalem.

Q. What did they do with their heads?

A. The fixed them on poles by order of Solomon, and exposed them to public view with that of Akirop, as an example to the people of the city and the workmen of the Temple.

Q. What was the name of the 1st Villain?

A. According to the Elected of 9 they call him ABYRAM, but that word is only an emblem, as it signifies either Villain or Assassin, his right name is JUBELLUM AKIROP, and was the eldest of the Brothers.

Q. On which gate were the heads exposed?

A. On the South, East and West gates. That of Akirop on the East Gate, that of Jubello Gravellot on the West Gate, and that of Jubella Gibs on the South Gate.

Q. For what reason were they thus exposed?

A. Because each of them had committed their crimes at these gates of the Temple. For when Jubella Gibs at the South Gate, had stuck Hiram Abiff with a 24 inch gauge, Jubello Gravellot, struck him with a square at the West gate, and Jubellum Akirop, made the finishing blow with a setting maul at the East gate, which killed our respectable Master Hiram Abiff.

Q. What is the word of the Grand Master Elected?

A. ZERBAL.

Q. What is the pass word?

A. ELOHIM, by which you enter the Chapter.

Q. What are the signs?

A. *(Here he gives the signs.)*

Q. What are the Tokens?

A. *(Here he gives the Tokens.)*

Q. What signifies the signs and Tokens?

A. That I am always ready to inflict the same punishment on those, who break their obligation, by revealing the secrets of this Degree.

Q. What's the clock?

A. Six in the Evening.

Q. Why six in the Evening?

A. Because it was at that hour when the two last assassins expired, by which the death of Hiram Abiff was revenged.

END OF THE LECTURE

§. *To Close.*

The Most Illustrious Master says—Brethren, since the death of our dear and respectable Master Hiram Abiff is revenged, by the death of his murderers, we ought to be satisfied and rest ourselves.—

He then Knocks————————*15*

The Inspector————————*15*

Then all the Brethren————*15 and* the Chapter is closed.

FINIS

Apron.—*White, lined and bordered with black, with strings of the same—on the flap 3 bloody heads on poles.*

Order.—*The same as in the 9th Degree.*

Jewel.—*with a poniard at the bottom, with this difference; instead of red roses, there must be painted or embroidered on that part of the order which crossed the right breast—3 heads on poles.*

11th Degree of the First Series (1801) of the Southern
Jurisdiction of the United States of America, called

12 Illustrious Knights, or
Chapter of Sublime Knights Elected

olomon presides in this chapter. A Grand Inspector and Grand Master of Ceremonies, instead of Wardens.

The Hangings of this chapter, the same as the 10th Degree, and lighted by 24 Lights.

Apron.—Apron White, lined and bordered black, and black strings. On the flap a flaming heart.

Order.—Broad black ribbon, from the right shoulder to the left hip. A flaming heart, painted or embroidered, on that part, which crosses the breast.

Jewel.—The Jewel is a sword of Justice suspended at the bottom of the order.

In all Lodges, Chapters &c. where Solomon presides, he must use a scepter, instead of the hammer of Hiram.

§. *To Open.*

The Thrice Puissant knocks 12 at equal distances, and is only answered by the Grand Inspector.

T.P.   What's the clock?

G.I.   It is twelve.

T.P.   It is now time to improve our labor by the Influence of the Greatest Light. This Chapter is open.

§. *Form of Reception.*

The Grand Master of Ceremonies goes out to the Candidate, and knocks 12 at the door, which, is answered by the Thrice Puissant, and then by the Grand Inspector, who goes to the door and demands—Who is there?

The Grand Master of Ceremonies answers—There is a Grand Master Elected of 15, who demands to enter into the Chapter of Illustrious Knights.

The Grand Inspector, reports this to the Thrice Puissant, who gives orders to introduce him, decorated with the Jewel, order &c. of his last Degree. He is then carried to the Grand Inspector, who examines him in all this former Degrees.

The Thrice Puissant asks
Q. What does the Grand Master of 15 want?
A. To be admitted to the Degree of Illustrious Knight, and to be recompensed for his labor and travels.
Q. I suppose my Brother you travel, with the sole view of Advancing your interest?

Candidate answers—My first view is, to do my duty, which I have done to the best of my abilities, and at my own expense to punish all traitors, and now I humbly solicit the recompense for honor.

The Thrice Puissant then says—Come and contract your

§. *Obligation.*

I — — do most solemnly and sincerely swear and promise, on the Holy Bible, never to reveal, either directly or indirectly the secrets of this Degree, nor receive any person into it, without full permission first had and obtained for that purpose from my superiors, nor to assist at any such reception, unless in a regular Chapter of this Degree, that I will be charitable to all my Brethren, and in failure of this my obligation, I consent to have my body opened perpendicularly and be exposed for 8 hours in the open air, that the venomous flies may feed on my entrails, my head to be cut off, and stuck on the highest pinnacle of the world, and always inflict the same punishment on those, who should disclose this Degree, and break their obligation. So God maintain me. Amen.

He kisses the Book.

§. *Sign, Token & Words.*

Sign.—The Sign is, To cross both your hands close upon your breast, your fingers clinched, and the thumbs upright.

Token.—The Token is to take each others thumb, and turn them reciprocally, and say, as in the Intimate Secretary, BERITH, the other NEDER, when the first answers SELEMOUTH.

Pass Word.—The Pass Word is EMETH, which signifies TRUTH, or a true man on all occasions.

Secret Word.—The Secret Word is, ADONAI, which signifies Supreme Lord of the Universe.

§. *History.*

After inflicting vengeance on the 3 Assassins of Hiram Abiff Solomon, in order to recompense the zeal and constancy of the 15 Grand Masters Elected, by giving them a higher Degree, that he might be enabled to raise some other deserving Brethren, from the lower Degrees, to that of Grand Master Elected. He created 12 out the 15, Illustrious Knights by ballot, that he might not give offense to any. All the names were put into an urn, and with the first twelve, that were drawn from thence, he formed a Grand Chapter, and placed them over the 12 Tribes of Israel. He gave them the name of Excellent Emeth, a Hebrew word signifying, a true man on all occasions, and shewed them the precious things in the Tabernacle, in which was deposited the tables of the laws, which were written by God, and given to Moses, near the Burning Bush on Mount Sinai.

He then decorated them with a broad black ribbon, on which was embroidered a flaming heart, and a sword of Justice was suspended therefrom.

These are, my Illustrious Brother, the chief objects in our draft, which you should make the constant subject of you reflections.

We flatter ourselves, as you have so fine a filed pointed out to you, for reflection, that you will pursue it, leaving those dangerous paths, which seduce you from the many great and important duties, which you have to fulfill.

The execution of them will be more easy, as your heart hath already felt the Justice and necessity of it. In short, keeping firm to your obligations and faithful to your promises, we shall find in you, a Brother, Zealous and Charitable, and worthy to bear the name of a Sublime Elected Knight which you have received.

§. *Lecture.*

Q. Are you an Elected Knight?

A. My name will convince you.

Q. What is your name?

A. Emeth is my name and profession.

Q. How many Illustrious Knights are in a Chapter?

A. There can by no more than 12, who compose the 12 Commanders over the 12 Tribes of Israel.

Q. Give me the Sign?

A. (*He gives it.*)

Q. Give me the Token?

A. (*He gives it.*)

Q. What signifies your signs?

A. That my faith is immovable, and my Trust in God.

Q. What did you see on entering the Chapter?

A. Twenty four Lights.

Q. What do they signify?

A. The 12 Masters Elected, and the 12 Tribes over which they presided, when building the Temple.

Q. What are the names of the 12 Masters Elected?

A. JOABERT, STOKIN,   TERCY

ZABUD,   ALQUEBART,   DORSON

KERIM,   BERTHEMER, and   TITO,

these were the 9 Masters Elected, who went with the stranger in search of Akirop, ZERBAL, BENACHARD, TABOR are the other 3, to complete the number of the 12 Masters Elected.

Q. Over what tribes, had these the Inspection?

A. Joabert over the tribe of ---Judah
   Stokin ----------------------Benjamin
   Tercy -----------------------Simeon
   Zabud-----------------------Ephraim
   Alquebart--------------------Manassah
   Dorson ----------------------Zebulon
   Kerim-----------------------Dan
   Berthemer-------------------Asher
   Tito ------------------------Naphthali
   Zerbal----------------------Reuben
   Benachard-------------------Issachar and
   Tabor ----------------------God.

These Masters superintended the working of the Tribes, paid them their wages, and rendered daily, an account of their proceedings to Solomon.

Q. Do the 24 Lights allude to any things else?

A. To the 12 princes of Solomon, and their governments, who furnished subsistence to the Workmen, and the Kings Household.

Q. What are the names, and the countries over which they preside?

A. HUR—the son of Hur, Intendant General in Mount Ephraim.

   ABINIDAB—Son of Abinidab, in the Reign of Dor, he was married to Taphath, Solomon's daughter.

   HESED—Son of Hesed, in Aruboth and all Hepher &c.

   DEKAR—Son of Dekar, in making Beth-shemesh &c.

   BAANA—Son of Ahihud in Taannach Megedo &c.

   AHINIDAB—Son of Iddo, in Mahanaim &c.

   AHIMAAZ was in Naphthali, he was married to Basmath Solomon's daughter.

   BAANAH—Son of Hushai, in Asher, Aloth &c.

   JEHOSHAPHAT—Son of Paruah in Issachar.

   SHIMER—Son of Elah in Benjamin.

   GEBER—Son of Uri, in the Country of Gilead &c.

Q. Give me the pass word?

A. EMETH.

Q. What signifies that word?

A. A true man on all occasions.

Q. Give me the Holy Word?

A. ADONAI—which signifies supreme Lord of all.

Q. Why is the Chapter sometimes open until midnight?

A. As some of the Sublime Knights are employed during the day, in their different avocations, and others of them being engaged in deeds of Charity and Benevolence, they meet at midnight to give an account of what they have done.

Q. Why is the Chapter closed at the dawning of day.

A. To execute such business, as be ordered by the Chapter.

END OF THE LECTURE

§. *To Close.*

Q. Are you an elected Sublime Knight?

A. My name will inform you.

Q. AMETH.

A. What is the meaning of that word?

Q. A true man on all occasions.

A. At what time do you close the Chapter?

Q. At the dawning of day.

A. What's the Clock?

Q. The day appears.

T.P.— As the day appears, give notice the chapter of Sublime Knight Elected is closed— *He then strikes 12— which is repeated by the Inspector— And the Chapter is closed.*

FINIS

12ᵗʰ Degree of the First Series (1801) of the Southern Jurisdiction of the United States of America, called
● ● ●
Grand Master Architect
⸸

This Chapter must be decorated with white, and red flames. The five orders of Architecture. In the North an Illuminated Star, and under it a table, on which is a case of Mathematical Instruments. Seven Stars around the Chapter, arranged as nearly as possible, in the form of the URSA MAJOR.

Solomon presides, adorned with the Jewels of perfection.— On the altar before his is a case of Mathematical Instruments.

Every Grand Master Architect must have a case of Mathematical Instruments.

Apron.—The Apron is white lined and bordered with black — on the flap must be painted a Compass, square and rule, formed in a triangle.

Order.—The order is a broad blue watered ribbon, from the left shoulder to the right hip, from which is suspended the

Jewel.—which is a gold square medal, on one side of which must be engraved 4 half circles, around 9 stars in each angle of the square—and in the center, a triangle with *AG* therein.— And on the other side must be engraved the 5 orders of Architecture, on the top a level, and below a square and compass across—in the middle of the square and compass R.M. the first and last letter of the word RABONIM.

§. *To Open.*

The Most Powerful strikes 1 and 2—the two Wardens repeat the same.

Q. Brother Warden do your duty.

A. Grand Master Architect, the Chapter is well tyled, and the profane cannot penetrate into our mysteries.

Q. Are you an Architect?

A. I know what is contained in a perfect case of Mathematical Instruments.

Q. What is contained in it?

A. A simple compass, a compass with 5 points, a parallel rule, a drawing pen, a scale or compass of proportion, a protractor, having engraved on it 180 Degrees.

Q. Where was you received an Architect?

A. In a white place figured with flames.

Q. What do the white and the flames mean?

A. The white signifies the purity of the heart, and the flames the zeal of the Master Architects ought to be possessed of.

Q. What does the Star in the North mean?

A. That Virtue should guide every Mason in his actions as the North star guide the mariner in their Navigation.

Q. What's the clock?

A. Lucifer, Morning Star.

Most Powerful—Since it is so, my dear Brethren, let us work. *He then strikes 1 and 2—the Wardens repeat the same.*

The Grand Master Architect then says—This Chapter is Open.

§. *Form of Reception.*

The Candidate must be decorated with the ornaments of the Sublime Elected Knights. The Grand Master of Ceremonies, knocks 1 and 2 on the door, on which he enters the Chapter with the Candidate, who goes immediately from the West to the South, where he remains for a minute or two, admiring the Star in the North. He then returns to the West, where he is interrogated in his former Degrees, by the Senior Warden, he is then ordered to take 3 square steps—first one—Then two quick, which brings him to the altar, where he kneels and takes the following

§. *Obligation.*

I —— Sublime Elected of the 12 tribes of Israel, do most solemnly and sincerely swear and promise to God, and this Chapter of Grand Master Architects, never to reveal, either directly or indirectly, the secrets of this Degree, which I am now about to receive, but to a true and lawful Grand Master Architect, knowing him to be such, and that, I never will give my consent, to receive or admit, any Candidate to these mysteries, but those whom I conscientiously believe, will be conformable to the laws, statutes, and the secret constitutions of the order. I do furthermore swear to pay due Obedience to all the regulations which may be given or sent to me from the Grand Council of Princes of Jerusalem, and if I fail in any of these my present engagements, I consent to suffer all the penalties which I have imposed upon myself, by my former obligations, my name to be wrote in red letters, and hung up in the Chapter, that posterity may remember me as an infamous and perfidious man. God grant that I may walk in righteousness and equity.—

Amen — Amen — Amen.

(He kisses the Bible.)

After this, the Most powerful gives the following

§. *Discourse.*

My dear Brother, Solomon determined to form a school of Architecture, for the instruction of those, who conducted the works of the Temple, to encourage and improve true Masons in the Sublime Sciences, and to promote from that school those, whose zeal and discretion should make them deserving of the highest perfection. For this purpose he created the 12th Degree, under the title of Grand Master Architect.

King Solomon, full of Justice, foreseeing the events, which were likely to take place was willing to recompense the zeal, knowledge and Virtue of the Sublime Knights Emeth, that they might approach nearer to the Celestial Throne of the Grand Architect of the Universe. This foresight made him cast his eyes upon those who were last made Illustrious Knights and Brothers in order to effect the promise which God had made to Enoch, Noah, Moses and David, that if through ardor, they penetrated the bowels of the earth, it would not avail, unless Divine providence permitted it.

The attachment which I make no doubt, you will evince in the study of Geometry, will procure you the means of unfolding the most sublime knowledge.

The Candidate is then ordered to walk to the Senior Warden, with 3 steps as before, to learn the Sign, Token and Word. After he has made the 1st step, he stops to admire the Star in the North, and then retreats 3 steps back, as if he was surprised at its brilliance, he then makes the other 2 steps, which brings him to the Warden.

§. *Sign, Token & Words.*

Sign.—Strike or slide your right hand over the inside of your left hand, then stop a little, the slide twice, somewhat quicker, the fingers close, and thumbs extended, after this you do as if you were drawing a plan with the right hand in the left, looking often at the Grand Master Architect, for a subject to draw your plan by.

Token.—Interlace the fingers of your right hand with the left of a Brother, at the same time, both placing their left hands on their hip.

Pass Word.—Is RAB BONE, that is, I am a Master builder, or Master Stone Cutter.

Sacred Word.—Is ADONAI, which is the 1st name of God.

Then the Senior Warden decorates him with the order and Jewel, and clothes him with the Apron, Embraces him, and wishes him joy upon his acquisition of this sublime Degree. He also tells him to go to the Grand Master Architect, and give him the Sign, Token and Word, and from thence to all the Brethren, after which he takes his seat and listens attentively to the following

§. *Lecture.*

Q. Which is the first of all the Arts?

A. Architecture, of which geometry is the key, as well as of all the sciences.

Q. How many kinds of Architecture are there?

A. Three, Civil, Naval, and Military—

Civil Architecture is the art of building houses, palaces, temples, Altars &c in order to decorate and embellish cities. Naval Architecture is the art of building ships of war, and all other kinds of Vessels of Navigation. Military Architecture is the art of fortifying cities, towns, &c. to sustain the attacks of greater numbers with less, and to throw up the works in such a manner, that they cannot be cut through, to strengthen them with trenches and outworks, in short, Military Architecture teaches us, to improve all the advantages, which the natural situation of places afford, to erect works which are easily defended, while at the same time, they are impenetrable to the assailants. In the art of Civil Masonry, it is only necessary for the Masters to be acquainted, with Civil Architecture, the other two, serve only as attributes to the Masons, but if possessed of a knowledge of them, it will evince their zeal and attachment to the Sciences.

Q. Which are the Sciences that a perfect Master Architecture ought to possess?

A. There are several which have a connection with each other, and cannot be dispensed with, if you wish to exercise Architecture in all its branches. Thus a Grand Master Architect ought to possess the following— vizt.

1st	Arithmetic	11th	Hydraulics
2nd	Geometry	12th	Geography
3rd	Trigonometry	13th	Chronology
4th	Optics	14th	Cutting of Stone
5th	Catoptrics	15th	Cutting of Wood
6th	Dioptricks	16th	Measure
7th	Designing	17th	Physics
8th	Perspective	18th	Music
9th	Mechanics	19th	Architecture
10th	Statics		

Q. What is Arithmetic, and in what manner does it serve a Mason?

A. It is the art of calculating, and is called Arabe, because the characters we make use of, come to us from the Arabians—and what we call Algebra, is also Arithmetic, but greatly abridged, and is not much likes, particularly by those who are not Masters of it, but those who have a perfect knowledge of it, delight in the use of it, as it affords the means of finding the incomprehensible quantities, unknown proportions and their roots, with much more case, and in short, to resolve by a little work, all the problems of Geometry. The Algebraic characteristics are $+ = V \Lambda$ more, less, equal, greater, smaller, &c. You may make use of the first letters of the Alphabet for the known quantities, and the last for the unknown, Arithmetic is the attribute of a good Mason, because it teaches him to multiply his benevolence and knowledge to all his Brethren and to look upon any recompense, as a cipher of Arithmetic, as he had only discharged a duty he owed to himself in doing a good action.

Q. What is Geometry, and why is that science an attribute to Masons?

A. Geometry is the first of the Sciences, founded on the preceding one, it came from the Egyptians, who were much embarrassed in the bounds of their lands, after every inundation of the River Nile, from which circumstance was suggested the discovery of Measure and limits, upon just and given principles, whereby they might ascertain their respective bounds, when the waters subsided. This art was called by the Greeks *Geometras*, or measure of land, so that geometry is the art of measuring land, on the surface or superfices but not solids, but from this is derived the art of measuring solids, having several superfices. That is to say, Height and depth. Geometry is an attribute of a good Mason, as he ought continually to measure his actions with the line of Justice, to circumscribe his desires by the bounds or reason, and be content with his portion of property, and not infringe on that of neighbor, that he may render Glory to the Grand Architect of the Universe, and be an example of virtue to his Brethren.

Q. Is Trigonometry also necessary, and is it an attribute of Masonry?

A. Yes, Grand Architect, this sciences is inseparable from the preceding, by it we measure angles, Tangents and secants, and by a knowledge of Triangles we find the ineffable measure of the unknown sides, Arithmetic and Algebra.

The discovery of this art, we owe to Pythagoras. The most essential explanation of the problems of Trigonometry, are cited in the 1st proposition of Euclid. This learned philosopher, sacrificed one hundred Oxen to the Gods, in acknowledgment of the discovery, he would have deserved applause among the Masons, if he had not been an Idolater. Trigonometry is rather an attribute belonging to the Grand Architect of the Universe; than to a Mason. All our actions put in signs, will form a triangle, of which two sides only will present themselves to our conscience, viz the Good and Evil but the Grand Architect of the Universe will find the other, and judge us in the aggregate.

Q. Of what do the Sciences of Opticks, Catoptrics, and Dioptrics treat, and how are they attributes of Masonry?

A. They treat of the reflection and refraction of the rays of light, and of the Science of Vision generally, both natural and artificial. They are attributes to masons, because every man should look at his own faults, with glasses which enlarge the object, and in viewing the faults of his Brothers, he should use glasses, which diminish and remove them.

Q. We know what drawing or designing is, but how are they likewise attributes of Masonry?

A. As the most perfect design, has been began by a sketch, so should Masons when they find any good qualities in a Brother, acknowledge him as a sketch. After which they should copy, and complete the picture of perfection. By imitating, the actions of a virtuous Brother, you render him honor, and yourself respectable.

Q. What is perspective, and how an attribute of Masonry?

A. perspective is the art of delineating objects in accurate proportion and color. So should Masons, setting out from the point of Virtue, observe a relative proportion and connection in all their actions and pursuits. As in a well drawn perspective, let their conduct in the foreground of their lives, be brilliant in the cause of Virtue, and as they retreat into the background of the piece, or sink into the gulf of time, the sweet recollection of a well spent life, will soften the pillow of death, and give them the sweet pledge of enjoying happiness hereafter.

Q. Let us go to Mechanics—

A. Mechanics is the science of motion, or the art of Machinery, by which we carry and raise to the most elevated places, burdens of great weight, with little seeming strength and by the aid of few people, by Levers, Vices, Rollers, Cranes &c.— By this art is constructed Mills, Clocks, Jacks &c. which receive motion by wheels, springs, weights &c. The great spring of a Mason, is in the heart. Here the first causes of his actions rise, and here the first impulse of his morals are felt. If he is so fortunate as to make Virtue the primum mobile of his pursuits, and adjusts with nice proportion, the equilibrium of his weights, and gives a due impulse to his moving powers. He may expect to receive that happiness which the Grand Architect of the Universe has promised to those who shall deserve it.

Q. Of what use is statics to Masons?

A. Statics has a connection with the science of mechanics, and is the knowledge of weights and moving forces, the art of steelyards and balances &c. The judgment of a Mason, should be preserved in so just an equilibrium, that no consideration of Interest or party spirit can make him deviate from Equity and Justice.

Q. What is Hydraulics and of what use to Masons?

A. It is the art of conducting, governing and draining water, necessary for the health and life of our fellow creatures, as well as for the purposes of Commerce, and to embellish palaces, gardens, &c. which a professor of this art conducts scientifically, through canals or pipes, and collect it, in Basins or Reservoirs for the several purposes for which he wants it. An Architect knows how to drain by canals, fields or meadows for Agriculture, and by cutting canals through the highest mountains, is enabled to connect together remote seas, for the purposes of Commerce and Navigation. In short by the use of Hydraulics we can convert into a place of elegance and pleasure, mud pool or a desert. The minds of Masons should be as brilliant canals, flowing with sweetness and ease, and not as remote seas separated by mountains, like two Brothers, whose affections are sometimes divided by misrepresentations, jarring interests or by the follies of youth— 'till some Mediator, generally, penetrates and divides the obstacles which separate them, and unites them together in the firm bond of reciprocal affection.

Q. What is Geography, and of what use to a Mason?

A. Geography is the knowledge and description of the Earth, comprising every place by Land or Sea, inhabited or uninhabited, of capital cites and inferior towns and villages, of every Kingdom and nation, of the rivers which water them, and of the seas which wash their shores; of the mountains which separate them, and in short of every thing which you see delineated on the face of a map or on the Terrestrial Globe. Though Masonry is the same in every part of the Earth, yet there are many Temples in divers places, where Masons Assemble to work at their mysteries, under the same statutes, and to sing the praises of the Eternal God. These Temples we call Lodges and Chapters, and a good Mason should possess a knowledge of Geography, that he may know where the different Lodges are held, that he may be able to correspond with them, to improve himself by their labor and talents, and render them the honor due to their merit.

Q. Do you know Chronology in the number of indispensable sciences to an Architect Mason?

A. Chronology being the science and knowledge of past events. A Mason should be possessed of it, that he may be ready to name those Masons, who have distinguished themselves since the Creation of the World; of Kings, Princes and Pontiffs, and all those in power who have supported Masonry, with honor to the Craft, and reputation to themselves, the various events and revolutions which Masonry has undergone, which should serve as a lesson to our patience, constancy and Resolution.

Q. What do you mean by cutting in Stone?

A. I mean the most essential science to a Mason, which is the art of describing by means of the square, all the stones which are to compose and edifice, so that when the workmen begin to lay them, they will be found, exactly to correspond, and require no alteration. No man, in any academy in the world, can attain the knowledge and conduction of an Architect, if he has not, himself, cut, dressed and fixed his stones. Thus in the Royal Art of Masonry, no Brother can attain the eminent Degree of Grand Master Architect, who has not disposed his heart to the cause of Virtue, and becomes himself one of the materials in the edification of the Temple, dedicated to the only true and living God.

Q. What do you mean by cutting in wood?

A. The only difference between cutting in stone and in wood, is in the materials. The timber should be ready prepared before it is brought into the edifice, that when they are going to use it. They will find the pieces correspond, and the points exactly adapted to each other. So should a Mason, in the right propriety of his conduct towards a Brother, endear himself to his affections, which forms the junction of Masons. The exactness and unanimity of their deliberations, the brightness of their works, and their sweet and innocent pleasures should always be in unison.

Q. What is measure?

A. As an Architect is always to be the Judge of Masons, he ought to know, by measuring their works, what pay is due to them for their labor—he must also measure the materials, to pay the provider agreeably to the quantity, and no Intendant of the Building can pay a farthing, but by order of a Grand Master Architect. For that reason, a Mason, who has attained by his knowledge, the measure in hand, should view it, as the center of Justice and benevolence, and for the use of which, he must render an account to the Grand Architect of the Universe, who will judge him accordingly.

Q. How can physic be of any use to a Grand Master Architect?

A. That he may be able to determine on the salubrity of a place before he erects his buildings, to avoid muddy or marshy places or stagnant waters—and arrange the windows in such a manner, that they may receive those winds, which bear health upon their wings. A Mason also, should physically vanquish, the difficulties, which an inordinate stomach, oppose to his health, and if he should be of a weak habit of body, prudently to deprive himself of some pleasures, which are prejudicial to him, though not to others.

Q. Of what use can Music be in Masonry and to an Architect?

A. The knowledge of Music was very necessary to and Architect in the time of the Ancient Romans, in constructing Saloons, Rotunda's and other places, in which was performed Vocal and instrumental music, for which reason, those Architects must have understood Music, as they placed Columns, vaults, ceilings &c. and even brass vessels in some places to produce an echo, and increase the sound and harmony of the performance. But in the present day, those buildings are made less, which presents the necessity of increasing the sound by art, the Ceilings are proportional to the extent of the rooms, by which the vibrations are kept at the required distance. Music is considered as an attribute of Masons, for as the harmony of the different sounds elevate the generous sentiments of the soul, so should concord reign among our Brethren, that by the sweet unison of friendship, the boisterous passions may be lulled and harmony reign throughout all the craft.

_Q._ Are these all the sciences, which a Mason should be possessed of?

_A._ Mathematics is a general term, by which one may comprehend, a great many other sciences, besides those, I have already given an account of. This term is also an attribute of a Mason, for when he says, he is Master of the Mathematics, it signifies, that he has a heart zealous in the cause of Masonry, and that, as he increases in knowledge, he will increase in Virtue.

_Q._ How many orders of Architecture are there?

_A._ There are 5; The Tuscan, Doric, Ionic, Corinthian and Composite.

_Q._ What difference is there in these orders?

_A._ The Tuscan and Doric, are the most revealed, and the less adorned, the Corinthian and Composite, are the finest and most adorned, and the Ionic is more adorned than the 2 first, but less than the two last. —

_Q._ Are there any other kinds of Architecture?

_A._ An infinite number—Viz^t—the Tostille, the Presstille, the DeEstille, the Lamphi prostile, the Pirintore &c. &c. and a vast many others.

_Q._ On what depends the stile of building?

_A._ On the proportion of the Columns, their distance according to their magnitude, the ornaments of niches, panels &c., in short, the standing rules of true Architecture must be adhered to, when raising a building, that it may appear elegant.

_Q._ You have told me my Brother, that Naval and Military Architecture, are necessary attributes of a Mason, how can that be?

A. They both are attributes, because masons should work at Sea, as well as upon land for the promotion of the Royal Craft, and the relief of his Brethren, and in Military point of view, he should serve as a rampart for Masons who are attacked.

Q. Did King Solomon possess a knowledge of the Science of Mathematics?

A. Without doubt, since the Grand Architect of the Universe, was graciously pleased to give him that wisdom, for which he was called the wisest Kings, and especially as God had chosen him to build a Temple to his name.

Q. What is the great attribute of a Grand Master Architect?

A. It is a case of Mathematical Instruments, in a small compass, which contains all the instruments necessary for the various designs, an Architect may invent.

Q. Explain these instruments and their uses to me?

A. The simple compass serves to take dimensions, dividing lines in equal parts, denote parallels, to make sections of triangles, equiangular and equilateral, in short, it may be used in an infinite number of Mathematical problems, too long to enumerate, but its use is well known to Mathematicians, and being the principle instrument in Mathematics, it is worn as a Jewel, by the Grand Master of a Symbolic Lodge of Masters. There is another Compass with five points, of which one is moveable and may be altered as occasion requires. This Compass serves to draw circles or parts of Circles, the immovable point being always the point or Center. On different occasion you may use a pencil, a drawing pen or a roller, on the moveable point. The Compass of proportion, is a solid rule, and is an instrument of great importance to an Architect. It saves an infinite deal of trouble, as the calculations of every operation are marked on it. It is a general table in which you will find a scale of parts, the planes, the polygons, the chords of solids, the weights of metals and of bullets, with their sizes &c. &c. The line of equal parts serves to divide a line pursuant to a line given; the line of planes, to diminish or increase it to his mind. The line of polygons is to describe a circle, or regular polygon of such numbers of planes or angles; the solid lines, to increase or diminish a solid, according to a reason given; the line, for metals to know the difference and proportion between six metals. The parallel rule and drawing pen are two instruments which must be used together, to draw a strait line which is also an attribute of Masons, as a Mason's conduct should always be fair and strait, and his inclinations should coincide with his duty and be connected together as these two instruments.

The protractor or Quadrate is generally is generally made of brass, and is used in opening of angles, to take their height, and to divide the roses of the simple Compass. This is the Jewel of a Perfect Master, which makes him who wear it, remember, never to make use of it on any occasion except he has a point of perfection in view.

END OF LECTURE

§. *To Close the Chapter.*

Q. Give me the Sign of a Grand Master Architect?

A. *He gives it, drawing a plan in his hand. Then the Grand master Architect opens his case of mathematical instruments, and says—*"Let us work," *when he arranges all the instruments on the table before him and puts his left hand on the Compass of proportion, and leaning on his right hand says—*

Q. Do you know only this work?

A. I comprehend another.

Q. Give me the Token?

A. He goes to the Grand Master and gives it.

Q. Give me the Pass Word?

A. RA.

Q. Go on.

A. Bo.

Q. Make an end.

A. NIM.

Then the Grand Master Architect makes a triangle with the Compass and says— "My Dear Brethren, we finish." *On which all the Brethren put up their instruments in their several cases and say—* "We finish."

Q. What is the Clock?

A. The beginning of night.

Then the Grand Master Architect strike 1 and 2 and says— "Give notice this Chapter is closed." *The Wardens repeat the same, and*

THE CHAPTER IS CLOSED

FINIS

BOOK 3rd

A true Copy of the M.S.S. belonging
to Ill^{trs} Brother Giles F. Yates,
R ✠ K—H, S.P.R.S. &
Sov. Gnd Ins. Genl of 33:rd—A.L. 5833

13th Degree of the first Series (1801) of the Southern Jurisdiction of the United States, called

♠ ♠ ♠
Royal Arch
¥

his Chapter should be holden in a most secret place. A vault under ground would be most proper, in the center of the top of which there must be a trap door, large enough to admit a man through. In the middle below, there must be a hollow triangular pedestal, the sides of which are white; on the top must be fixed a hollow cubical triangle, made of oil cloth, inside of which must be placed a light, and on the top and sides must be placed יהוה in Hebraic characters in letters of gold.

To form a chapter of this degree, five persons at least must be present. They are—

1st.—The Thrice Puissant Sublime Grand Master, representing Solomon in the East, seated in a chair of State, under a rich canopy, with a crown on his head and a scepter in his hand. He is dressed in Royal Robes of yellow, and an ermined vestment of blue satin, reaching to the Elbows; a broad purple ribbon from the right shoulder to the left hip, to which is hung a triangle of Gold.

2nd.—The Grand Warden, representing Hiram King of Tyre, on his left hand, seated as a stranger, clothed in a purple robe, and a yellow vestment.

3rd.—The Grand Inspector, representing GIBULUM in the West, with a drawn sword in his hand.

4th.—The Grand Treasurer, representing Joabert in the North, with a golden key to his fifth button hole, and upon it the letters I.V.I.L., JUVENIS VERBUM INTRE LEONIS.

5th.—The Grand Secretary, representing Stokin in the South.

The four last mentioned officers to be ornamented with the same ribbon and jewel as the M:P: and to sit covered. The three last to have robes of blue without vestments.

No person can be admitted to this degree without having previously taken all the preceding degrees.

§. *To Open.*

The Thrice Puissant knocks 9 times (3 by 3).

Hiram King of Tyre repeats the same.

The Grand Inspector calls—"To order, Brethren."

The remaining brethren repeat the 9 knocks in the same manner.

After which, the two Kings make the Sign of Admiration, and the Brethren repeat the same.

The two Kings then kneel respectfully at the pedestal. Solomon rises first, and seeing Hiram King of Tyre still kneeling, he raises him up. Then all the Brethren pay obedience on their knees, admiring the grand △ *and raising each other by the order of Solomon, who says—*"This Royal Arch Chapter is Open."

§. *Reception.*

No more than 3 candidates can be made at a time. Should there be but on applicant, two of the brethren must undergo the ceremonies with him.

They must be placed over the vault, near the trap door, and the Guard near them, who must demand of the Chapter, for the three zealous Brethren, the favor of being admitted to the degree of Royal Arch, having regularly passed their other preceding degrees.

The Guard is answered, that it is not possible for them to be received, they must offer up their petitions to God, to admit it.

On which the Guard retire, and after some time, again demands it, when they again receive a negative—they withdraw—then a third time ask the favor. [Each time they knock 3 times 3 on the door.]

The Inspector demands from within, whether the Candidates are willing to descend into the Abyss, in search of the greatest treasures. They consent, & have a rope tied round the middle of one of them, who is let down through the trap door, he is desired if he sees anything, to shake the rope, & he will be immediately hauled up. Meeting with some obstructions, they are twice hauled up. When going down the third time, a lighted taper is put into his hand, some stone & mortar is thrown down upon him, and a brother (who is placed in the vault for that purpose) suddenly blows out his light and instantly uncovers the pedestal. When the Candidate sees the illumined words, he falls on his knees, in which position he remains until the other two are introduced in a similar manner. The Grand Inspector then informs then, that they are going to receive, in that position, a solemn obligation which will unite them to our Mysteries.

§. *Obligation.*

I — — do promise and vow in the most solemn and inviolable manner, on the Holy Bible, and in the presence of the Great and only One, Most Holy, most puissant, terrible, Just and most Merciful Architect of the Universe, that I will redouble my zeal in love and friendship for my brethren who have arrived to this Royal Degree. I promise never to receive any Brother to this Royal degree, nor consent to his being received, except in a Chapter regularly established, unless permission shall have been first obtained from legal authority, or a proper patent for the same purpose. I promise never to give the word or words, except in the presence of 3 Brethren, and those being properly and previously examined. I promise never to receive, or give my consent to receive, any Brother to this Royal degree, who has not regularly passed his other degrees, and is a Member of a Regular Lodge, and has been a Master of the same, and having demonstrated his zeal, fervor and constancy in Masonry, Charity and benevolence for his Brethren. I promise to observe and keep all the laws, Rules and Regulations that shall appear, & be approved of by this Royal Chapter, and will also keep inviolably secret, every transaction of this Chapter with its Bye-laws. I further promise that I will never lay with the wife of my Brother, nor dishonor his mother, Sister, nor any female of his family; and in failure of this, I hereby consent to receive in this place, the whole tenor of all my former obligations, with this condition, that my body shall be exposed to the wild beasts of the Forest, for their food. So God maintain me in my present obligation with Equity and Justice.

Amen. Amen. Amen. Amen.

§. *History.*

My worthy Brethren, it is my intention at this time to give you a clearer account than you have yet been acquainted with, of Masonry; of which you at present barely know the elements.

In doing this it will be necessary to explain to you some circumstances of very remote antiquity.

Enoch, the son of Jared, was the sixth son in descent from Adam, and lived in the fear and love of his maker; God appeared to him in a vision, and thus deigned to speak to him: As thou art desirous to know my name, attend, and it shall be revealed unto thee. Upon this, a mountain seemed to rise to the heavens, and Enoch was transferred to the top thereof, where he beheld a triangular plate of gold, most brilliantly-enlightened, and upon which were some characters which he received a strict injunction never to pronounce.— Presently he seemed to be lowered perpendicularly into the bowels of the earth, through nine arches; in the ninth, or deepest of which, he saw the same brilliant plate which was shewn to him in the mountain.

Enoch, being inspired by the Most High, and in commemoration of this wonderful vision, built a temple under ground, in the same spot where it was shewn to him, which like that consisted of nine arches, one above another; and dedicated the same to God. Methusaleh, the son of Enoch, constructed the building without being acquainted with his father's motives.

This happened in that part of the world which was afterwards called the land of Canaan, and since known by the name of the Holy Land.

Enoch, in imitation of what he had seen, caused a triangular plate of gold to be made, each side of which was a cubit long; he enriched it with the most precious stones, and encrusted the plate upon a stone of Agate, of the same form. He then engraved upon it the same ineffable characters which God had shewn to him, and placed it on a triangular pedestal of white marble, which he deposited in the ninth, or deepest arch.

When Enoch's temple was completed, he received the following command, viz.—"Make a door of stone, and let there be a ring of iron therein, by which it may be occasionally raised; and let it be placed over the opening of the first arch, that the sacred matters enclosed therein may be preserved from the universal destruction now impending." And he did so, and none but Enoch knew of the precious treasure which the arches contained; nor knew the right pronunciation of the great and sacred name יהוה.

And behold the wickedness of mankind increased more, and became grievous in the sight of the Lord, and God threatened to destroy the whole world. Enoch perceiving that the knowledge of the arts was likely to be lost in the general destruction, and being desirous of preserving the principles of the sciences, for the posterity of those whom God should be pleased to spare, he built two great pillars on the top of the highest mountain, the one of brass, to withstand water, the other of marble, to withstand fire; and he engraved on the marble pillar, hieroglyphics, signifying that there was a most precious treasure concealed in the arches under ground, which he had dedicated to God. And he engraved on the pillar of brass the principles of he liberal arts, particularly of Masonry.

Methuselah was the father of Lamech, who was the father of Noah, who was a pious and good man, and beloved by God. And the Lord spake unto Noah, saying, "Behold I will punish the sins of mankind with a general deluge; therefore build an Ark, capable of containing thyself and family, as also a pair of every living creature upon earth, and those only shall be saved from the general destruction which I am about to inflict, for the iniquities of the people."—

And God gave unto Noah a plan by which the ark was to be constructed. Noah was one hundred years in building the ark; he was six hundred years old when it was finished, and his son Seth was ninety-nine. His father Lameth had died a short time before, aged 777 years. There was not at this time any of the ancient patriarchs living, save Methuselah, the grand father of Noah, who was about 969 years old, and it is supposed that he perished in the general ruin.

The ark being finished, Noah, agreeable to the instructions he had received from the Most High, went into it with his family, and took with him such things as he was commanded.

The flood took place in the year of the world 1656 and destroyed most of the superb monuments of antiquity. The marble pillar of Enoch fell in the general destruction; but by divine permission, the pillar of brass withstood the water, by which means the ancient state of the liberal arts, and particularly Masonry, has been handed down to us.

We learn from holy writ, the history of succeeding times, till the Israelites became slaves to the Egyptians; from which bondage they were freed under the conduct of Moses. We also learn from the Annals deposited in the Archives of Scotland, that in a certain battle, the Ark of Alliance was lost in a forest and was happily recovered by the roaring of a Lion, who couched at the approach of the Israelites—and who had destroyed a number of the Egyptians who attempted to carry it away.— He had kept in his mouth the key of the Ark, and which he dropt at the approach of the High Priest, retiring to a distance without offering any violence to the chosen people.

The sacred Bible also informs us, that Moses was beloved of God, and that the Most High, spoke to him on Mount Sinai, in the B.B. To Moses God communicated his divine law, written on tables of stone; with many promises of a renewed alliance. He also gave him the true pronunciation of his sacred name; which he told him should be found by some of his descendants, engraved upon a plate of gold. It was at this time that Moses replied "Who art thou?" and God said יהוה is my true name, that is, I am that I am, a strong and Jealous God, Most mighty, Puissant.— God gave a strict command unto Moses, that no one should pronounce his sacred name; so that in process of time the true pronunciation was lost.

The same divine history particularly informs us of the different movements of the Israelites, until they became possessed of the land of promise, and of the succeeding events until the divine Providence was pleased to give the scepter to

David; who, though fully determined to build a temple to the Most High, could never begin it; that honor being reserved for his son.

Solomon, being the wisest of Princes, had fully in remembrance the promise of God to Moses, that some of his descendants, in fullness of time, should discover his holy name; and his wisdom inspired him to believe, that this could not be accomplished until he had erected and consecrated a temple to the living God, in which he might deposit the precious treasures.

Accordingly, Solomon began to build, in the fourth year of his reign, agreeably to a plan given to him by David his father, upon the ark of alliance.

He chose a spot for this purpose, the most beautiful and healthy in all Jerusalem. In digging for a foundation they discovered the ruins of an ancient, edifice, amongst which they found a very considerable quantity of treasure, such as vases of gold and silver, urns, marble, porphyry, jasper and agate columns, with a number of precious stones.

All the treasures were collected and carried to Solomon, who, upon deliberation, concluded them to be the ruins of some ancient temple erected before the flood; and possibly to the service of idolatry; he therefore declined building in that spot, lest the worship of the Deity should be profaned by the place. He then made choice of another place where the Temple was erected.

You have already been informed by the history of Masonry which you have, at different times received, and by the melancholy death of our much respected Master Hiram Abiff, that the Temple of Solomon was constructed by the Craft; but there are some particulars respecting it with which you have not yet been made acquainted.

Solomon caused a Cavern to be built under the Temple, to which he gave the name of the SECRET VAULT. He erected in this vault a large pillar of white marble, to support the Sanctum Sanctorum and which by inspiration, he called the pillar of Beauty, from the beauty of the ark, which it sustained.

There was a long, narrow descent, which led from the palace of Solomon to this vault, through nine arches, in regular succession; and to this place he used to retire privately, in company with Hiram of Tyre and Hiram Abiff when they had occasion to enter upon things of a secret and important nature.

There were none else then living, qualified to enter this sacred vault. The loss of Hiram Abiff disordered their system for a time, as two were not permitted to enter the vault, there being absolutely necessary, and as they were consulting in what manner to supply his absence, application was made to them by some Intendants of the Building, Elected Knights, and Grand Master Architects, who well knew there was a secret place under the Temple, in which the King, &c. before-mentioned, used to meet, soliciting the honor of being admitted there; to whom Solomon replied with an open air "My Brethren, it cannot now be granted. God will permit you one day to arrive at the knowledge which you now solicit."

Some days after this circumstance, Solomon sent for the three Grand Master Architects, JOABERT, STOKIN, and GIBULUM, and directed them to go and search once more, amongst the Ancient ruins, where so much treasure had been already found, in hopes of discovering more. They accordingly departed, and one of them, namely Gibulum, in working with the pick-axe amongst the rubbish, came to the large iron ring, which he immediately made known to his companions, who all concluded that it might lead to some curious discovery; and accordingly they worked with redoubled ardor, to clear away the earth around it, which, when they had done, they found it fixed in a large stone, perfectly square. With much difficulty they raised it, when the mouth of a deep and dismal cavern appeared.

Gibulum proposed to them that he would descend. A rope was accordingly tied round his body, to facilitate his return—he told them, that when he shook the rope violently, they should immediately draw him up. He descended, and presently found himself in an arched vault, in the floor of which was a secret opening, through which he also descended, and in like manner through a third. Being now in the third vault, he found there was an opening for descending still farther; but being afraid to pursue his search, he gave a signal, and was hoisted up by his two companions.

He recounted to his companions what he had seen, and proposed to them to descend by turns, which they refused; upon this he determined to descend again, and told them, that through every arch he passed, he would gently shake the rope. In this manner he descended from arch to arch, until he was lowered into the sixth arch; when finding there was still another opening, his heart failed him, and, giving the signal, he was again pulled up.

He acquainted Joabert and Stokin with the particulars of his second descent, and now earnestly urged that one of them should go down, as he was very much fatigued; but, terrified at his relation, they both refused. Gibulum then receiving fresh courage, went down a third time, taking a lighted flambeau in his hand. When he had descended into the ninth arch, a parcel of stone & mortar suddenly fell in, and extinguished his light; and he was immediately struck with the sight of a triangular plate of gold, richly adorned with precious stones; the brilliancy of which struck him with admiration and astonishment, on which he made the Sign of Admiration, which was the same that Solomon and Hiram King of Tyre made to him, when he came first with his two companions, and requested to be admitted into the sublime degrees. Gibulum fell prostrate on his knees, with his right hand forming the sign of the Intimate Secretary, his left hand behind him, shaking the rope three times, his companions assisted him in re-ascending.

Gibulum related to his two companions the whole astonishing scene he had been witness to; and they now being desirous of witnessing the discovery, all concluded to go down together, by means of a rope ladder, which they made on that occasion. When they had descended into the ninth arch, Joabert and Stokin were struck with admiration and astonishment, and prostrated themselves with Gibulum. When Joabert and Stokin had recovered themselves, they got up, and seeing Gibulum still prostrate, they went and raised him, and said HAMALACH GIBULUM, (which signifies, Gibulum is a good man, or, more properly, Gibulum is an Angel) we must help him. After recovering themselves they examined the plate more particularly, and found it was encrusted by an agate of a triangular form. They also observed certain characters engraved thereon, of the meaning of which they were then ignorant; they therefore determined to carry the treasure to Solomon, and solicit the honor of being admitted to the knowledge of this sublime mystery.

Early in the morning they arrived at the apartment of Solomon, who had the King of Tyre with him. To them they presented the precious treasure they had found. When the two Kings beheld it, they were struck with amazement, and made the same Sign of Admiration to the 3 Masters, as they had made in the ninth arch, and falling down on their knees, remained some time in ecstasy. Solomon recovering from his surprise & seeing the King of Tyre still on his knees, raised him and said HAMALACH GIBULUM. They then examined the sacred characters with attention, and immediately knew them to be יהוה, but would not explain them to the three Grand Master Architects. Solomon told them that God had bestowed upon them a particular favor, in having permitted them to discover the most precious jewels of Masonry; by which he seemed to intimate their election, and as a reward for their zeal, constancy & fidelity, he elected them Knights of the Ninth Arch, afterwards called The Royal Arch. He further promised them an explanation of the sacred and mysterious name and characters of the golden plate, when it should be fixed in the place designed for it; and that he would then confer on them the most sublime and mysterious degree of Royal Arch Masonry.

Solomon then explained to them, how the promise of God, made to Noah, Moses and his father David, was now accomplished. That promise which assured them, that in fullness of time his name should be discovered, engraved upon a plate of gold; that they were bound to defend the sacred characters, and that they were not at liberty to pronounce the sacred name.

The Kings informed the three Knights, that until that time they knew nothing of that word but by tradition, and that in the course of its being handed down, through a succession of ages, it had been much corrupted; but since they were now in possession of the true characters, he would soon give them the true pronunciation, to which honor they seemed to be so justly entitled, both on account of personal merit, as also being so particularly elected by the Almighty, to finish this great work.

The sacred name of the Eternal God must never be pronounced; it must be lettered, & that with the greatest circumspection.

From the corruption of the said name, springs the Juba of the Moors, the Jupiter of the Romans, and many others of a like nature. The true name is said to have been visible in the Temple, at the time St. Jerome flourished, written in the ancient Samaritan characters, and is still preserved in the hearts of sincere Masons.

The two kings, accompanied by the three Knights, then took the sacred treasure, and descended by the private way, through nine arches, into the secret vault. They worked there together, and encrusted the golden plate upon the pedestal of the pillar of beauty, happy in being employed in so glorious a work.

After having finished the work, they prostrated themselves before the Grand Architect of the Universe, paying him homage, adoration & praise for his signal decrees in their favor.

The brilliancy of the plate and jewels were of themselves sufficient to give light to the place, and to make and mark the principal ages of Masonry, 3, 5, 7 and 9, which when multiplied by our well known calculation, makes 81, which will be more fully explained in our general instructions.

The two Kings then changed the name of the place, from the SECRET to the SACRED vault; a place known only to the Grand Elect Perfect and Sublime Masons.

It was now time to recompense the virtue of the three elected Masters and Knights of the Royal Arch, Joabert, Stokin and Gibulum; the two Kings gave the degree of Grand, Elect, Perfect, Master and Sublime Masons, explaining to them the sacred word engraved on the golden plate, that which was, and is, the name of the sacred Omnipotence, a pronunciation which has suffered much and been greatly corrupted. This is the manner of pronouncing it— remark the number of Letters which compose these words, they are the mysterious numbers of Masonry, which will be explained to you in the degree of Perfection.

The names of the syllables which compose the mysterious name are as follows.

3	JUB.	All Puissant.
3	JEA.	Divine Light.
3	JNO.	Striking Light.[1]
5	HOYAH.	It is, that it will be.
5	GOTHA.	God himself alone.
5	JEEVA.	God eternal.
7	JEKINAI.	O God by your great force that we may aid & assist each other.
7	ADOUNAI.	O you that is eternal.
7	JEHOVAH.	Brilliant God.
9	ELINIHAM.	Mercy of God or God my Comforter.
9	JEHABULUM.	In God is my faith.
9	יהוה	The Grand name, I am that
72		I am The Lord Almighty.

The last is the appellation which you will know when you are initiated into the degree of Perfection. This mysterious word is covered by 3 pass words, 6 covered words, and by 3 touches, preceding the figurative signs, before you arrive at the true one.

The three newly elected Masters took their obligations before God, never to pronounce openly the sacred word—and, never to admit any Mason, to this sublime degree, who had not given proofs of his zeal and attachment to the Craft and always to use the same ceremony in commemorating the mysterious history of the divine יהוה was the Burning Bush where God made the Patriarch Moses promise the same.

---

[1] On the authority of Ancient M.S.S. of Albany Br. Yates changes *Jno* to *Jua*.

The number of the grand and sublime elected, were at first three, and now consisted of five; to wit Solomon—Hiram King of Tyre, Joabert, Stokin and Gibulum; and continued so until the Temple was completed and dedicated; when king Solomon, as a reward for their faithful services, admitted to this degree the twelve Grand Masters, who had faithfully presided over the twelve tribes of Israel, since the death of Hiram Abiff also one other Grand Masters, eminent for their virtue, were chosen Knights of the Royal Arch, and shortly afterwards were admitted to the sublime degree of Perfection.

The nine Knights of the Royal Arch tyled the nine Arches, which led to the sacred vault; the most ancient, stood in the Arch next the vault, and so on in regular progression; the youngest taking his station in the first Arch, which was near to the private apartment of Solomon. None were suffered to pass, but those who proved themselves to be properly qualified, by giving the following pass words.—

THE WORDS OF EACH ARCH ARE

1st	JUB	4th	HOYAH	7th	JEKINAI
2nd	JEA	5th	GOTHA	8th	ELINIHAM
3rd	JNO	6th	ADOUNAI	9th	JEHABULUM.

The brother who gives the sacred word in the inside of the sacred vault, is obliged to give another pass-word—vizt. SHIBOLETH, 3 times with an aspiration.

You have been informed in what manner the number of the Grand Elect was augmented to twenty-seven, which is the cube of three; they consisted of two Kings, three Knights of the Royal Arch, twelve Commanders of the twelve tribes, nine elected Grand Masters, and one Grand Master Architect.

There were living at that time, 3568 other ancient Masters, who had wrought in constructing the Temple. These began to be extremely jealous of the pre-eminence shewn to the twenty-five brethren, for they often saw them admitted to the apartment of the King, which was shut to them. They deputed therefore, a certain number to wait on King Solomon, with their compliments, to request that similar honors might be conferred on them. The King heard them with attention and with the most benign air imaginable, gave them for answer, that the twenty-five Masters were justly entitled to the honors conferred on them, for their unceasing ardor, and inviolable fidelity in the work that had been committed to them. Go, said he, in peace. God may one day permit, that you may be rewarded according to your deserts.

Upon this, one of the deputies, by no means satisfied with this mild reply, turned round to his companions saying (with an unbecoming degree of warmth) what occasion have we for an higher degree? we know the word has been changed; we can travel as Masters and receive pay as such.

Solomon was much moved at this, but would not rebuke them, but spoke in the following terms; The ancient members whom I have advanced to the degree of perfection, have in a particular manner deserved this favor from me. They have wrought hard in the ancient ruins, and although the undertaking was difficult and full of horror, they penetrated into the bowels of the earth, from whence they brought in immense treasure to enrich and beautify the temple of God; go in fear, wait with patience, & aspire to perfection by good works.

The Deputies returned and made report of their reception to the Masters, who were assembled to hear it. These Masters, hasty and impatient, in their dispositions, and of consequence vexed at the refusal, determined, one and all, to go to the ancient ruins, and search under ground, with a view of arrogating the merit, so necessary for attaining their desires.

Accordingly they departed next morning, and presently after their arrival, discovered the iron by means of which they raised the square stone, and found the entrance into the arches. They immediately prepared a ladder of ropes, and descended, with lighted flambeaux; but no sooner had the last descended, than the nine arches fell in upon them, and they were no more heard of.

The Ancient Word that was corrupted was lost with them, no person having known it since.

Solomon soon heard of this dreadful accident, and sent Joabert, Stokin and Gibulum to inform themselves more particularly of the matter. They accordingly departed at break of day, and upon their arrival, were perfectly astonished at the strange appearance of the place. There were no remains of the arches to be seen; nor could they learn, that one single person of all those who had descended, escaped the destruction.

They examined the place with diligence, but found nothing of note, except a few pieces of marble, upon which were engraved certain hieroglyphics; these they carried back with them to Solomon, and related what they had seen. The King sent for some persons skilled in hieroglyphic knowledge, and from their interpretation, was fully assured, that those pieces of marble were a part of the marble pillar that had been erected by Enoch; and the ruins in which they had found so much treasure, were those of the Temple which he had consecrated to God before the flood. Solomon ordered the pieces of marble to be carefully put together, and deposited in the sacred vault.

I exhort you, my dear Brethren, to meditate on the grandeur of out mysteries; you have not arrived at the summit of our knowledge, and which, you can only expect by zeal, fervor and constancy.

END OF THE HISTORY

§. *Lecture.*

Q. Where are you?

A. In the center of the most holy place in the Earth.

Q. How came you to be introduced into this holy place?

A. By aid of Divine providence.

Q. Explain that to me?

A. I dug in the Ancient ruins of Enoch, I penetrated through the nine Arches under ground, and in the end found the △ which was promised to the patriarchs.

Q. What is the △ ?

A. A Gold triangular plate replenished with a great light, on which was engraved by Enoch, the great and mysterious name of the Grand Architect of the Universe.

Q. Who are you?

A. I am that I am, my name is Gibulum.

Q. Do you know the real pronunciation of the name of the Grand Architect of the Universe?

A. It is a sacred word, known only to the Grand, Elect, Perfect and Sublime Masters.

Q. What is your quality?

A. A Knight of the Royal Arch.

Q. How was you received in that quality?

A. Solomon, with Hiram King of Tyre, to recompense me in my zeal, fervor and constancy, conferred this degree upon me, and also upon Joabert and Stokin.

Q. Give me the signs, token and word?

A. The first is, of Admiration, which is to extend the arms with hands open, the head resting, on the left shoulder.

Q. The second it, to fall on your left knee, the right hand on the back.

A. The token is, to raise and help a brother, with both hands on the elbows of the Brother raised. The word is HAMALACH GIBULUM.

Q. What signifies those words?

A. O! THOU ART AN ANGEL GIBULUM! which was exclaimed by Joabert and Stokin after the brilliant discovery made by Gibulum.

Q. Have you any other desire?

A. To receive the sublime degree of Masonry, called Perfection.

§. *To Close.*

Q. What is the clock Brother Inspector?

A. It is evening.

Q. Acquaint the Brethren that I am going to close this Royal Chapter by the most perfect & mysterious number.

A. Venerable Brethren, the Thrice Puissant is going to close the Royal Chapter by the most perfect and mysterious number.

Solomon strikes	*3 times 3.*
King Hiram —	*3 times 3.*

The Grand Inspector 3 times 3, then the Grand Secretary the same. After which the Grand Inspector says "To order brethren." When the two Kings & all the brethren fall on their knees, and give the sign with their right hand to their back, after which they help each other to raise—the two Kings begin, and the rest follow the example, and make their obedience to the two Kings. The Solomon says—

This Royal Chapter is closed with all its honors.

FINIS

Apron.—The Apron is lined with yellow on the front a triangle.

Order.—The Order is a broad purple ribbon worn from the right shoulder to the left hip.

Jewel.—The Jewel is a medal of God or silver gilt, on one side is represented two people letting down a third with a rope through a square hole into a Arches, and around the edge of that side these initials RSSGI and SIPATSRE Anno Lucis 2995 (id est) REGNANTE SAPIENTISSIMO SOLOMON GIBULUM JOABERT AND STOKIN INVINCIENT PRETIOSSISSIMUM ARTIFICIUM THESAURUM SUBTER RUINES ENOCH ANNO MUNDI 2995.

On the reverse of the Medal, a Delta or triangle *in the middle of the rays of the sun with the letter HEY in it.*

This Jewel to be worn round the neck, by a red ribbon.

END

14ᵗʰ Degree of the First Series (1802) of the Southern Jurisdiction of the United States of America, called
Grand, Elect, Perfect & Sublime Mason

§. *Form of the Lodge*

he Lodge of Perfection represents a subteraneous vault, and must be painted red, with many columns of fiery color. Behind the Master must be a transparent Light, which illumines the Lodge and shines through a Delta or , and for the appearance of the Burning Bush with the Hebraic characters יהוה therein, under which are ruins, and before the Master a broken pedestal. Lights are arranged according to the several stages of Masonry, vizt, three behind Junior Warden, five behind Senior Warden, seven in the south, and nine behind the Master.

The Right Worshipful and Most Perfect Master represents Solomon, seated in the east, dressed in royal robes and having a crown and scepter placed on a pedestal before him. The two Wardens must be placed in the west, and on the right hand of the Right Worshipful sits the Grand Treasurer with a table of perfumes before him, on which is a silver hod and a gold trowel. On his left hand sits the Grand Secretary with a table before him with shew bread with 7 loaves, a cup of red wine for libation, and also jewels for the candidates at their reception.

The Brethren must be dressed in black with drawn swords in their hands.

Jewels.—The Jewels of this degree are a crowned compass, extended to 90 degrees, or a quadrate with a sun in the center—and on the reverse of which is a blazing star, enclosing a Delta or , hung to a broad fiery ribbon of triangular form, around the neck. A gold ring for each candidate with this inscription therein—"Virtue unites, what death cannot separate."

Apron.—*The Apron is a white skin bordered and decorated with red, and a blue ribbon round the edge and the Jewel painted on the flap.*

The passage to the sacred vault is long and narrow, having a lamp to light it. It is guarded by three Brethren, with drawn swords in their hands, viz[t], the first is at the Entrance, the second in the center, and the third at the door of the sacred vault.

§. *To Open.*

Q. Most Venerable Wardens, are we well tyled?

A. Right Worshipful and Most Perfect, we are.

Master.—Let us pray.

§. *Prayer.*

Almighty & Sovereign Architect of the Universe, who by thy divine power dost penetrate the most secret thoughts of mortals—purify our hearts by the sacred fire of thy love. Guide & direct us, in the path of Virtue, cast from thy adorable sanctuary all impiety & perverseness. We pray thee to entirely occupy our thoughts with the grand work of our perfection, which will be a sufficient price for our travel, & that peace & Charity may closely link us together in the bond of union; & that this Lodge may be a faint resemblance of what the Elected will enjoy in thy heavenly Kingdom. Give us a spirit of holy discernment, to distinguish the good & refuse the evil & that we may not be deceived by those, who are not to be marked with the formidable zeal of perfection, & finally, that we may have no other design, but thy Glory & an advancement on the good works in the reign of true Masonry. Amen. Amen. Amen. God bless us, & our works.

Q. Venerable Brother, Senior Warden what brings you here?

A. Most Worshipful & Most Perfect, the love of Masonry, my obligation, & a desire for perfection.

Q. What are the properties & qualities for acquiring it?

A. The two first lead to the third & are three to happiness.

Q. What have you brought here?

A. A heart zealous in virtue and friendship.

Q. What is the disposition of an Grand, Elect, Perfect & Sublime Mason?

A. To have a heart divested of jealous revenge and iniquity, & always ready to do good and keep his tongue from calumny, and detraction.

Q. How are you to behave in this place?

127

A. With the most profound respect.

Q. Whence comes it, my Brother, that men of all ranks and conditions are in this place, & are termed Brethren together, and are all equal?

A. Because there is something in that Delta (*pointing to it*) repeated on the pedestal and firmament, puts us in mind that there is one infinity, that is superior to us all.

Q. Why is respect paid to that Delta?

A. Because it contains the name of the Grand Architect of the universe.

Q. What are you?

A. I am 3 times 3, the perfect number of 81, according to our mysterious number.

Q. Explain that.

A. I am a Grand, Elect, Perfect and Sublime Mason, my trials are finished, and it is now time that I should reap the fruit of my labor.

Q. What did you contract when you was made Grand, Elect, Perfect & Sublime Mason?

A. I contracted an alliance with Virtue & the virtuous.

Q. What mark have you to show for it?

A. This Gold ring, or symbol of Purity.

Q. What is the Clock?

A. High twelve.

Q. What do you understand by high twelve?

A. Because the sun darts its rays into this Lodge, which is the time we should avail ourselves of, to profit by his influence.

Q. Venerable Senior Warden announce that I am about to open this Lodge of Grand, Elect, Perfect & Sublime Masons by the mysterious number of 3, 5, 7, and 9.

This being announced by the Senior Warden, the Junior Warden strikes 3— then the Senior Warden 5, & the Master 7, after which a profound silence reigns for a minute. The Master says—

To order Brethren, *when he strikes 3 slow, on which all the Brethren make*

1ˢᵗ Sign.—Bring the right hand from left to right, horizontally, across the abdomen.

He then makes 3 other strikes when they give the

2ⁿᵈ Sign.—Bring the back part of the open right hand to the left cheek, supporting the elbow with the left hand. This represents Moses at the Burning Bush, guarding his eyes from the brilliancy thereof.

He then gives 3 more strikes & they make the

3ʳᵈ Sign.—or that of Admiration, by raising the arms & hands to heaven with the head inclined & eyes looking upward, after which put the 3 first fingers of the right hand on the lips.

The Right Worshipful and Most Perfect then says—Brother Senior Warden, this Lodge of Perfect Masons is open.

Junior Warden says—This Lodge of Perfect Masons is open—*& the Master salutes the Lodge with the first sign, which they all return. Then all cover their heads and take their places.*

§. *Form of Reception.*

When the Candidate wishes for admission to the vault, he gives the following pass word, vizt.—1st MAHABIN, 2^ndly ELENEHAM, 3^rdly SHIBBOLETH; pass word repeated thrice.

Candidate is in preparation room separated from the Lodge by a long narrow passage, with all the ornaments of his former degrees. Master of Ceremonies directs him to knock 3, 5, and 7, at the first door of the passage, and to give the first pass word to the first Guard, who says, "pass," at the middle door he gives the second pass word to the second guard who says "pass" at the door of the sacred vault he gives the third pass word, and knocks 3, 5, 7, and 9, which are answered from within, alternately by the Junior Warden, Senior Warden and Master, who says—

Brother Grand Junior Warden, who knocks there in the manner of a Grand Elect, Perfect and Sublime Mason?

*Junior Warden goes and says—*Who is there?

*Master of Ceremonies answers—*A Knight of the Royal Arch, who is desirous of arriving at Perfection, and being admitted to the second vault.

*Junior Warden reports, and Master says—*Admit him according to ancient form.

The door is opened and the Master of Ceremonies and all the Brethren presenting swords to his breast, & thus place him between the two Wardens, when he gives the Sign of Admiration to the Master. Silence follows for two minutes.

*Master—*What do you want here, my Brother?

*A.—*Right Worshipful & Most Perfect, I ask the perfection of Masonry.

*Master—*Respectable Brothers, do you consent that he shall be admitted? *(Affirmative by uplifted hands.)*

Master.—My Brother, before you are initiated into our sacred mysteries, you must answer the following questions, otherwise you must be sent back until you are better qualified.

Q. Are you a Mason?

A. My Brethren all know me as such.

Q. Give me the sign, token, and word.

A. (*Candidate gives those of an Entered Apprentice.*)

Q. Are you a Fellow Craft?

A. I have seen the letter G and know the pass.

Q. Give me the pass, sign, token and word.

A. (*Given.*)

Q. Are you a Master Mason?

A. I know the sprig of acasia, and what it means.

Q. Give me the pass, sign, token, and word.

A. TUBAL CAIN. MAHABON.

As soon as he speaks the word, all the Brethren present their swords to him and the Master says—What you have done affrights us, my Brother, in speaking this word so loud. We are always ready to punish the indiscretion of the person who pronounces this word aloud, lest some profane person hear it— but, as you intended no harm, we will forgive you.

Q. Are you a Secret Master?

A. I have passed from the square to the compass, and have seen the tomb of our respectable Hiram Abif and have shed tears on his grave.

Q. Give me the sign, token and word.

A. (*Given.*)

Q. Are you a Perfect Master?

A. I have seen the 3 circles & the perfect square placed on the two columns across.

Q. Give me the sign, token and word.

A. (Given.) As soon as he gives the word JEVA, all the Brethren present their swords to him and the Master says—

What you have done affrights us, my Brother, when we hear this word so loud. We are always ready to put to death the person who pronounces the least syllable of the sacred Word and mysterious name of the Great Architect of the Universe—but, as you intended no harm, let us pass to the 6th degree.

Q. Are you an Intimate Secretary?

A. My curiosity is satisfied, but it nearly cost me my life.

Q. Give me the sign, token and word.

A. (Given.)

Q. Are you a Provost and Judge?

A. I render justice to all workmen without exception.

Q. Give me the sign, token, and word.

A. (Given.)

Q. Are you an Intendant of the Building?

A. I have made the 5 steps of exactitude; I have penetrated into the innermost parts of the Temple; I have seen a great light, in the middle of which I saw 3 mysterious letters I.S.I. in Hebraic characters, without knowing what they were.

Q. Give me the sign, token, and word.

A. (Given.)

Q. Are you an Elected Knight?

A. One Cavern received me, one lamp lighted me, and a spring refreshed me.

Q. Give me the sign, token and word.

A. (Given.)

Q. Are you a Grand Master Elected?

A. My zeal and my works, have procured me that honor.

Q. Give me the sign, token, and word.

A. (*Given.*)

Q. Are you an Elected Knight?

A. My name will convince you.

Q. What is your name?

A. EMETH is my name & profession.

Q. Give me the sign, token, and word.

A. (*Given.*)

Q. Are you a Grand Master Architect?

A. I know what is contained in a perfect case of Mathematical Instruments.

Q. Give me the sign token, and word.

A. (*Given.*)

Q. Are you a Knight of the Royal Arch?

A. I have penetrated the bowels of the earth through 9 arches, and have seen the brilliant triangle.

Q. Give me the sign, token and word.

A. (*Given.*)

Q. What is your name?

A. ·GIBULUM.

Q. What do you desire further, my Brother?

A. To be exalted to the Degree of Perfection.

The Master makes the sign of admiration, and says—"Retire, my Brother, God will permit that you receive what you so earnestly desire."

Master orders Master of Ceremonies to take Candidate out till he shall be wanted. When he has retired, the Most Perfect says—"Brethren, you are still of opinion that this Knight of the Royal Arch shall be admitted to the Degree of Perfection?"

(The Brethren signify their assent by uplifted hands.) The Candidate is ordered to be admitted by the mysterious number. The Master of Ceremonies places him below the Wardens, and the Master says—

"Does your conscience, my Brother, accuse you of committing any offense against your Brethren, which may render you unworthy of this degree?"

A. It does not.

Q. Have you ever communicated, or revealed any of our mysteries to Cowans? What would you have done to the assassins of our respectable Master Hiram Abiff, had you lived in those days? Would you have revenged his death? Be sincere—Answer me, do not hesitate.

A. I would have done as Joabert did.

Q. Have you been always mindful of the obligations which you have contracted in the presence of the Grand Architect of the Universe? Answer me?

A. I have.

Q. Did you ever find anything in your Obligations which was contrary, and against your religion, the State, yourself, or anything that might hurt your delicacy? Answer me?

A. Never.

The Master then continues, and says—"Remember now, my Brother, if you approach cool & indifferent to our sacred mysteries you will be more blamable after receiving this degree of Grand, Elect, Perfect & Sublime Mason than you could have been heretofore, and will have more to answer for, at the great and awful day of Judgment, where the secrets of all hearts shall be disclosed. This degree, my Brother, is the end, and full measure of Masonry, to which you are now going to be attached, particularly by some indispensable obligations, which are as yet unknown to you. So I hope you will fix them in your heart, when communicated and demonstrated to you. Your goodness by a steady pursuit of virtue, and close united love, for all your Brethren particularly for us, who are your fellows and superiors, will be the only means to exemplify your attachment to this sublime degree.

Q. Do you desire to be contracted to these new Engagements?

A. I do most cordially.

The Master then says—"If you do, then go my Brother, and wash your hands in the Brazen Sea, to prove your innocence, & that you have not violated any Engagements that you have solemnly made; remember that our fore-fathers used the same Ceremony, when they were accused of crimes, & by that means proved themselves guiltless."

Then the Master of Ceremonies shews the Candidate the Brazen Sea, to which he goes and washes his hands. He then returns between the two Wardens and the Master proceeds—

"You are now introduced, my dear Brother, into the most sacred place of Masonry; the most sacred mysteries of which are now going to be revealed to you. The rampart of this degree has been properly guarded by the strictest care of the Grand Elect against every vile discover; when the 3 first degrees has been laid open to the public eyes of the world. We are now going to confirm you in our Grand secrets, as we are certain of your discretion, & have no doubt among us concerning you. Come then, my dear Brother, and add to our tranquillity, by swearing inviolable fidelity to us."

Then the Master of Ceremonies makes him take 8 quick and 1 slow step to the Master—with the sign of Elected Master on him, he kneels and takes the

§. *Obligation.*

I — — do promise and vow on the Holy Bible, in the presence of the Grand Architect of the Universe, & before this respectable Lodge of Grand, Elect, Perfect & Sublime Masons, to be eternally faithful in my Religion. I promise never to take up arms against the State, nor to enter into any conspiracy against the same, or to know of such without making it known. I further promise never to reveal the mysteries of this degree to any person whatsoever, to whom it doth not belong, the mysteries of this most high degree, or any other matter that shall occur in this Lodge, or any laws or regulations of this degree. I further promise to have an equal regard for my Brethren of this royal degree without distinction of riches, poverty, noble or ignoble birth or parentage, nor any other distinction but that of virtue. I will never make, nor assist in making in my presence, any person to this degree who is not, or has been an officer in a regular and legitimate Lodge, & not unless permission shall have been first obtained from legal authority, or a proper patent for the same purpose. And in failure of this my obligation I condemn myself to have my body cut open, and the bowels torn out and given to vultures for food. So God maintain me in my present obligation with Justice and Equity. Amen. Amen. Amen. Amen. Amen.

The Candidate remains on his knees, while the Master of Ceremonies carries the hod and trowel, to the Master who anoints his head, lips, and heart, with the holy oil which anointed David and the wise Solomon, and says—"By the power committed to me, which I have acquired by my assiduity, labor, constancy & integrity—I make sacred your eyes, lips and heart with holy oil which anointed the penitent David and the wise Solomon. I stamp you with an ardent zeal of the Great Architect of the Universe to the end that you will always live in his adorable presence and that he may always be in your mind and heart—that zeal and constancy may always rule your actions."

Then raising the Candidate the Master presents him with the bread and wine, saying—"Eat with me this bread, and drink this wine, in the same cup with me, and learn therefrom to succor each other mutually & graciously."

He then presents him the gold ring, saying—"Receive this ring as a token of alliance, and to shew that you have made a contract with virtue and with the virtuous. Do promise me, my dear Brother, never to give it to any, but your wife, your eldest son, or your nearest friend."

After this ceremony the Brethren all eat of the bread and drink the wine, and make a Libation according to the ancient custom that was practiced at sacrifices. This being finished, the Master decorates the Candidate with the ornaments of the degree, and says—"I now salute you, my dear Brother, and give you title of Grand, Elect, Perfect & Sublime Mason, & with inexpressible pleasure I decorate you with the symbols thereof. Receive this ribbon of the Order, the triangle appended thereto, represents the Delta on which was engraved by Enoch, the holy name which is the principle object of our mystery, and which was accomplished by the utmost labor, trouble & danger without having a knowledge of what it was. The red color represents to you two things—first, the rays that encompass the Burning Bush when Moses received the first time the sacred name, and secondly the preeminence of the Grand, Elect, Perfect & Sublime Masons over all other Brethren of inferior degrees.

The Jewel that hangs around your neck gives us a great deal of useful instruction—first, the Crown designs the Royal origin of Masonry.

2ndly—The compass and circle of 90 degrees represents the operation of the most important things which the Grand, Elect, Perfect and Sublime Masons profit by, and

3rdly—The sun designs the superiority of their rank, and the triangle represents the sacred name of the Divinity or Delta which was found by the Knights of the Ninth Arch—all of which is suspended on your breast, to the end that you may continually see the ornaments of our dignity, so that we should never fail in the duties imposed on us by the instruction of an History. The matters which I shall now confer on you will perfect you in the study of Masonry.

There are three signs, three guards words, and three pass words, which belong to this degree, besides the mysterious word.

§. *Signs, Tokens & Words.*

1st Sign.—Bring the right hand from left to right, horizontally, across the abdomen.

1st Token.—Take each other's right hand, as in the token of the 6th degree, & say BERITH, NEDER, SHELOMOTH.

1st Covered Word.—is GABALON, which signifies Elected favorite & zealous Master.

1st Pass Word.—is SHIBBOLETH, with an aspiration, & signifies Abundance.

2nd Sign.—Bring the back part of the open right hand to the left cheek, supporting the elbow with the left hand. This represents Moses at the Burning Bush guarding his eyes from the brilliancy thereof.

2nd Token.—Begin with the Master's grip—Then ask, "Can you go further?" Then slip the hand to the middle of the arm below the Elbow, & then to the Elbow. Then put your left hand on the other's right shoulder, then balance three times as the Secret Master does 7 times.

2nd Covered Word.—is MAHABIN, which signifies Silence & respect.

2nd Pass Word.—is ELINIHAM, which signifies Mercy of God.

3rd Sign.—or that of Admiration, is by raising the arms and hands to heaven with the head inclined & eyes looking upward, after which put the 3 first fingers of the right hand on the lips.

3rd Token.—Seize each others right hand, grasp his shoulder with your left hand & pass your left hand behind his neck as if to raise him.

3rd Covered Word.—is ADONAI, which is O, God Eternal.

3rd Pass Word.—is MAHER MAHERBUCK, which is God be praised we have finished it, & Quick! quick! destroy it and make away with it!

Grand or Mysterious Word.—is יהוה, JEEHOOVAH.

After this the Master has the plan of the Lodge laid before the Candidate, which he inspects, while he listens to the following

§. *History*

My dear Brother, your good conduct, zeal and discretion, have been the cause of our determining you give you, in the end, the true knowledge of perfection. You have now received the name of Grand, Elect, Perfect & Sublime Mason—we are also happy to, my venerable Brother, in having a circumspection in giving you this knowledge, without which we should be liable to the same fatality that the 3 first degrees has been subject to. You know, my Brother, when the temple at Jerusalem was finished, the Masons had achieved great honor, their society was established into an order and the extreme niceness of the Brethren in their choice of fit objects rendered them respectable for merit—and merit only proved as yours has been—procured them this advantage. The Grand, Elect, prefect and Sublime Masons were not by any means to be seduced to determine in favor of Candidates who were unworthy, but received those (of at the utmost hazard to themselves) who appeared deserving of that Honor. The principal members of the Grand, Elect, perfect and Sublime Masons, being able workmen, passed from Jerusalem after the dedication of the Temple, and dispersed themselves among the neighboring nations, to instruct them in the Truth of the Royal Craft, but with the precaution of only initiating the males, and those of a free and eminent understanding. Notwithstanding this resolve, Masons in the inferior degrees multiplied over the face of the earth—their numbers increased beyond measure, by which means their secrets were disclosed; their knowledge was made common, and they were held in no high esteem. The Grand, Elect, Perfect & Sublime Masons only, had the precaution to conceal the higher Mysteries, by coming to a resolution not to raise any higher than a Master and if such were not circumspect in their words, actions and lives, to give them no further knowledge. As it was through the imprudence of some of the Brethren in the 3 lower degrees, that Cowans frequently obtained their Signs and tokens. These disorders chagrined the Perfect Masons (who luckily at that time were but few in number,) they took great pains to stop the contagion but all their endeavors were in vain, the Craft degenerated Insensibly. Receptions were obtained too easily, the intervals between degrees were broke into too hastily and were scares separated at all. In the end they were not preferred by merit, but preferring amusement to Instruction, innovations increased and new doctrines arose, which destroyed the old (that they ought to have adhered to). These differences occasioned disputes, quarrels, heart burnings, and dissensions, which in the end produced a total discovery of our works—for which we grieve, and by which masonry suffered in the three first Degrees. Happy it is for us who have the consolation of knowing the secret of the Grand, Elect, Perfect & Sublime Masons—let us endeavor to render it impossible for this degree to share the same fate as the three lower; let us be animated with zeal to procure that Ancient perfection. We travel to obtain their science and to follow their direction, in order to get a full knowledge of their noble occupation. The study and initiation of the Grand Architect of the Universe were always their principle object, and his holy name was the Ancient Masters Word. Solomon chose that word expressly in order to fill the principle workmen with due reverence for the great God, to whom the temple was dedicated, and also to excite them never to neglect the Execution and Duties of their office; so that the Masters uniformly followed their Occupation with this their Grand secret: The Sign, Token and Words of which make a parts of this degree. The sage King knew all the force of this Holy Name—he knew that the Grand Architect of the Universe appeared to Moses in the Burning Bush (near which our Lodge is kept) and declared to him that this was his name, and that he was the only one of the patriarchs that knew it; and further that he would be invoked by no other name in the Temple, which he would order to be built in the land of promise, upon the plan and design of the Tables of the law to be deposited therein. This his holy name having so great a report in, and to, the construction of the temple, was the reason of its being made the Masters Word. When Hiram Abiff was killed, we being convinced of his courage and discretion in never disclosing this secret. It was resolved never to entrust a matter of this importance in the future to a single person; therefore the Master's Sign, Token and Word were changed ass it is before related, and not other than the Ancient Masters knew it, until it was taken by the Knights of the Royal Arch from the Delta in the ruins of Enoch, where was wrote the true name that was made the principle object of the perfection of Masonry. Solomon and Hiram King of Tyre being satisfied in having placed in safety the precious deposit of the Grand, Elect, Perfect and Sublime Masons under the S:S: he named this place the Sacred vault, a denomination truly just; because there was nothing on the Pedestal, save the Divine Delta, and this column was the third that supported the Temple of which you know everything but indifferently, and have always been kept ignorant of the true situation of the Hebraic name thereof, which is that of the Grand Architect of the Universe, and which is called the pillar of perfection and sustains wonderfully the most beautiful place in the Universe. The curious Cowans have not been able to discover the place were this sacred word was deposited, as it was always kept a secret from all Masons, but those of the Royal Arch and of this degree. A strict guard was ever kept at the door, to prevent admission to any but the Grand, Elect, Perfect & Sublime Masons, who repaired there to contemplate the mystery of the sacred word, and there was one substituted in its place for the Inferior degrees, so that it was not possible for any greater precaution to be taken by this wise prince, to preserve this great name from all profane persons, and which rule has always been observed by the Grand Elect, who lived after him, and were possessed of this zeal, and which has been handed down to each other. Then Commenced the unity of the fraternity, which was sworn by the grand, Elect, to which this word was a seal. The Temple was finished in the year of the world 3000, being six months and six days from Solomon's laying the first stone, and finished with the utmost pomp, brilliancy, and magnificence.

This ceremony being over, Solomon gave audience for three days successively to all the Brethren. The first day was to the Elected Masters who were introduced into the sacred vault—the Knights of the Royal Arch took care of the Arches of the vault, & guarded the entrance thereto, at the same time the Grand Masters Architect were in the kings Apartment. He qualified with the Degree of Perfection, the most virtuous among the two orders, & made them promise solemnly, to live by themselves in peace and union and benevolence in

Imitation of their deceased Chief, and that the basis of their actions might like him, be that of Wisdom, justice and equity, and to keep a profound silence relative to their mysteries, & never to reveal them to any one who did not deserve this signal favor by their zeal, fervor & constancy, & to assist mutually each other by their works, and to punish severely treason, perfidy & injustice. On which he gave them his blessing 7 discovered to them the Ark of Alliance open, from which the grand Architect of the Universe used to deliver his oracles. He ordered many sacrifices and admitted them to a holy Libation, he embraced them and gave to each gold ring, as a proof of the alliance they had contracted with virtue and the virtuous. He gave them many present with permission to stay or retire as they should choose.

The second day Solomon gave admittance to the Masters and Knights Elected in the heart of the Temple, & made them promise as the others had done, that they never would depart from the principles of virtue, of which their ancient chief was a model; always to live united & to help each other in their works. He bestowed on them the degree of Grand Master Architect & decorated them with all the honors relative thereto, & made them promise that they would be faithful guardians of their mysteries & never to communicate them to any who did not merit them. He bestowed on them many favors and permitted them to stay or retire at their discretion.

The third day Solomon gave audience to the Fellow Crafts and Apprentices in the Eastern part of the Temple. He gratified the Fellow Crafts who appeared to him to be virtuous, with the degree of Master, and the Apprentices with that of Fellow Craft. He introduced them into the porch of the Temple, and made them of both degrees, promise never to depart from the principles of virtue, of which their Ancient Chief was their pattern, and to be always united, assisting each other mutually, and to keep secret among them, the Sign, Token and Word of each Degree, and never to communicate them to any but those who should merit it, by their goodness, and were known to be virtuous: he loaded them with presents, and permitted them to stay or go where they pleased, he also gave order to his Intendants to defray their expenses, until they should arrive at their own Countries and homes.

King Solomon so wise and so just, in all that he had done, became in his latter days deaf to the voice of the Lord, proud of knowing himself to be the greatest Monarch on earth, and having built a Temple so large, that the structure and magnificence of it was the admiration of the Universe: Soon the king did forget the goodness of God, and gave himself up to licentiousness & idolatry; his shameful & excessive complacency to his wives, led him into their vices, and by that means destroyed the piety of his former life, and drew upon him the displeasure of the Almighty. He also profaned the holy temple by offering the incense to the idol Moloch, which should have been burnt in the S:S: This conduct of the King was soon imitated by a great part of the nation, and was viewed with a great deal of concern, anxiety and detestation by all good men and Masons, who brought up their children in his paths of virtue , & according to the tenets they had received by the holy and respectable union that substituted among them. They also endeavored by their counsel and good example to deter & dissuade their fellow citizens from that impiety and sacrilege, which they was so guilty of, but despairing of being able to succeed, they remembered in the bitterness of their hearts the vengeance that god had taken on their forefathers for their disobedience. They imagined that lightning would fall on their heads, and that the superb Temple would be laid low, that Jerusalem would be destroyed, & that their children would suffer for the iniquities of the nation, by a dreadful slavery. These expectations determined the greatest part of the good masons to banish themselves voluntarily out of Judea, so that they might not be inspectors, & sharers in the expected horror & destruction, whenever it should happen.

The crime of the name having arrived at their utmost pitch, & the time come, when god had resolved to deliver them into the hands of their Enemies— Nabuchadnezzar, King of Babylon, by means of Nebuzaredan his General, laid siege to Jerusalem which he took, and having Mastered all Judea, he razed the walls and destroyed to the foundation the Temple of the living God, took the inhabitants with their King Zedekiah captive into Babylon, exporting with him all the riches of thier Temple. This event happened according to Josephus 470 years 6 months and 10 days after its dedication.

The Grand, Elect, Perfect & Sublime Mason who was left at Jerusalem, defended it with intrepidity, but could not resist the force & vivacity of the conquerors, they were not under any concern about the riches of the place, nor had they any inquietude concerning the Treasure thereof, but only, least the sacred vault should be ransacked, these lively apprehensions remained in the bitterness of their hearts to see the temple ruined and destroyed.

They intrepidly exposed themselves to the fury of the soldiers who guarded the door, till they penetrated through the ruins in the sacred vault, and search with great ardor, till they found the golden plate, on the cubic triangular stone of agate. They also found there the body of Galahad, the son of Sophoris, who was a man of note among the Perfect masons, & chief of the Levites.

Galahad was, at the time, chief guard of the sacred vault, to take care of the burning lamps, and to adore and contemplate the Ineffable Word. He was a man equal to Hiram Abiff who 400 years earlier had lost his life rather than disclose the secret of the Master. This Galahad preferred being buried alive in the ruins of the Temple rather than discover (by his departure) the Treasure to be defiled by the hands of the barbarians. They all cried MAHA MAHARABAC, God be blessed, we have found it—and this is the 3rd pass word and the most necessary to be known by the faithful guardians of the sacred treasure.

It is difficult to express the other demonstrations of joy, with which they were filled at this time. The immediately set to work to efface this sacred name, that it should no more be legible, to run any risk of it being discovered by the impious. They put said golden plate in the ark which contained the tables of the Law & other precious treasures, broke down the cubic agate stone (as they found it impossible to carry it off) oversetting the column or pedestal, on which the sacred name had been deposited. They dug 27 feet deep and there sunk the Ark of Alliance with its covering and contents. They took from Galahad the robes of chief of the Levites, consisting of a tiara and vestment of fine linen, and covered him with the marble tables which were deposited in the sacred vault, and found also by Gibulum, Joabert & Stokin in the ruins of the holy patriarch Enoch, when they retired satisfied, resolving never to trust in the future to anything, but their memory of carrying down to posterity by tradition that Ineffable Name, from which comes the custom of spelling letter by letter the holy name of names, without ever joining a syllable—an usage afterwards observed when the Temple was rebuilt under Cyrus, & has been particularly observed among us. The Grand priest in the middle of a small number of Perfect Brethren who formed a circle like a chain, used to spell it once a year in the Temple, giving orders to the people to make a great noise, less they should be head by them.

By their having so great a circumspection, they lost the method of writing & pronouncing this great name. They were uncertain of the number of letters which composed it, & by stopping and giving the syllables, the true pronunciation, which has securely rested to this time only with the Grand, Elect, Perfect & Sublime Masons. As God permitted the Ancient Masters, who were not Elected, and who had the knowledge of this word, before the death of Hiram Abiff, & who had treated Solomon so ill, to form the blamable project of penetrating into the ancient ruins of Enoch, by which means they were all destroyed. The Grand, Elect, Perfect & Sublime Masons who had penetrated into the ruins of the Temple at Jerusalem for the purpose of securing this inestimable treasure, & who had so happily succeeded—left Judea & traveled into strange lands & new Countries into Egypt, Syria and Scythia, even to the deserts of Thebias, others passed the Seas and took shelter in the southern climes, principally in England, Scotland & Ireland, where they continued faithful in virtue, assisting each other, and knowing no superiority among them, but only of those who excelled in virtue and good works, by this means they became the Admiration of the people among whom they had taken refuge, & excited them to the practice of their virtues, which determined many to enter the society of good Masons, beseeching them to be initiated into their mysteries.

The good Brethren chose among them the most eminent & acquainted them with their History, and exhorted them to deplore the uncertainty of human affairs, of which King Solomon was a remarkable example; to shun vice and practice virtue, in imitation of their Master Hiram Abiff, & to crown their zeal and constancy by imitating them in their mysteries. Some of the few who preserved themselves from the general corruption, having with a regret of heart seen some of their Brethren depart from the road of virtue, took a resolution of keeping & preserving their secrets, & remembering certain Signs, which the folly of their Brethren made them forget—they separated themselves from them as if they were not countrymen.

The time arrived when the Christian princes combined together for conquering the holy land, and delivering Jerusalem out of the hands of the Turks, who had it in possession. The good & virtuous Masons worthy of the heritage of those who built the Temple, voluntarily contributed to the execution of so holy an enterprise, & offered their service to the confederate princes on these conditions, that they should have no other Chief but one of their own choosing. The princes accepted their offer & they hoisted their own Standard and departed. In the tumult and disorder of the war they still retained the principles of virtue of which their father had given them the model; they lived perfectly united, lodging together in the same tents without any distinction of rank they knew any general, but in time of battle, retiring on an Equality & giving mutual assistance to each other, and extending their charity to the indigent & even to their Enemies. In all their actions they sustained & gave proof of their great valor & frequently resisted the whole force of the enemies troops. The confederates themselves could not withstand the violent impetuously of the Turks. But the Brethren reestablished the combat and courage and intrepidity. On signal given they would attack, open, close, rally & fall on the enemy with such impetuosity & firmness that nothing could resist them. These prodigies of valor succeeded alternately—the south wing did not destroy so fast, as did the Masons, on every occasion; Their order, their intrepidity in all dangers, joined to the wisdom, the union, the charity & the disinterestedness of the Brethren in refusing to partake of the spoils of the field, awakened with the attention, principally of the Knights of Jerusalem, when they came to have a knowledge of the heroes, & saw them entreated their Alliance.

What a moving spectacle was it to see those Illustrious Knights, such worthy defenders of religion, throwing themselves into the arms of those Masonic heroes, calling them their fathers, & offering them the tribute of a grateful acknowledgment. The generous Mason replied that tribute was only due to the Grand Architect of the Universe. That they took up arms to defend the common cause, that Judea was their ancient country, & that their fathers had been obliged to abandon it for many years, the particular circumstances of which, when they reflected on, brought tears from their eyes.

The princes were surprised to meet with so great virtue among the Brethren, and requested to be admitted into their society, & to be particularly initiated into their mysteries. The Masons replied that wisdom, justice & probity, peace, good manners & equity, friendship & union, were the principal laws which charmed them, & their zeal & fervor were recompensed, by partaking of the mysteries of which they had become worthy by their constancy.

The Knights of St. John of Jerusalem readily assented to what the Masons had laid down to them, & were initiated into all their mysteries, instructed in the History, & learnt of them the Grand Mysteries of universal religion & benevolence, & by the Instructions of the Ancient Masons, Masonry in general has been gloriously perpetuated from age to age in all Europe & part of America; & although there has been many revelations in the form of Empires & Kingdoms, yet have they never affected our glorious profession, which has been handed down to us, my dear Brethren, in all its primitive purity.

Let us therefore offer up our prayers at the footstool of the Grand Architect of the Universe, that we may never be divided, & that Masonry may continue throughout all ages. Amen. Amen. Amen.

§. *Lecture*

Q. Who are you?

A. I am what I am and more. I am a Grand, Elect, Prefect & Sublime Mason, and nothing is unknown to me.

Q. Where were you admitted to this degree?

A. In a place where the light of the sun or moon was not necessary.

Q. Where is that place situated?

A. Under the Holy of Holies, in a vault called the sacred vault.

Q. Who received you in that sacred place?

A. The wisest and most powerful of kings.

Q. How did you enter?

A. Through nine long arches.

Q. How did you gain admission?

A. By three knocks.

Q. What did they signify?

A. The age of the Entered Apprentice, and the number of Elected Knights, who penetrated the bowels of the earth and took from thence the inestimable treasure.

Q. What was produced by the three knocks?

A. Five other knocks.

Q. What is their signification?

A. The age of the Fellow Craft, and also the number of the Grand Elect when the treasure was first placed in the arch.

Q. What were their names?

A. SOLOMON, HIRAM, GIBULUM, JOABERT & STOKIN.

Q. What followed these five knocks?

A. Seven other knocks.

Q. What do they signify?

A. The age of the Master Mason, the seven expert Brethren chosen to replace one, and the seven years the temple was building.

Q. What answer was given to these seven knocks?

A. Nine other knocks.

Q. What is signified by those nine knocks?

A. The age of the Perfect Master.

Q. What did they produce?

A. The opening of the ninth vault, and I penetrated into the most holy place in the world, where I heard pronounced, the word SHIBBOLETH.

Q. What is signified by the three lights behind the Master?

A. The three Fellow Crafts, who slew Hiram Abiff.

Q. Who were they?

A. The three Brothers of the tribe of Dan.

Q. How do you enter the Lodge of Perfection?

A. With the character of virtuous firmness and constancy.

Q. How do you stand in the Lodge of Perfect Masons?

A. In an attitude of Admiration.

Q. Why so?

A. Because Moses stood so when he saw God; Solomon and Hiram stood so when the precious treasure was brought before them from the vault of Enoch.

Q. What are the tools of Grand Elect Masons?

A. The shovel, crow, and pickaxe.

Q. How long were the Israelites in bondage in Babylon?

A. Seventy years.

§. *To Close*

Master. — Acquaint the Grand, Elect, Perfect & Sublime Masons that I am going to close the Lodge by 3, 5, 7, and 9.

S. W.   Venerable Brethren, the Right Worshipful & Perfect Master is going to close this Lodge of Perfect Masons by 3, 5, 7, and 9.

This is announced by Junior Warden, when they strike 3, 5, 7 & 9 and give the Sign.

Master. — Venerable Brothers Wardens, respectable officers of this Lodge of Grand, Elect, Perfect & Sublime Masons, I charge you to retire in peace to practical virtue, and live always impressed with a just sense of duty that the Grand Architect of the Universe, may always be present with us. May he bless us and all our work.

FINIS

15ᵗʰ Degree of the First Series (1801) of the Southern Jurisdiction of the United States, called
🌸 🌸 🌸
Knight of the East, or Sword
⚜

he hangings of the Council should be of a bluish green, or water color, in remembrance of those events which happened at the river Euphrates, called SATARBUZANAI on the return of the Israelites from captivity, of which a particular account will be given in the History. The Hangings should also be sprinkled with red, in memory of that river.

The Lights which Illuminate the Council should be 72 in memory of the 72 years captivity of the Israelites—but may be done with 7 Large and 2 small, the two last years of Sairedes's reign, the time the siege lasted, and the 70 years. The captivity lasted from the time that the Israelites were carried to Babylon by Nebuzaradan under the reign of Nabuchadnezzar, who destroyed the Temple, until the rebuilding of it in the reign of Satrabuzzanes King of Persia. 2ˡʸ on account of the 72 letters which compose the words of the order and those of the Grand Elect Perfect & Sublime Mason, as may be seen in the following example.

151

Words of the Knts of the E.		*Words of G.E.P.& Sub∴ Mas∴*	
YAVERON HAMAIM	13	BERITH	6
RAFODOM	7	NEDER	5
BENJAMIN JEHUDA	14	SHELOMOTH	9
GABAON	6	SHIBBOLETH	10
LIBERTAS	8	ELINIHAM	8
TYR	3	MAHER MAHARBUCK	14
		GABALON	7
JACHIN	6	MAHABIN	7
BOAZ	4	ADONAI	6
	72		**72**

All the Knights are decorated with a broad green watered ribbon, from the right shoulder to the left hip, a wooden Bridge painted on that part of it which rests on the right shoulder with the letters YH in gold. These letters signify YAVERON HAMAIM—Liberty of passage for Free Masons.

Order.—The ribbon must be strewed with heads and limbs of bodies newly slain, broken pieces of swords, crowns, scepters &c. &c. and the word Starbuznai in large letters one half on each side of the Badge.

Jewel.—At the bottom of the order must be suspended a small Eastern Saber in a sheath of crimson.

There must be no deaths heads or dry bones, nor any black colors, which have the appearance of mourning. The Knights of the east should never go in mourning for any person, and why should he? On considering the happy revolution of Masons, when they triumphed victoriously in a Combat, wherein some were slain but those under Surturates who endeavored to oppose their passage, contrary to the orders of the greatest King in Persia.

The Green water colored ribbon is the only proper on for them, as well on account of the victory they obtained, as the color of the river on which banks they triumphed. The interspersion of Limbs, heads &c. is a natural representation of what happened on the banks and bridge of the river Euphrates, whose green water after the bloody battle, was tinged with Assyrian blood, and covered with their limbs, heads and bodies. The River is called by the Knights of the East, SATARBUZANAI, the name of the Chief of the adversaries who opposed the building of the temple; which signifies recovered Art, as we are taught in the Talmud, a signification which agrees with the proposition of the Knights of the East, a name composed of 12 Letters which being added to the other words of the order, form the mysterious number 81 as shall be fully explained hereafter.

Apron.—The Apron is a white skin, lined with red bordered with green. On the flap a bloody head between 2 swords in the form of St. Andrews cross. On the area of the Apron 3 heaps of broken Triangular chains.

§. *Explanation of the Draft*

At the upper end in the east, stands an Eagle upright on his legs, his wings extended, his head fiercely erected, staring at the sun at his right side, at his left is the moon—by his right foot a large *I* and by his left a *B*, and at an equal distance on either side of him the two initial letters of the compound word *Y* and *H*.

Immediately under the eagle is a great oblong square, representing the 2nd Temple constructed according to the dimensions of King Cyrus.

In the east part of the oblong square is represented the Holy of Holies where the ark of the Covenant is deposited, covered by the wings of two Cherubims, which sustains the Delta, on which is the name of the sacred Architect of the Universe and never to be pronounced without terror.

The Holy of Holies is to be separated from the rest by a curtain or veil.

In this sacred places is to be an altar of sacrifices in the middle of which is a flaming heart, with the letters *R.O.* the initials of two words, which signify, Free or true Masons, such as those who devote the hearts to God and the general good of the Order *RAF ODOM*. On this altar are likewise all the tools and implements of Masonry, which were employed in the constructions of the Temple.

At the West door is the grand stair case of 7 steps.

Beneath the Altar of sacrifice is the square of 9 which multiplied 3 times make 27 and multiplied again by 3 makes the favorite number of 81, of which, you have here the first example referring the explanation to another occasion, when we will shew you why the number 81 is so peculiarly dear to the perfect Masons. This square of 9 which gives 3 times 27 explains the triple triangle, of which we shall give you the figure. Its explanation is 9 virtuous attributes, to the 3 first of the triangle compose the numbers 81.

Boundless Mercy	Creation	Almighty
Justice	Omniscience	Perfection
Immensity	Beauty	Eternity

3 ---------------------------- 3 ---------------------------- 3 Virtues

which added together makes	9
applied to the triple triangle	27
and in letters make	81

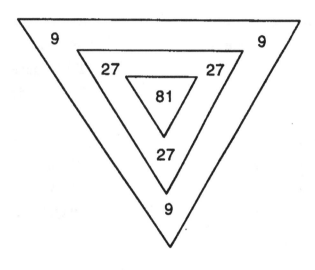

B	E	T	E	A	H	B	B	J
E	R	H	T	M	E	A	I	E
R	S	S	H	M	R	L	N	E
I	H	H	E	A	B	O	A	H
T	E	I	L	H	U	N	D	O
H	L	B	I	E	C	M	O	O
N	O	B	N	R	K	A	N	V
E	M	O	I	M	G	H	A	A
D	O	L	H	A	A	A	I	H

3 Words of Engagements.

B ---------------- 6 Letters

N ---------------- 5

S ---------------- 9

3 Pass Words

S ---------------- 10

E ---------------- 8

M ---------------- 14

3 Covered Words

G ---------------- 7

M ---------------- 7

A ---------------- <u>6</u>

          72

Gr^d Wr^d <u>9</u>

          81

Explanation of Engagements.

1st Alliance

2nd Promise

3rd Perfection

3 Pass Words

1st Abundance

2nd Mercy of God

3rd Quick, quick destroy it
     or make away with it.

3 Covered Words

1st Favorite or Zealous &
     Elected Master

2nd Silence & Respect

3rd O Thou who art Eternal.

156

Within the Temple, on a line with the Ark, and below the Sun, stands Mount HOREB—Known by all Masons, represented by the Initial letter of its name H.— Under the Moon in the left side stands Mount GABALON, marked by the initial G.— On this mount the sacrifices were made before the Temple was built.

At the south gate is a hand holding a trowel and 5 steps, opposite the gate, in a hod for carrying of mortar, under the 5th step are a heap of Cubic Stones fit for use, and a little further off, a heap of unhewn stones to fortify the building.

At the north gate is a hand armed with a sword and 3 steps, under which is a trophy of arms for the use of the builders in case of urgent necessity.

Lower down are figured the vases, urns, and other sacred ornaments of both Temples, the Molten Sea, the Table of bread of proportion, the Candlesticks with 7 branches, the altar of perfumes, placed immediately below the steps, and surrounded by the instruments of the sacrifice.

In the center of the draft below the 7 steps is the Bible, Square and Compass.—

Somewhat lower on another Line, on the right hand, are represented a shovel, laver & Cutting hammer, and on the 3rd line on the above side, a Level, perpendicular, cube, Triangle and a quadrangle, so disposed that they may occupy the whole Lodge from North to South on the same line.

Upon another line is placed triangular wise a rule, chisel, & mallet and in the center of the void upon the bank of the river, the word Judea or the initial I.

You see in the north a square stone with a ring in it, and the opening of it covered, being the representation of Enoch's Temple, which was built under ground and was composed of 9 Arches—and in the south you see an Egyptian pyramid.

The draft towards the west end is traversed from North to South by the River Euphrates, called by the Knights of the East STARBUZANAI, over the middle of which is a wooden bridge, for the passage of Free Masons to get to Judea. On the bridge are seen the 2 Initials Y & H which means, a free passage to Free-Masons. You see floating in the river heads, trunkless bodies & Limbs, broken crowns & Scepters. —

On the west side of the river, opposite to the bridge is the word Syria, and at each extremity of the river, on the same side, is represented a Column of chains & Triangular links, and in the middle of these chains, the Candlestick of 7 branches overset.

On the right is a mountain, on which is the letter T representing the quarry of Tyre from whence the stone was taken for the construction of the Temple — and on the left is a mountain with the Letter L representing Mount Lebanon, from which the timber was taken. Below the Mount is, a small oblong square Tomb of Sedicias,[2] the last King of the race of David.

On the West side of the Bride, and opposite to it, are the two broken Columns of B & J crossing each other.

At the bottom of the draft is represented the plan of the City of Babylon in ruins. — Underneath the Quarry of Tyre, is a heap of triangular chains broken. —

Each article of the explanation of the draft includes a mysterious sense, which will be explained to you in the instructions which will be hereafter given to you—at least, such a part of it—as is consistent with the degrees you have received. The rest must remain an enigma, until the moment when truth shall be wholly unveiled to you in the higher degrees. Happy moment! When Free masons shall be wholly attached to the first principles of the Craft, as that only can give us any rational arrangement, on a solid and permanent situation of happiness. Happy are they who are initiated into our mysteries, but happier are they whose virtues render them deserving of it.

---

[2] Zedekiah.

158

END OF THE EXPLANATION OF THE DRAFT

All the members are styled princes, by the Sovereign, and among themselves they have the title of Excellency.

The Candidate represents ZERUBABEL. The door of the Council must be guarded by the two youngest Knights, armed with their pikes, one stands within the other without. All the Knights are to be armed with Javelins, and when the Sovereign enters the council they form an Arch therewith, for him to pass through.

1st.—The Sovereign represents CYRUS, or DARIUS, ARTAXERXES or LONGIMANUS whose names he assumes indifferently—he is placed in the east, under a canopy, on a Throne dressed in his royal robes.

2nd.—The Grand Keeper of the Seals is called NEHEMIAS, he is placed on the right hand of the Sovereign, and should never leave his place even for a visiting Prince of Jerusalem, who are able to take their seats on his right.

3rd.—The Grand General called SATARBUZANES takes his stand in the west of the Council on the right side.

4th.—The Grand Treasurer called MITHRIDATES is placed in the west, on the right of the Grand General.

5th.—The Grand Orator, of Minister of State, called EZDRAS, is placed on the left of the Sovereign.

The other Brethren, princes, place themselves indifferently on either side. it is not forbidden the council to nominate the 5 Grand officers from among the Brethren in case of the absence of all or either of the officers.

There are no Wardens in this Council.

§. *To Open.*

The Grand General of the Army in the West shall open the Council by saying, "Brother Knights, the Sovereign assembles us to hold a Council, here he comes, let us be attentive to which he proposes to us."

The Sovereign then enters suddenly & passes in the manner already mentioned to his Throne—he strikes his foot stool with his drawn sword, and says— "Princes the Council is Open."

He salutes the Knights by putting his right hand on his heart, and bowing, his crown or hat on.

All the Princes return the salute in the same manner, holding their hats in their left hands, putting the point of their lances to their heart, bowing, when they take their seals.

§. *Reception*

The Candidate stands on the outside of the Council door, covered with a large black crape from his head to his breast, and stands so sear that the Guard within can hear his sighs.

As soon as the Inner Guards hear his sighs he half opens the door, to see what is the matter, and seeing him to be a man in mourning, he shuts the door briskly, and goes and acquaints the Grand General of the Army with it, who leaves his seat without speaking, goes to the Candidate and asks him the following questions, which he answers, being prompted by the Guard without (In a severe tone of voice)—What do you want here?

A. I beg you will procure me the honor of speaking to the King.

Q. Who are you?

A. A Jew by nation, a Prince by blood, descended from the reigns of David of the tribe of Judah.

Q. What is your name?

A. Zerubabel.

Q. What is your age?

A. Eighty One years.

Q. What motives bring you hither?

A. The fears and distresses of my Brethren.

Then the General of the Army says—"Wait awhile. I will go to the King, and intercede for you."

He then strikes the bottom of the door with his foot, it is opened by the guard who recognizing the general gives him admittance, who goes to the foot of the Throne, and relates to the Sovereign what he had heard—who orders him to admit Zerubabel with his face veiled with a crape.

The General, bowing profoundly, goes to Zerubabel and says to him—"You have found grace before the greatest of the Kings of the Earth, he suffers you to appear in his presence veiled."

The General of the Army then gives on stroke on the door, which is opened, and he introduces the Candidate, covered with black crape. The Guards having previously examined him, that he conceals no arms, with which he might attempt the life of the Sovereign.

As the Candidate passes through the council all the Knights stand, with their swords drawn or their lances in their hands, and their hats on.

The general conducts the Candidate to the foot of the Throne where he kneels. The Minister of States, unveils the face, and asks him the following questions—

Q. What brings you hither?

A. I come to implore the Bounty & Justice of the King.

Q. On what occasion?

A. To beg a grace for my Brethren masons, who have been in captivity these 72 years.

Q. Who are you?

A. Zerubabel, a Hebrew Prince, of the blood of David.

Q. What is the grace you ask?

A. To set my Brethren free, to suffer us to return to Judea, and restore the temple, revive the laws of the God of battles, and the ordinances of Moses.

A signal is made to Zerubabel to withdraw, who is conducted to the door by the general of the Army, and is escorted out by some of the Guard, the others shut the door.

The Sovereign then addresses the Knights as follows— Princes, I have for a long time past meditated on giving the Captive Masons their liberty, it troubles me to see these people in chains. Their God, whom they call their Mighty God,

162

has appeared to me in a vision, and me thought this god, threatened me, like a raging Lion, ready to fall on & devour me. Me thought I heard two words from his mouth, which signifies in our language "Give my people their Liberty, or thou shalt surely die." From you, therefore beloved Princes, I expect council, what must I do with the people of Zerubabel.

The King having ceased speaking, the whole Council observes a profound silence. The Minister of State, gathers the suffrages of each Knight, and reports the same in the Kings right ear, who commands the General of the Army to introduce Zerubabel. After introducing him with a white robe, girded with a broad green ribbon, and in this situation he brings him up to the throne, when falling on his knees, the King says—

Rise, I grant your request, I consent that Israel be set at liberty, and that they may be permitted to return to their own Country, or remain in my dominions. And that you may be enabled to build a temple to the Mighty God, all the vases & ornaments of the old Temple, shall be restored for the adornment of the new. Furthermore, I appoint you Chief of all the Jewish Nation, and command that they obey you as such, and as an authentic mark of my good will I shall arm you with a terrible sword to combat your enemies and make you formidable to such of your Brethren as might arouse the Country to cabul against you. I command my general Satarbuzanes to instruct you in the art of war.

As soon as the King has armed Zerubabel with a sword, he is conducted by the General of the Army to one side of the Council, where he teaches him the method of making himself known, and asks him the following questions, the answers to which are prompted by Mithridates.—

Q. Where is your Country situated?

A. Beyond the River Euphrates to the East of Syria; its name is Judea.

Q. What are the names of those who are captive?

A. Israel. Divided into tribes, that of Benjamin and Juda.

After these questions Starbuzanes says to him—My dear Brother, I rejoice at the favor you have received from our Sovereign. By his bounty you and your nation are now become free. He has armed you with a sword, to defend against yourself against the attacks of your enemies; by the authority he has given me, I will decorate you with a ribbon to which is suspended the Jewel of the order, a sword. You must wear it from the right shoulder to the left hip.

§. *Signs, Token & Words.*

Sign.—Carry your right hand to your right shoulder, and in a serpentine manner bring it down to the left hip where the saber hangs, which you draw and raise, as if you were going to engage an enemy. The other answer the same.

Token.—Clinch the fingers of the left hand with a Brothers left hand, as if you were repulsing each other, to obtain a free passage, putting the points of the sabers reciprocally on each others heart. One says JUDAH, the other answers BENJAMIN.

Pass Words.—The Pass Words are YAVERON HAMAIM, Liberty of Passage.

Grand Word.—In order to make yourself known in a Council you must give the Grand Word, which is RAF ODOM, which signifies a true Mason.

The Candidate is then led to the altar where he kneels and takes the following

164

§. *Obligation.*

I — — do swear and solemnly promise and engage in the presence of the grand Architect of the Universe and before all the Brethren Knights of the East, here assembled, on the faith of an honest man and Free Mason, to be faithful to my religion, and to the laws of the country I live in, as far as in my power, and that I never will reveal the mysteries of the order of the Knights of the East or Sword, and never to consent to receive or to initiated any to this degree, but a Brother who I am convinced, will be strictly conformable to the ancient statutes & constitutions of the order, under the penalty of being dishonored, and losing the title of a Free Mason, and of being deprived of the advantages of the Council. I also promise to recognize in any part of the earth, the Princes of Jerusalem, as the Chiefs of Masonry, to render them as such all the honor & homage due to their dignity, and to do my best to merit & aspire to that eminent degree. So may God maintain me in uprightness & Justice. Amen. Amen. Amen.

After which the Candidate has the Draft explained to him. The Grand Orator then relates the following

§. *History.*

The Knights of the East date their origin from the captivity of Babylon, where the Israelites remained 70 years, & after the siege of 2 years, they had their liberty granted them by Cyrus King of Persia, by the solicitations of Zerubabel, a Prince of the tribe of Judah, descended from the race of David, and Nehemias, as Holy Man, and of a distinguished family. Cyrus permitted them to return to Jerusalem, and to rebuild the temple, for which purpose, he restored to them all the ornaments which had been carried away at the distinction of Solomon's Temple by Nebuzaradan, General of Nebuchadnezzar's Army. The ornaments & utensils restored to them amounted to 7410.

He entrusted the whole to Zerubabel, commanding him to build the new temple 70 cubits high, and as many broad. He issued an edict, enjoining all his subjects, to let the Free Masons, pass through his dominions without giving them any molestation, under the pain of death to those who should infringe his commands. He ordered Satarbuzanes, his General, teach Zerubabel the art of war, he armed him as a Knight, and gave him powers to confer the same degree on such of the masons whom he should judge worthy of so distinguished an honor.

Zerubabel then assembled all the Israelites to the number of 42,360, exclusive of slaves. He selected those Free Masons who escaped the general slaughter & fury of the soldiers at the destruction of the Temple, and assembled 7000 of them. he armed them all Knights, and placed them at the head of the people, to fight such as should oppose their passage on the road of Judea. The march of the Israelites was prosperous, until they arrived at the banks of the Euphrates or Starbuzanai, which separates Judea from Syria. The Knights masons who arrived there first, found armed troops disposed to hinder them, from passing the bridge, on account of the treasure of the Temple, which they carried along with them. Neither the remonstrances of the Knights, nor the edict of Cyrus was able to restrain their insolence. They fell upon the Knights, who repulsed them with such ardor, that while they were all, either drowned, or cut to pieces, on the bridge.

After this victory, Zerubabel caused an altar to be erected on the field of battle, on which he offered sacrifices to the God of Armies, who had fought for Israel. He took YAVERON HAMAIM for a Pass Word, as it signifies Liberty of Passage.

The Israelites passed the river, and arrived at Jerusalem, after a four months march, on the 22nd of June, at 7 o'clock in the morning.

After a rest of 7 days, the Architects with their associates, began to lay out the New Temple. They divided the workmen into classes, each of which had a chief, and 2 assistants. Each degree in every class, was paid according to their rank in the work, and each had his respective word.

The word of the 1st Class was JUDEA, and were paid at the Column which stood at the entrance to the Temple. the word of the 2nd Class was BENJAMIN, and received their wages at the Portico. The 3rd Class received theirs in the middle of the Temple, after pronouncing YAVERON HAMAIM. The same order was observed at the construction of the new temple, as was practiced in the building of the first.

The work was begun when the Knights Masons were disturbed by false Brethren from Samaria, who jealous of the glory, which the tribes of Judah and Benjamin would acquire, being now free, resolved to make war against them, and defeat their design of re-building the Temple. But Zerubabel, being informed of their intentions, immediately gave orders that all the workmen should be armed, with the trowel in one hand and the sword in the other, that whilst they worked with the one, they might defend with the other, and be able to repulse the enemy if they should present themselves. The construction of the new temple lasted 40 years. It was began in the reign of Cyrus, and was finished in that of Artaxerxes—this Temple was consecrated in the same manner as the first was, by Solomon.

The Decalogue and the ordinances of Moses were observed a new, and a chief was appointed to govern the nation. He was chosen from among the Knights Masons, called Knights of the East, because they were freed and created Knights, by Cyrus, King of Persia.

Their 2nd Temple having been destroyed by the Romans, the Knights Masons of the present age, are descendants of those who constructed it, were obliged, under the conduct of Zerubabel to raise a third to the glory of the Grand Architect of the Universe.

END OF THE HISTORY

§. *Lecture.*

Q. Are you a Knight of the East?

A. I have received that character, my name, my robes, my sword and my firmness will assure you thereof.

Q. By what means did you arrive at this high degree.

A. By my humility my patient & frequent solicitations.

Q. To whom did you apply?

A. To a King.

Q. What is your first name?

A. Zerubabel.

Q. What is your origin?

A. I am an Israelite of the tribe of Judah.

Q. What is your profession?

A. Masonry.

Q. What buildings have you erected?

A. Temple and Tabernacles.

Q. Where did you construct them?

A. In my heart.

Q. What is the surname of a Knight of the East?

A. What of a most Free Mason.

Q. Why are you a most Free Mason?

A. Because the Masons who worked in the Temple of Solomon were qualified as such, and of course, they and these descendants were declared exempt from every charge of duty, even that of going to war—their families being called free by excellence. But in process of time, having been subdued, and only recovered their right through the bounty of king Cyrus, who confirmed it to them, and therefore they are called most free.

Q. Why did Cyrus give the Israelites their Liberty?

A. Because God appeared to him in a dream and gave him a charge to set his people at liberty that they should rebuild the Temple that had been demolished.

Q. What are the duties of the Knights of the East?

A. To Love God and are him, to hold tradition in honor. to succor our Brethren in necessity, to anticipate their wants, to receive with friendship, strangers who are Brethren; to visit the sick and comfort them, to aid in burying the dead, to pray for those who are under persecution, Love mankind in general, avoid the vicious, never frequent places of debauchery, not women of infamous lives, to be religious in adoring your maker, and an exact observer of all the laws of the Country in which I live, and in short to follow the precepts of Masonry in all its points, render Justice and honor to the princes of Jerusalem and respect to all the superior orders.

END OF LECTURE

§. *To Close.*

The Sovereign says—"Princes the Council is over."

He then strikes the steps 7 times with his sword, upon which, all the Knights say together—"Glory to God, Honor to our Sovereign and prosperity to the Knights of the Order."

The Sovereign is saluted by all, by bowing and putting their right hand on their hearts.

THE COUNCIL IS THEN CLOSED

§. *Festivals.*

The feats of Obligations of the Knights of the East.—

The Thrice Excellent Knights of the East celebrate the feat of the re-edification of the Temple of the Living God on the 22nd March and the 23rd of September. At the Equinoxes or the renovation of the long and short days, in commemoration of the Temple, having been built twice by the Masons.

When a Knight of the East visits a Lodge of Perfection or Royal Arch chapter, they are to be received with the honors of the Arch, and if the Master of the Lodge is not a Knight of the East, he offers the Hiram & his seat to the visiting Knight, who may accept it or not. If he accepts it, he keeps it for but a few minutes, & then returns them, he then seats himself at the right hand of the Thrice Puissant who offers him Inspection of the Minutes and transaction—if more Knights than one should visit at a time, they take their seats on the right & left of the Thrice Puissant but he who has the superiority of degrees, has the honor of the Hiram and seat offered to him.

FINIS

16th Degree of the First Series of the Southern Jurisdiction of the United States, called

⚜ ⚜ ⚜
Prince of Jerusalem
⚜

§. Form of the Council.

The Council must be divided into two apartments, with an arch in the middle. The first part in the west must be decorated with red, and represents the city of Babylon, where the Most Illustrious and most valorous King Darius is seated on a throne under a red canopy, a small table before him on which is a naked sword, an hand of justice with a roll of paper, a balance, and a scepter in the Kings hand.

The 2nd part, in the east, must be decorated with yellow and represents Jerusalem. The Sovereign is seated on a throne under a yellow canopy, before him a small triangular table on which are a naked sword, a balance & shield, a scepter & a candlestick with 5 branches, & a broad yellow ribbon on from his left shoulder to his right hip.

The 2 Grand Wardens represent the general of the Army & the grand Treasurer. They are seated under a small canopy in the western part of the room, on the right side of the Arch in the same manner as the Sovereign, except the crown. The Grand keeper of the Seals is called Nehemias and sits on the right hand of the Sovereign. The Minister of State is called Esdras & is seated on the left hand of the Sovereign.

The other Princes are placed to the right and left by graduation, and the door of the Grand council must always be guarded by the two youngest Princes, who receive their orders from the general of the Army, and they must be armed with a

172

spear instead of a sword. All the princes who are in office ought to be armed with a shield and lance.

The council must be illumined by 125 lights distributed by fives, representing the embassy which was compose of 5, and the 2nd room or apartment of the council mist be lighted with several lights, placed without the order, to represent the bonfires made at the City of Jerusalem upon the return of the Ambassadors. In one corner of the apartment must be a cabinet, where King Darius worked with Satrap.

Apron.—The apron is red, lined & bordered with yellow, on the flap a balance equal held by the hand of Justice. On the area a Temple, on each side of which is a Cross and shield with the letter T: on one side and A: on the other.

Order.—The order must be worn from right to left, 4 inches wide & yellow, bordered with red, to the end of which must be appended a gold medal, on which must be 5 stars, one sword double edged, in the middle of the stars, on each of the sword the letters D:Z:

Gloves.—The gloves are red.

§. *To Open.*

*The most Illustrious and Valorous prince Zeruababel says to the Wardens in the west—*Thrice Illustrious Princes, how came it that this place is divided into two parts, and that the east part is decorated with yellow, and the west with red?

A. The eastern parts represents Jerusalem with yellow or gold colored hangings, & is the holy place where the first temple dedicated to the service of the Living God was constructed; the western part, which is adorned with red represents the great city of Babylon—the red hangings are the emblem of the blood that was spilt in the different combats that were fought on the road between Babylon & Jerusalem, by the Knights Masons when they returned from their captivity.

Q. Who presides in this our Grand Council?

A. The prince Zerubabel, under the title of Equitable.

173

Q. Who are the grand Wardens?

A. Two of the Princes under the title of Most Profound, or Most Enlightened.

Q. If that is so, Thrice Excellent Brothers princes Most Enlightened, grand Wardens, acquaint the Thrice valorous Brethren here present that I am going to open the Grand council.

A. Most Excellent Brothers, most Valorous Princes & Most Illustrious Princes, the Sovereign of Sovereigns hereby acquaints you, that the grand Council is opened, and you will therefore be attentive to what he proposes.

Q. What is the O Clock?

A. it is the hour of 5 in the Evening.

The Sovereign strikes 5, one by itself and 4 quick on the steps of the Throne, & says—"Most Valiant Princes, the Council is opened," which is repeated by the grand Wardens, as also the 5 knocks.

§. *Form of the Reception.*

The Candidate must be in the Anti-Chamber where, after he has remained for some time, the Master of Ceremonies goes to him, blindfolds him & conducts him to the door, and announces him by 5 knocks, when the door is opened, he introduces and carries him to the east to Zerubabel, who demands for what purpose he comes before him. He answers that he comes on an Embassy to the Great King Darius to complain against the Samaritans. Zerubabel answers that the great King Darius was not there, but that will be the road he must follow. They then give him a light and arm him with a naked sword & buckler. They also give him the ornaments of the Knights of the East, when he is conducted to their Great King Darius, brandishing and flourishing his sword as if fighting his way. he must also be accompanied by 4 Princes. When he arrives before the Great King Darius, he delivers the subject of his embassy as follows—

"I am come with my 4 companions Knights Princes of Jerusalem, with a deputation from the people of Jerusalem, & as their ambassador to pray for

Justice against the Samaritans, who refuse to contribute to the rebuilding of the holy temple, & to furnish the requisites for the sacrifices & other necessities."

The Great King Darius then gives him a letter, which having received, he takes his leave of the King, & returns back by the same road he came, brandishing his sword as if fighting with his enemies, when he arrives he is conducted to Prince Zerubabel & delivers him the letter, who orders it to be read and is as follows—

"We, Darius, King of Kings, willing to favor & protect our dear people of Jerusalem after the example of our Most illustrious predecessor king Cyrus, having heard the complaint against the Samaritans, we will and do ordain that they shall continue to pay the tribute which they owe for the support of the sacrifices of the Temple, otherwise we shall punish their further disobedience. given in our Grand Court, the 4th day of the 2nd Month in the year 3534 & in the 3rd year of our reign."

After which Zerubabel congratulates them on their success & orders that the people be informed thereof, and then gives the following

§. *Obligation.*

I — — do promise & engage on my sacred word of honor, in the presence of Almighty god, and the Most Excellent Princes of Jerusalem of the Grand Council here present never to reveal to the Knights of the East, or Sword, or any other person below this degree the secrets which are now going to be communicated to me, under the penalty of being destroyed for ever, to be divested of all my clothing, & my naked body exposed to every affliction, torture & hardship that can be inflicted on me, my heart to be pierced with a dagger until my blood is drawn forth. I further promise & swear never to fight or combat with any Brother of this degree, nor dishonor him, but to do him all the good in my power. So God maintain me in uprightness & Justice. Amen.

After he has taken this obligation he is conducted out of the Council, & goes from Jerusalem, accompanied by 4 of the Princes, in imitation of Prince Zerubabel, whim he represents at the head of the Embassy; the road that he traveled in the council represents the road which Zerubabel traveled from Jerusalem to Babylon, the combating & fighting which he performed is figurative of that which Zerubabel performed against the Samaritans in his route—his travels being finished he is presented to Prince Zerubabel to whom he gives an account of his Journey and the subject of his embassies.

He returns by the same road, where he meets with the same obstructions, which he combats and overcomes, in this he imitates the celebrated deputation which was sent from Jerusalem to the Great King Darius—being returned from his journey he is again presented to Zerubabel to whom he delivers the letter he received from the Great King Darius, which indicates the return of the embassy from Babylon to Jerusalem, Zerubabel reads & gives orders that the people be informed of the success of the embassy. He departs the Council to return against with honor when he is shewn by particular friendship the magnificent with which the embassy was received at Jerusalem, when the mysteries are made known to him, which represents the power given by the people of Jerusalem to their ambassadors.

As a recompense for their glorious success, that being finished, the signs, tokens, the pass word and sacred word are given to him, with the manner of entering the Grand Council at the time of his knocking at the door for admission.

§. *Sign, Token & Word.*

Sign.—The Sign is the right arms extended horizontally as his as the shoulder.

Token.—The Token is by taking each others left hand & placing the thumb on the middle joint of the little finger, striking 5 times.

Pass Word.—The Pass Word is TEBETH, which signifies the 20nd day of the 10th month, on which day the ambassadors made their entry into Jerusalem.

March.—The march is to take 5 steps on the square.

Sacred Word.—The Sacred Word is ADAR, signifying the 23rd of the 12th month, on which day thanks were given to the Almighty, for the reconstruction of the Temple.

Age.—The age of a Prince of Jerusalem is 5 times 15.

§. *History.*

The Samaritans having refused to pay the tribute for the sacrifices of the Temple, Zerubabel sent 5 ambassadors of Knights of the East to the Great King Darius whose residence was at Babylon to prefer his complaints to him. The Samaritans having notice thereof assembled to oppose their passage, but those Knights being filled with zeal and courage valiantly fought and forced a passage to Babylon, where they made known the subject of their embassy to the Great King Darius.

The king, to render them Justice, gave them a latter in which he ordered the Samaritans to submit themselves and pay a tribute to the Jews, his allies. On their return to Jerusalem they were received in royal pomp and magnificence. The people met them without the city & accomplished them, singing songs of joy and praise for their happy return.

They proceeded to Zerubabel to whom they delivered the letter of the Great King Darius—Zerubabel read it with a loud voice and gave orders to inform the people of the embassy, & that the Great King Darius had graciously granted their request & in consequence of their fidelity & courage they were appointed Governors and Princes of Jerusalem to render Justice to the people. They were ornamented with habits of gold stuff, most rare and precious. They were decorated with a yellow ribbon which hangs from the right shoulder to the left hip, to which was suspended a medal of gold upon which was engraved a balance, to shew that they ought to conduct themselves with Justice and Equity. There was also a hand of Justice on the reverse side of the medal, as a mark of their authority over the people, as Princes of Jerusalem, which dignity was offered to them as a recompense for their services rendered & the courage they manifested in protecting the workmen in the construction of the Temple, & on the embassy. They assembled in the two chambers of the Temple to render justice to the people. This, my dear Brother, is an exact abridgment of the origin of the Princes of Jerusalem.

§. *Duties & Privileges Of Princes Of Jerusalem*

Princes of Jerusalem are chiefs of Masonry—they have a right to inspect all Lodges, & councils, as far as the Knights of the East, they can revoke & annul all the work done in such, if found repugnant to the Constitution and Laws of Masonry.

When a Prince visits a Lodge or Council of Masonry, he must be decorated with his proper clothing & order to make himself known, that he is a Prince of Jerusalem—upon which the Sovereign or Venerable Master must depute a Brother of that Degree (if there is such in the Lodge) to try & examine him, this done he enters into the council or Lodge to give an account that the visitor is such as has been announced. If it is in a Council the Sovereign orders the door to be thrown wide open, he calls to order, to form the Arch of Steel, & places him to his right hand, and does him all the honors due to him. If it is in a Symbolic Lodge, the visitor must be known as a Prince of Jerusalem to some Brother in the Lodge of the same degree, otherwise he must pledge his word of honor that he is such. The Worshipful deputes 4 of the most eminent Brothers if the Lodge, at the same time he ought not to deprive those of their places who are in office. Those deputies accompany him to the door, which is then opened, & the Arch of Steel is formed. They give him the most eminent place, & if the Worshipful is not a *Prince of Jerusalem*, he must offer him his place and mallet to the visitor, who is at liberty to accept or refuse it, when he leaves the Lodge, the same ceremonies is performed as at the time of his entry.

§. *Lecture.*

Q. Are you a Prince of Jerusalem?

A. I know the road to Babylon.

Q. What were you formerly?

A. A Knight of the East.

Q. How came you to arrive at the dignity of Prince of Jerusalem?

A. By the Grand Zerubabel and the courage I have manifested in many conflicts.

Q. How do the Princes of Jerusalem travel?

A. From Jerusalem to Babylon.

Q. Why?

A. On account of the Samaritans having refused to pay the tribute for the sacrifices of the Temple, they were appointed to go in an embassy to Babylon to the Great King Darius to make known their complaints.

Q. How many Knights composed that embassy?

A. Five.

Q. Who presided at that embassy?

A. The Grand Architect of the Universe & myself.

Q. Did they meet with any enemies on the road with whom they combated?

A. The Samaritans against whom they were going to complain, armed themselves to oppose their passage, whom they encountered & vanquished.

Q. What did they obtain from Darius?

A. A letter, in which he ordered those people to pay the tribute, on failure of which he should punish him.

Q. How were they received in Jerusalem?

A. With royal and magnificent pomp, the people went out of the city to meet them & accompanied them to the Temple with songs of joy, thanking the Grand Architect of the Universe for their safety & success, & they were elected princes & Sovereigns of Jerusalem.

Q. Where did they assemble to administer Justice to the people?

A. In the two chambers of the Temple.

Q. How were they clothed?

A. In gold, to decorate princes so respectable the choice was made of the cloth that was most precious.

Q. Was there nothing more remarkable or conspicuous in their decorations?

A. They had a yellow sash hanging from their right shoulder to the left hip, at the end of which was engraved a balance, a two edged sword, 5 stars with the letters D:Z: which signifies DARIUS & ZERUBABEL.

Q. Why all those attributes?

A. To remind them, that they ought at all times to conduct themselves with equity.

Q. What does their habit represent?

A. The Temple of Solomon—the courage that was displayed in the rebuilding; the square and compass & trowel were the tools which were made use of; the sword and the shield are the arms of the Princes Knights, made use of to defend the workmen while they were constructing the Temple, the hand of Justice shews the power of the Princes of Jerusalem.

Q. Why is the habit commonly called an apron?

A. To remember that it was by its means they arrived to the high degree of Prince of Jerusalem.

§. *To Close.*

Sovereign. —Thrice Illustrious Brethren Valorous Princes Most Enlightened, what hour is it actually?

General. —Most Illustrious Most Valorous & Most Equitable Sovereign, the sun has traversed half his career, and Justice has been done to the people.

Q. Thrice Illustrious & most Enlightened princes, proclaim that I am going to close this Grand Council by the mysterious numbers.

A. Thrice Excellent & most valorous Princes, the Sovereign of Sovereigns announces that the Grand Council is about to be closed.

A short silence then ensues, after which they all arise, then the Sovereign strikes 5 with his sword on the Table 7 says—"This Council is closed," *which is repeated by the Grand Wardens with the 5 strokes, then all the Brethren strike 5 and the Council is closed.*

17th Degree of the First Series (1801) of the Southern Jurisdiction of the United States, called

🌹 🌹 🌹
Knights of the East & West

§. *Form of the Grand Council.*

The Grand Council of Knights of the East & West must be hung in red spread with Gold stars. In the east of the council Chamber must be a canopy elevated by 7 steps, supported by 4 Lions or Eagles, and between them an animal of the Human form with 6 wings. On one side of the throne must be a transparent painting of the sun, and on the other side, the moon—below the moon is stretched a Rainbow. In the East a Basin with perfume and water and a skull. On the south side there must be 6 small canopies and on the north side 5, elevated by 3 steps, for the Venerable ancient, and opposite the throne in the West are two canopies, elevated by 5 steps for the two ancient officers, who act in this Council as Grand officers or Wardens.

A full Grand Council must be composed of 24 Knights. The Venerable Master is called "All Puissant", the Wardens and the 21 other Brethren, are called Respectable Ancients. If there are more Brethren present, they are styled Respectable Knights, and are placed North and South, behind the small canopies. The first canopy at the right side of the Puissant is always vacant for the Candidate.

All the Brethren are clothed in white, with a zone of gold round their waist, long white beards, and golden crowns on their heads.

The Knights in their ordinary habits, wearing a broad white ribbon from the right shoulder to the left hip, with the Jewel suspended thereto. They also wear the cross of the Order to a black ribbon round their necks.

The All Puissant has his right hand on a large Bible, which lays on the pedestal, and from which is suspended seven large seals.

The Draft of the Council is an Heptagon in a circle, over the angles these letters, B.D.W.P.H.G.S. In the center, a man clothed in a white robe, with a girdle of gold round his waist, his right hand extended and surrounded with 7 stars, he has a long white beard, his head surrounded with a glory, a two edged sword in his mouth—seven candlesticks round him, and over them the following letters H.D.P.I.P.R.C.

Jewel.—Is an heptagon of silver, at each angle a star of Gold, and one of these letters B.D.W.P.H.G.S. In the center, a Lamb on a book with 7 seals. On the reverse, the same letters in the angles, and in the center, a two edged sword, between a balance.

Apron.—White lined with red, bordered with yellow or gold, on the flap is painted a two edged sword, surrounded with the 7 holy letters, or the apron may have the plan of the draft painted on it.

§. *To Open.*

The All Puissant, with his right hand on the Bible sealed with seven seals, demands—"Venerable Knights Princes, what is your duty?"

A. To know if we are secure.

Q. See that we are so.

A. All Puissant, we are in perfect security.

The All Puissant strikes 7 times and says—"Respectable Knights Princes, the Grand Council of Knights of the East and West is open. I claim your attention to the business thereof."

A. We promise obedience to the all Puissant commands.

They rise and salute him, when he returns the compliment and requests them to be seated.

§. *Reception.*

The Candidate must be in the Antechamber, which must be hung with red, and lighted by 7 lights, where he is clothed with a white robe, as an emblem of the purity and innocence of his life and manner. The Master of Ceremonies brings him barefooted to the Council Chamber door, on which he knocks 7 times, which is answered by the All Powerful, who desires the youngest Knight to go to the door, and demand who knocks.

The Master of Ceremonies answers—It is a valiant Brother and Most Excellent Prince of Jerusalem, who requests to be admitted to the Venerable and All Puissant.

The Knight reports the same answer to the All Puissant, who desires the Candidate to be introduced.

The Most Ancient Respectable Senior Grand Warden then goes to the door, and takes the Candidate by the hand, and says—"Come, my dear Brother, I will show you mysteries worthy the contemplation of a sensible man. Give me the Sign, Token, and Word of a Prince of Jerusalem."

After which the Candidate kneels on both knees, about 6 feet from the throne, when the Most Ancient Respectable Senior Grand Warden says to him—"Brother, you no doubt have always borne in memory the obligations of your former degrees, and that you have, as far as in the power of Human Nature, lived agreeably to them?

Cand.—I have ever made it my study, and I trust, my actions and life will prove it.

Q. Have you particularly regarded your obligations as a Sublime Knight of Perfection, Knight of the East and Prince of Jerusalem; Do you recollect, having injured a Brother in any respect whatsoever? Or have you seen or known of his being injured by others, without giving him timely notice, as far as was in your power? I pray you answer me with candor.

Cand.—I have in all respects done my duty, and acted with integrity to the best of my abilities.

The All Puissant says—"You will be pleased to recollect, my Brother, that the questions which have now been put to you, are absolutely necessary for us to demand, in order that the purity of our Most Respectable Council may not be sullied; and it behooves you to be particular in your recollection. As the indispensable ties which we arc going to lay you under, will, in case of your default, only increase your sins and serve to hurl you sooner to destruction, should you have deviated from your duty.—Answer me my dear Brother.

Cand.—I never have.

The All Puissant says—"We are happy, my Brother, that your declaration coincides with our opinion, and are rejoiced to have it in our power to introduce you into our society. Increase our joy by complying with our rules, and declare if you are willing to be united to us by taking a most solemn obligation?"

Cand.—I ardently wish to receive it and to have the honor of being united to so respectable and virtuous a society.

The All Puissant orders one of the Knights to bring an ewer containing some perfume, a basin of water, and a clean white napkin to the Candidate, who washes his hands.

The All Puissant says—"It is necessary my Brother we should always appear in the presence of the Grand Architect of the Universe, with pure hands and hearts."

Then the Candidate is brought close to the foot of the throne, where he kneels on both knees, and placing his right hand on the Bible, his left hand between the hands of the All Puissant, in which position he takes the following

§. *Obligation.*

I — — do promise and solemnly swear & declare, in the awful presence of the only One Most Holy, Puissant, Almighty, and Most Merciful Grand Architect of Heaven & Earth, who created the universe and myself through his infinite goodness, and conducts it with wisdom and justice—and in the presence of the Most Excellent and Upright Princes and Knights of the East and West, here present in convocation and Grand Council, on my Sacred Word of Honor and under every tie, both moral and religious, that I never will reveal to any person whomsoever below me, or to whom the same may not belong, by being legally and lawfully initiated, the secrets of this Degree which are now about to be communicated to me, under the penalty of not only being dishonored but to consider my life as the immediate forfeiture, and that to be taken from me with all the tortures and pains to be inflicted in manner as I have consented to in my preceding degrees.

I further promise and solemnly swear, that I never will fight or combat with my Brother Knights, but will, at all times, when he has justice on his side, be ready to draw my sword in his defense, or against such of his enemies who seek the destruction of his person, his honor, peace or prosperity—that I never will revile a Brother, or suffer others to reflect on his character in his absence, without informing him thereof, or noticing it myself, at my option; that I will remember on all occasions, to observe my former obligations, and be just, upright, and benevolent to all my fellow creatures, as far as is in my power.

I further solemnly promise and swear that I will pay due obedience and submission to all the degrees beyond this, but particularly to the Princes of the Royal Secret, and the Supreme Council of Grand Inspectors General of the 33rd, and regulate myself by their determinations, and that I will do all in my power to support them in all justifiable measures for the good of the Craft, and advantage of Masonry, agreeably to the Grand Constitutions.— All this I solemnly swear and sincerely promise, upon my sacred word of honor, under the penalty of the severe wrath of the Almighty Creator of Heaven and Earth, and may he have mercy on my soul, on the great and awful day of judgment, agreeably to my conformity thereto.— Amen. Amen. Amen.

The All Puissant then takes the ewer filled with perfumed ointment, and anoints his Head, Eyes, Mouth, Heart, the tip of his right Ear, hand, and foot, and says—"You are now, my dear Brother, received a member of our society. You will recollect to live up to the precepts of it, and also remember that those parts of your body, which have the greatest power of assisting you in good or evil, have this day been made Holy."

The Master of Ceremonies then places the Candidate between the two Wardens, with the draft before him.

The Senior Warden says to him—"Examine with deliberation and attention everything which the All Puissant is going to show you."

After a short pause, he says—"Is there mortal here worthy to open the book with the 7 seals?"

All the Brethren cast their eyes down and sighing.— The Senior Warden, hearing their sighs, says to them—"Venerable and respectable Brethren, be not afflicted—here is a victim [*pointing to the Candidate,*] whose courage will give you content."

S.W. to the Candidate—"Do you know the reason why the ancients have a long white beard?"

Cand.—I do not, but I presume you do.

S.W.—They are those who came here after passing through great tribulation, and having washed their robes in their own blood—will you purchase your robes at so great a price?

Cand.—Yes I am willing.

The Wardens then conduct him to the basin, and bare both his arms—they place a ligature on each, the same as in performing the operation of blood-letting. Each Warden being armed with a lancet, makes an incision in each of his arms, just deep enough to draw a drop of blood, which is wiped on a napkin, and shown to the Brethren.

The Senior Warden then says—"See, my Brethren, a man who has spilled his blood to acquire a knowledge of our mysteries, and shrunk not from the Trial."

Then the All Puissant opens the 1st Seal of the Great Book and takes from thence a bone quiver, filled with arrows, and a crown, and gives them to one of the Ancients, and says to him—"Depart and continue the conquest."

2nd.—He opens the 2nd Seal and takes out a sword and gives it to the next aged, and says—"Go, and destroy peace among the profane and wicked Brethren, that they may never appear in our Council.

3rd.—He opens the 3rd Seal, and takes a balance, and gives it to the next aged, and says—"Dispense rigid justice to the profane and wicked Brethren."

4th.—He opens the 4th Seal, and takes out a skull, and gives it to the next aged, and says—"Go, and endeavor to convince the wicked that death is the reward of their guilt."

5th.—He opens the 5th Seal, and takes out a cloth, stained with blood, and gives it to the next aged, and says—"When is the time, that we shall revenge and punish the profane and wicked, who have destroyed so many of their Brethren by false accusations.

6th. He opens the 6th Seal and at that moment the sun is darkened and the moon stained with blood.

7th.—He opens the 7th Seal, and takes out Incense which he gives to a Brother, and also a vase with 7 Trumpets, and gives one to each of the seven aged Brethren. After this the 4 old men, in the 4 corners, shew their inflated bladders, representing the 4 winds, when the All Puissant says—"Don't strike the profane and wicked, until I have selected the true & worthy Masons.

Then the 4 winds raise their bladders,

1st.—And one of the trumpets sounds, when the 2 Wardens cover the Candidates arms, and take from him his apron & jewel of the last degree.

2nd.—The second trumpet sounds, when the Junior Warden gives the Candidate the apron and jewel of this degree.

3rd.—The third trumpet sounds, when the Senior Warden gives him a long white beard.

4th.—The fourth trumpet sounds, and the Junior Warden gives him a crown of gold.

5th.—The fifth trumpet sounds, and the Senior Warden gives him a girdle of gold.

6th.—The sixth trumpet sounds, and the Junior Warden gives him the sign, token, and words.

7th.—The seventh trumpet sounds, on which they all sound together, when the Senior Warden conducts the Candidate to the vacant canopy.

§. *Signs, Token & Words.*

Sign.—One looks to the right shoulder, and is answered by the other looking to the left shoulder.

Token.—One puts the right hand to the left shoulder and looks to the right, the other his left hand to the right shoulder and looks to the left.

Words.—One says ABADON, the other answers JABULUM, which signifies angel of Abyss.

§. *Origin of this Degree.*

When the Knights and Princes were embodied to conquer the Holy Land, they took a cross to distinguish them, as a mark of being under its banners. They also took an oath to spend the last drop of their blood to establish the true religion of the Most High God. Peace being made, they could not fulfill their vows, and, therefore, returning home to their respective countries, they resolved to do in theory what they could not do by practice—And determined never to admit or initiate, any into their mystic ceremonies, but those who had given proofs of Friendship, Zeal, and Discretion. They took the name of Knights of the East and West, in memory of their homes and the place where the order began; and they have ever since invariably adhered to their ancient customs and forms of Reception. In the year 1118, the first Knights, to the number of Eleven, took their vows between the hands of Garinus, Patriarch and Prince of Jerusalem, from whence the custom is derived of taking the obligation in the same position.

§. *Lecture.*

Q. Are you a Knight of the East and West?

A. I am.

Q. What did you see when you were received?

A. Things that were marvelous.

Q. How were you received?

A. By water and the Effusion of Blood.

Q. Explain this to me?

A. A Mason should not hesitate to spill his blood for the support of Masonry.

Q. What are the ornaments of the Grand Council?

A. Superb thrones—sun, moon, perfumed ointment, and a basin of water.

Q. What is the figure of the Draft?

A. An heptagon within a circle.

Q. What is the representation of it?

A. A man vested in a white robe with a golden girdle round his waist—round his right hand 7 stars, his head surrounded with a Glory—a long white beard, a two-edged sword across his mouth, surrounded by 7 candlesticks, with these letters; H.D.P.I.P.R.C.

Q. What signifies the circle?

A. As the circle is finished by a point, so should a Lodge be united by Brotherly love and affection.

Q. What signifies the Heptagon?

A. Our mystic number which is enclosed in seven letters.

Q. What are the seven letters?

A. B.D.W.P.H.G.S., which signifies Beauty, Divinity, Wisdom, Power, Honor, Glory and Strength.

Q. Give me the explanation of these words?

A. BEAUTY, to adorn; DIVINITY, that Masonry is of divine origin; WISDOM, a quality to invent; POWER to destroy the profane and unworthy Brethren HONOR is an indispensable quality in a Mason, that he may support himself in his engagements with respectability; GLORY that a good Mason is on an equality with the greatest prince, and STRENGTH is necessary to sustain us.

Q. What signifies the seven stars?

A. The seven qualities which Masons should be possessed of—Friendship, Union, Submission, Discretion, Fidelity, Prudence and Temperance.

Q. Why should a Mason be possessed of these qualities?

A. Friendship is a virtue that should reign among Brothers. Union is the foundation of society; Submission, to the laws and regulations, and decrees of the Lodge, without murmuring; Discretion, that a Mason should always be on his guard, and never suffer himself to be surprised; Fidelity, in observing strictly our obligations; Prudence, to conduct ourselves in such a manner that the profane, though jealous, may never be able to censure our conduct; and Temperance, to avoid all excesses that may injure either body or soul.

Q. What signifies the 7 candlesticks, with their 7 letters?

A. Seven crimes, which Masons should always avoid; viz: Hatred, Discord, Pride, Indiscretion, Perfidy, Rashness, and Calumny.

Q. What are the reasons that Masons should particularly avoid these crimes?

A. Because they are incompatible with the principles and qualities of a good Mason, who should avoid doing an injury to a Brother, even should he be ill treated by him, and unite in himself all the qualities of a good and upright man. Discord is contrary to the very principles of Society; Pride prevents the exercise of humanity; Indiscretion is fatal to Masonry; Perfidy should be execrated by every honest man; Rashness may lead us into unpleasant and disagreeable dilemmas; and Calumny, the worst of all, should be shunned as a vice which saps the very foundation of friendship and society.

Q. What signifies the two-edged sword?

A. It expresses the superiority of this degree over all others that precede it.

Q. Are there any higher degrees than this?

A. Yes; there are several.

Q. What signifies the book with 7 Seals which none but one can open?

A. A Lodge or Council of Masons, which the All Puissant alone has a right to convene and open.

Q. What is enclosed in the first seal?

A. One bow, one arrow, and one crown.

Q. What in the second?

A. A two-edged sword.

Q. What in the third?

A. A Balance.

Q. What in the fourth?

A. Death's head.

Q. What in the fifth?

A. A cloth stained with blood.

Q. What in the sixth?

A. The power to darken the Sun, and tinge the Moon with Blood.

Q. What is in the 7th Seal?

A. Seven trumpets and perfumes.

Q. Explain these things to me.

A. The bow, arrow, and crown, signifies that the orders of this respectable Council should be executed with as much quickness as the arrow flies from the bow, and be received with as much submission, as if it came from a crowned head, or chief of a nation. The sword, that the Council is always armed to punish the guilty. The balance is a symbol of justice. The skull is the image of a Brother who is excluded from a Lodge, or Council. This idea must make all tremble, when they recollect the penalties they have imposed on themselves under the most solemn obligations. The cloth stained with blood, that we should not hesitate to spill ours for the good of Masonry. The power of obscuring the sun and tingeing the moon, with blood, is the representation of the power of the Superior Councils—in interdicting their works, if they are irregular, until they have acknowledged their error, and submitted to the rules and regulations of the Craft, established by the Grand Constitutions. The seven Trumpets and perfumes, signify that Masonry is extended over the surface of the Earth, on the wings of fame, and supports itself with honor—The perfumes mark that the life of a good Mason should be free from all reproach.

Q. What age are you?

A. Very Ancient.

Q. Who are you?

A. I am a Pathmian.

Q. From when came you?

A. From Pathmos.

END OF THE LECTURE

§. *To Close.*

Q. What is the Clock?

A. There is no more time.

The All Puissant strikes 7 and says—"Venerable Knights, Princes, the Council is closed."

The two Wardens repeat the same and the Council is closed.

FINIS

BOOK 4th

Copy of the M.S.S. belonging
to Ill^trs Brother Giles F. Yates,
R ⚓ K—H, S.P.R.S. &
Sov. G^nd Ins. Genl of 33:^rd—A.L. 5833

18th Degree of the First Series (1805) of the Southern Jurisdiction of the United States, called

⚅ ⚅ ⚅
Knight of the Eagle, or Pelican
Sovereign Prince of Rose Croix de Heroden
🌹

§. Form of Reception

 hen a Brother wishes to receive this high degree, he must produce his certificate of Knight of the East, Prince of Jerusalem, and Knight of the East & West. The following articles must be read to him, to which he must agree before he can be received.

1st.—He must present at the door of the Chapter the following petition, & must kneel while one of the Brethren reads it—

"Brother —— who is a Knight of the East, Prince of Jerusalem, & Knight of the East & West, begs leave to represent to the Sovereign chapter the earnest desire he has, to arrive to the Sublime Degree of Rose Croix, the point of Perfection of Masonry, & that you will be pleased [being at present assembled,] to admit him among the number of Knights, if he is found worthy. And your petitioner shall never cease to make vows to Heaven, for the prosperity of the order & good health of all the Brethren."

After the petition is read the Candidate must sign it.

2nd. The Candidate must remain on his knees, at the door of the Chapter, until the answer is thrown to him on the floor by a Knight, when he rises & reads it. In the answer he will find the day appointed for his reception, and the name of the Knight who is to give him the necessary instructions. The Knight who is named in the answer, directs the Candidate to procure three pairs of gloves, [one pair of which must be women's] & two sticks of fine sealing wax for the seals. He also directs him to present to each of the Brethren, one pair of men's, & one pair of women's gloves, and two sticks of sealing wax.

3rd. He must make a donation of at least 6 dollars to the Superior Lodge, Chapter or Council of the Sublime Degrees, which must be done before he is received, & may be appropriated either to defray the expenses of the order or be given to the poor. He must also present to the Lodge three white wax candles for the Master, & two to each of the Knights, at his reception, previous to his entering into the third apartment.

4th. He must solemnly engage on his honor, never to reveal the place where he was received, who received him, nor those who were present at his reception.

5th. He solemnly promises to conform to all the ordinances of the Chapter, & keep himself uniformly clothed as far as he is able.

6th. He must promise to acknowledge his Master at all times & in all places; never to confer this degree without permission, & to answer for the probity & respectability of those whom he proposes.

7th. That he will be extremely cautious in granting this degree, that it may not be multiplied unnecessarily. If the Candidate promises to perform these requisitions he may be admitted.

§. Title of the Order

This order, which is the NEC PLUS ULTRA of Masonry, has different titles. It is called Rose Croix from the rose on the cross of the jewel, being emblematical of the Son of God, who is compared to a rose by the evangelist—Knight of the Eagle, because of the eagle represented in the jewel. Knight of the Pelican, emblematical of the Son of God, who shed his blood for the great family of mankind.—De Heroden, because the first Chapter of this degree was held on a mountain of that name, situated between the west and north of Scotland, and where there is at this day the Superior Lodge and residence of the Sovereign Grand Chapter.

They meet in an old castle belonging to the Knights of the Rose Croix. It is from this circumstance that three-fourths of the Lodges of England took the name of the Rose Croix de Heroden, and the other fourth the name of Rose Croix, Knights of St. Andrew, because the first Masons of Scotland made a procession every year on the festival of that Saint—and because it is the day of their regular constitution, which has induced many to call it St. Andrews, which also is in commemoration of the troubles of that country. The form of the true jewel being lost, they substituted the cross of St. Andrew, though the ceremonies of this degree have no Connection with that jewel. They are yet worn in the Lodge of Cologne, suspended to a red ribbon in the form of a collar. In Berlin to a green ribbon—they also wear it to a button hole.

Jewel.—The jewel of this degree is a compass of gold extended to 60 degrees. The head of the compass is a covered rose, the stock of which comes to a point. In the middle of the compass is a cross, the foot of which rests on the middle of the circle, and the head touches the head of the compass. On one side an eagle, touching a quarter of the circles, the wings and head reclining. On the other side a pelican picking its breast to nourish its young which must be in a nest under it. On the head of the compass must be a crown. On the circle must be engraved on one side, the Knight in hieroglyphics, on the other side the pass word. The jewel must be of gold—the eagle and pelican of silver. It is worn to a collar of a bright red color, of at least three inches broad, edged with black—a rose at the lower end and a black cross on each side. The Knights must wear this jewel in every Lodge, and announce themselves at the door as Knights of Rose Croix, that they may receive the honor due to them.

Apron.—For the first chamber, white leather lined, and bordered with black, three red roses placed triangularly on the flap—a human skull with two thigh bones placed across each other, also on the flap. At the bottom of the apron must be a globe, surrounded by a serpent, and on the pocket of the apron a large I.

For the second chamber, red lined and bordered with the same. On the middle of the flap must be embroidered a triple triangle, with three squares within three circles, an I in the middle, which forms the jewel of the second chamber. On each side of this must be embroidered two compasses; the point of one stands in one square of the circle, and the other stands on a triangle, with the point down.

Jewel & Order.—For the 1st chamber, a broad, black ribbon from the left shoulder to the right hip, (3 inches broad.) On the breast a small cross of red ribbon—below this must be a red rose and a small rose of black below this, to which must be suspended a gold cross.

For the 2nd chamber, the order and jewel of this degree.

Clothing of the Knights, Jewels, & Titles of the Officers.—All the Brethren must be dressed in black clothes, with their swords on. The Master must be decorated with a brilliant star of seven points, which he wears on his breast over his heart. In the middle must be a circle and in its center the letter G. The following three words must also be engraved within the circle around the G.—Faith, Hope & Charity.

The Master is called, "Ever Most Perfect Sovereign." The Senior Warden wears a triangle, and is called, "Most Excellent and Perfect." The Junior Warden wears the Square and Compass, one above the other, and is called "Most Excellent and Perfect." The Brethren are called "Most Respectable Knights Princes of Masons."

1st Apartment.—The 1st apartment is a representation of Mount Calvary. It must be hung with black tapestry, and lighted with 33 yellow was candles, in 3 candlesticks and eleven branches each. There must be three columns of 6 feet high & on the chapiter of each must be written one of the following words, in large characters of gold—Faith, Hope & Charity. These columns may serve as candlesticks.—At the east end of the Chapter there must be a hill or bank raised to represent Mount Calvary, upon which must be placed three large crosses, and upon each a human skull and two thigh bones across. In the front of this must be the altar covered with black, on which must stand a cross and two yellow wax candles lighted. Behind the altar must be a black curtain to intercept the view of the Mount. It must extend to the top of the Chapter, and be made to open in the middle, and be drawn to each side. The Master must be seated on the last step of the altar, having a small table before him, on which is a lighted wax candle, a Bible, square & compass, and triangle. There must be no chairs or benches in the Chapter, but all the Brethren must be seated on the floor. All the Brethren must wear over their black clothes a white satin chasuble, bordered with black ribbon, two inches in width. A red cross, two inches in width, must reach from the top to the bottom of it. It must be made as the chasuble of a Catholic priest which he wears over the alb, when celebrating mass.

2nd Apartment.—The east end of the 2nd apartment must represent in transparent painting, the resurrection of Jesus Christ, the Savior of mankind—over which must be a brilliant triangle surrounded with glory. The hanging must be of transparent painting, representing the light blue æther of the sky, interspersed with glory. The altar must be splendidly decorated and illuminated with transparent lights.

There must be no candles in this apartment, as all the light must be received through the transparencies. No other figure must be painted on the hangings but the representation of our Savior at the resurrection. At the east, and behind the hangings, at some little distance, must be an organ or a band of music.

3rd Apartment.—On the hangings of the 3rd apartment must be represented, in transparent paintings, all the horrors which we attach to the idea of Hell, or of a place formed for the punishment of the worst of crimes; such as human figures & monsters with convulsed muscles, engulfed in flames, &c. &c. On each side of the door a human skeleton, with an arrow in his hand. Each apartment must be separate, only connecting with a narrow door.

§. *To Open.*

M.—My Perfect brothers, Knights Princes of Masons, assist me to open this Chapter.

The Wardens repeat the same one after another. The Master then knocks 3 & 4, which is repeated by the Wardens.

M.—Most Excellent and Perfect Wardens, what is our care?

S.W.—Most Wise, Perfect and Sublime Master, it is to ascertain whether the Chapter is well covered, and all the Brethren present are Knights of the Eagle and Rose Croix.

M.—Convince yourselves, my Perfect Brethren, one from the south and one from the north.

This the Wardens do by demanding from each Brother in rotation the sign, token, and word, after which they give an account to the Master, who says, "Most Perfect Senior Warden, what is the o'clock?"

S.W.—The moment when the vail of the Temple was rent; when darkness and consternation covered the earth; when the Blazing Star disappeared and the lamp of day was darkened; when the implements of Masonry were lost and the Cubic Stone sweat blood and water—that was the moment when the great Masonic word was lost.

M.—Since Masonry, my Brethren, has sustained so great a loss, let us employ ourselves by new works, to recover the word which was lost, for which purpose let us open the Chapter of Rose Croix.

S.W.—My Brethren let us do our duty; the Sovereign Chapter of Rose Croix is open.

Junior Warden repeats the same, after which all the Knights bend their right knees to the altar, repeating the same words seven times, a short interval between the 6th and 7th.

M.—What is the cause of our assembling here, Most Excellent Senior Warden?

S.W.—Ever Most Perfect and Sovereign Master, the propagation of the order & the Perfection of the Knight of the East, who demands to be received among us.

Then Brethren proceed to ballot for the Candidate.

§. *Form of Reception.*

When the Candidate has given satisfactory answers to all the conditions proposed to him, he must be placed in the chamber of reflection, which must be painted black, with a small table in it with a Bible and several human bones on it. The only light is received from a candle or lamp placed in the skull of a human skeleton. The Master of Ceremonies goes to the Candidate and decorates him in the attributes of the last degree he has received, & also with his sword and white gloves on.

He then says to him—"All the temples are demolished; our tools are destroyed with our columns; the sacred word is lost, notwithstanding all our precaution; and we are in ignorance of the means of recovering it, or of knowing each other. The order, in general, is in the greatest consternation— Will you assist us in recovering the word?"

The Candidate replies—"Most cheerfully."

The Master of Ceremonies says—"Follow me, if you please"—*when he conducts him to the door of the chapter, whereon he knocks as a Knight of Rose Croix.*

The Senior Warden demands—"What do you want?"

A. It is Brother Knight of the East and West, who is wandering in the woods & mountains, & who, at the destruction of the second temple, lost the word and humbly solicits your aid and assistance to recover it.

The door is opened & the Candidate is introduced. All the Brethren are seated on the floor, their right hands on their necks, their left covering their face, their heads down, their elbows on their knees, and their jewels covered with black crape.

The Master is in the same position at the table. The Senior Warden knocks as a Rose Croix, and announces him to the Master, who says—

"My Brother, confusion has come on our works, and it is no longer in our power to continue them. You must perceive from our looks and the consternation which prevails among us, what confusion reigns on the earth. The vail of the temple is rent, [*at this moment the black curtain is withdrawn*] the light is obscured and darkness spreads over the earth; the flaming star has disappeared, the cubic stone sweats blood and water, and the sacred word is lost; therefore it is impossible we can give it to you, nevertheless it is not our intention to remain inactive: we will endeavor to recover it. Are you disposed to follow us?

A. Yes, I am.

M.—Brother Wardens make the Candidate travel for 33 years [*alluding to the years of the Savior's life*] to learn the beauties of the new law [*which is reduced to 7 times round the Lodge.*]

The Wardens lead him slowly around the Lodge, and when he passes before the altar he must kneel, and when passing in the west he bends his right knee, they make him observe the columns and repeat the name of each as he passes them. After he has performed this ceremony, the Wardens knock one after the other and announce him to the Master, who says—

"My Brother, what have you learned on your journey?"

A. I have learned three virtues by which to conduct myself in future, Faith, Hope, Charity—inform me if there are any others.

Master.—No, my Brother, they are the principles and the pillars of our new mystery. Approach near to us and make an engagement never to depart from that faith.

The Brethren rise. The Candidate kneels on the last step of the altar and places his hands on the Holy Bible and takes the following

§. *Obligation.*

I —— do most solemnly and sincerely promise and swear, under the penalty of all my former obligations, which I have taken in the preceding degrees, never to reveal either directly or indirectly, the secrets or mysteries of Knight of the Eagle, Sovereign Prince of Rose Croix, to any Brother of an inferior degree, nor to any in the world besides, who is not justly and lawfully entitled to the same, under the penalty of being forever deprived of the true word, to be perpetually in darkness, my blood continually running from my body, to suffer without intermission, the most cruel remorse of soul; that the bitterest gall mixed with vinegar, be my constant drink; the sharpest thorns for my pillow; and that the death of the cross may complete my punishment, should I ever infringe or violate in any manner or form, the laws and rules which have been, are now, or may be hereafter made known or prescribed to me; and I do furthermore swear, promise and engage on my sacred word of honor, to observe and obey all the decrees which may be transmitted to me by the Grand Inspectors General, in Supreme Council of the 33rd degree, that I never will reveal the place where I have been received, nor by whom I was received, nor the ceremony used at my reception, to any person on earth, but to a lawful Prince of Rose Croix; that I never will initiate any person into this degree but by a lawful patent obtained for that purpose, either from this Chapter, or from a superior Council—so help me God, and keep me steadfast in this my solemn obligation. Amen.

He kisses the Bible.

The Master says—"My Brethren, all is accomplished!"

The Brethren all place themselves on the floor & cover their faces with their hands, except the Wardens who continue with the Master, and the Candidate whom they deprive of his apron and order. The Master invests him with the chasuble and says—

"This habit, my Brother, teaches you the uniformity of our manners and our belief, and will recall to your recollection the principal points of our mysteries. The black apron with which I invest you, is to mark our sincere repentance of those evils which were the cause of all our misfortunes, and it will also serve to show you those who are in search of the true word. The ribbon is the mark of our constant mourning, till we have found it. Pass to the west and assist us to search for it."

The Wardens conduct him to the west. The Master knocks 6 and 1, as a Knight—The Wardens repeat it. All the Brethren rise and place themselves in the sign of the Good Pastor.

The Master demands—"Brother Master Wardens, what is the motive of our assembling?"

A. The loss of the word, which, with your assistance, we hope to recover.

Q. That must we do to obtain it?

A. To be fully convinced of the three virtues which are the basis of our columns and our principles.

Q. What are they?

A. Faith, Hope, Charity.

Q. How shall we find those three columns?

A. By traveling three days in the most profound obscurity.

The Master says—"Let us travel, my Brethren, from east to north, & from west to south."

All the Brethren travel in silence, bending their knees as they pass the altar in the east, and go 7 times round. At the third time of going round, the Master passes to the 2nd apartment; at the 4th time the Wardens; at the 5th time all the officers; at the 6th time, all the Brethren; at the 7th time, the Master of Ceremonies stops the Candidate and says—

"You cannot enter unless you give me the word."

The Candidate answers—"I am in search of the word, by the help of the new law and the three columns of Masonry."

During this time the Brethren in the 2ⁿᵈ apartment take off their black decorations, and put on the red, and also uncover their jewels. The Candidate knocks on the door, and the Warden, for answer, shuts the door in his face.

The Master of Ceremonies says—"These marks of indignity, are not sufficiently humiliating, you must pass through more rigorous proofs, before you can find it."

He then takes off the Candidate the chasuble and black apron, and puts over him a black cloth covered with ashes & dust, and says to him—

"I am going to conduct you into the darkest and most dismal place, from whence the word shall triumphantly come to the glory and advantage of Masonry; place your confidence in me."

He then takes him into the 3ʳᵈ apartment, and takes from him his covering, and makes him go three times around, [showing him the representation of the torments of the dammed,] when he is led to the door of the Chapter and the Master of Ceremonies says to him—

"The horrors which you have just now seen, are but a faint representation of those you shall suffer, if you break through our laws, or infringe the obligation you have taken."

The Master of Ceremonies knocks on the door of the Chapter, and the Warden reports to the Master, who orders him to go and see who knocks. The Master of Ceremonies, answers—

"It is a Knight, who, after having passed through the most profound and difficult places, hopes to procure the real word as a recompense for his labor."

The Wardens give an account to the Master, who says—"Introduce him to the west of the Chapter with his eyes open."

The Wardens bring him in & then cover him again with his vail.

Master.—From whence came you?

Cand.—From JUDEA.

Q. By what road have you passed?

A. By NAZARETH.

Q. Who conducted you?

A. RAPHAEL.

Q. What tribe are you of?

A. Of the tribe of JUDAH.

Q. Take the initial letters of each of these words, and tell me what they form?

A. J, N, R, J.

Master.—My Brethren, what happiness! The word is recovered; give him the light.

The vail is taken off, and all the Brethren striking with their hands seven times, cry—"Hosanna in the highest; on earth peace, good will towards men."

The music immediately plays the following anthem, which is devoutly sung by all the Knights.

ANTHEM

Grateful notes and numbers bring
While the "name of God" we sing
Holy, holy, holy Lord,
Be thy glorious name adored.
Men on earth, and saints adore—
Sing the great Redeemers lore.
Lord, thy mercies never fail,
Hail celestial goodness hail!
While on earth ordained to stay,
Guide our footsteps in thy way:
Mortals raise your voices high
Till they reach the echoing sky.

After the anthem is sung, the Master says to the Candidate—"Approach, my Brother, I will communicate to you our perfect mysteries."

The Wardens conduct him to the Master, who says—"I congratulate you, my Brother, on the recovery of the word, which entitles you to this degree of Perfect Masonry. I shall make no comment or eulogium on it. Its sublimity will, no doubt be duly appreciated by you. The impression which, no doubt, it has made on your mind, will convince you that you were not deceived when you were informed that the ultimatum of Masonic perfection was to be acquired by this degree. It certainly will be a source of very considerable satisfaction to you, that your merit alone has entitled you to it. And I hope, my Brother, that your good conduct, your zeal, your virtue and discretion, may always render you deserving of the high honor which you have received, and I sincerely wish that your life may long be preserved, to enable you to continue an useful member, & an ornament to our society."

§. *Signs, Token & Words.*

1st Sign.—The first Sign is called the Sign of the Good Pastor or Shepherd. Cross the arms on the breast, the hands opened & eyes raised to Heaven. This is the Sign of the Order.

2nd Sign.—The second Sign is called the Sign of Recognition. Raise the right hand with the fore-finger pointing to Heaven. The answer is to point to the earth with the same finger. These two signs are given alternatively.

3rd Sign.—The third Sign is that of Help. Cross the legs, the right behind the left. The answer is to cross the left behind the right.

Token.—The Token is to give the sign of the Good Pastor, facing each other, bow & reciprocally put the hands crossed on the breast, giving the fraternal kiss, & pronouncing the pass word.

Pass Word.—The Pass Word is EMANUEL.

Sacred Word.—The Sacred Word is I.N.R.I. [J.N.R.J.], pronouncing the letters alternatively. They are the initials of JESUS NAZARENUS REX JUDÆORUM, Jesus of Nazareth, King of the Jews.

The Sovereign Master then says—"Go, my Brother, and make yourself known to all the members of the Sovereign Chapter, and return again."

The Candidate goes and whispers in the ears of the Knights the pass word; he then returns, and kneels before the altar. All the Brethren place their right hands on him.

The Sovereign Master takes the ribbon, to which is suspended the true jewel uncovered, and says to him—"By the power which I have received from the Sovereign Chapter of Rose Croix de Heroden, I receive and constitute you Prince Knight of the Eagle, Perfect Free Mason de Heroden, under the title of the Rose Croix, that you may enjoy, now & forever, all the privileges, prerogatives, & titles attached to that sublime degree, as virtue and humility are the foundation of it. I hope, my Brother, never to see you dishonor the ribbon with which you have been invested, & which a Perfect Mason should never quit but at his death."

§. *Lecture.*

Q. Are you a Knight & Prince of Rose Croix?

A. Most Wise and Perfect Sovereign, I have that happiness.

Q. Where was you received?

A. In a Chapter where reigned decency & humility.

Q. Who received you?

A. The most humble of all.

Q. How was you received?

A. With all the formalities requisite on that great occasion.

Q. How was you presented to the Chapter?

A. Of my own free will and accord.

Q. What have you seen on entering the chapter?

A. My soul was in ecstasy at the sight of our ineffable mysteries & silence reigned in the Lodge—and the situation of the Knights gave me a high idea of what was going to be communicated to me.

Q. What did they do with you afterwards?

A. They made me travel for 33 years. [*This number of years alludes to the age of the Savior when he was crucified.*]

Q. What did you learn in your travels?

A. I learned the name of the 3 columns which support our edifice, & as they are 3 great virtues, they are the foundation of this degree.

Q. When your journey was over, was your labor, pains & work finished?

A. The Most Wise ordered me to be conducted to the altar & there to kneel in the presence of Him before whom all nations bow & to take a most solemn obligation—which I did with as much respect as possible—my heart was penetrated with what I was saying, with a firm resolution of observing the same.

Q. What was done with you after that?

A. I was clothed with marks of grief & repentance, and was taught the reason thereof—All the knights then made a journey, by which we passed from misery to happiness; the dark & obscure road by which we traveled, was overcome with firmness, and we received as a recompense the object of our desire.

Q. What was you seeking for in this journey?

A. The word which was lost, and which our perseverance enabled us to recover.

Q. Who gave it to you?

A. It is not permitted to any person to give it; but having reflected on what I was seeing & hearing I found it myself with the help of Him who is the author of the word.

Q. Give it to me?

A. I cannot—interrogate me.

Q. What country are you of?

A. Of Judea.

Q. Where have you passed?

A. By Nazareth.

Q. What was the name of your conductor?

A. Raphael.

Q. What tribe are you of?

A. The tribe of Judah.

Q. I am not better instructed.

A. Most Wise, enable me to assemble the initial letters of the word, and you will find the subject of our joy & our mysteries.

Q. J, N, R, J, JESUS NAZARENUS REX JUDÆORUM.

A. It is very just, Most Wise.

Q. Did they give yon any thing else?

A. The pass word, and the signs and tokens to make myself known.

Q. Give me the first sign?

A. (*given.*)

Q. What do you call it?

A. The Good Pastor or Shepherd.

Q. After having given you all this, what did they do with you?

A. The Most Wise and the Knights constituted me Prince Knight of the Eagle, Perfect Mason, under the title of the Sovereign Knight of Rose Croix, and decorated me with the ribbon & jewel, and gave me the explanation of them; after which I made myself known to all the Knights, and took my place in the chapter.

Q. What was done with you afterwards?

A. The Most Wise made an exhortation, after which the business of the chapter was gone through and a convocation made for the next, and the chapter was closed in the usual form.

§. *To Close.*

The Most Wise knocks 7 times on the step of the altar. The Wardens repeat the same. The Knights rise up.

*The Master asks the following questions—*Most Excellent Brother Senior Warden, what's the o'clock?

A. The moment when the word was recovered; when the cubic stone was changed into a mystic rose; when the flaming star appeared in all its splendor; when our altars resumed their ordinary form; when the true light dispelled darkness, and the new law becomes visible m all our works.

Then the Most Wise takes the charity box to distribute to the ordinary servants, or the Brethren, who are in necessity, after which, he demands if any of the Knights have anything to offer for the good of the order and this chapter, and says—

"Brother Wardens, give notice that this chapter is going to be closed."

This done, they knock the same as the Master, and make the ordinary acclamations. The Master leaves his place, makes his obeisance, embraces all the Knights, and says—"Profound Peace."

All the Brethren so the same. The Most Wise then says, [having first saluted with his mallet]—

"My Brethren, this Sovereign Chapter of Rose Croix is closed—let us do our duty."

*They all exclaim—*VIVAT!

The Master says—"Let us go, my Brethren, and make the reflection which our work requires—let us go & return in peace."

The Brethren then take the buckles out of their shoes, and wear their shoes in the form of slippers.

The only banquet, or ceremony of the table, used in chapters of Rose Croix, is the following, which is indispensably necessary, being in commemoration of the repast of our Savior, which he gave at Emmaus, when he made himself known to his disciples after his resurrection.

The Most Wise orders the youngest Knight to go and prepare every thing for their repast—he goes into an apartment appropriated to this purpose, and covers the table with a white cloth, and places thereon a loaf of which bread in a plate in the center of a triangle, formed with 3 candlesticks, in which must be candles of white or yellow wax. He then takes to the Master wands of six feet high, who receives them and returns them to the Candidate, who presents one to each Knight. They then follow the Master to the banquet, where they place themselves round the table, and standing with their heads uncovered, except the Master, who puts on his hat after prayer.

§. *Prayer.*

Sovereign Creator of all things, who provides for all our necessities and wants, bless this food of which we are now going to partake, that we may receive it for thy honor and glory, and for our satisfaction and refreshment. Amen.

The Master breaks the bread and takes a piece, then passes it to the right for the rest, and when all are provided, they eat it. The young admitted Knight brings a goblet of wine which he places in the middle of the table. The Master take it, and makes the sign of Rose Croix, drinks, and presents the goblet to the Brother next to him, who drinks and passes it round till it comes to the Master again, who goes with all the Knights and throws what is left into the fire, being all kneeling on one knee, in the manner of making an offering.

The all rise, when the Master embraces them, and says—

"Peace be unto you"

They answer—"Be it so. Amen."

They go to the other chamber, where they put their buckles in their shoes and retire.

The feast of this chapter is on Shrove Tuesday, which cannot be dispensed with; and if there is but one Knight in a place, he must absolutely perform the ceremony of this festival, that he may reunite himself in spirit with his Brethren who do the same. If he is traveling on the road and meets a Brother, they are obliged to go to some convenient house to celebrate it.

§. Ordinances.

The Knights of the Rose Croix have the privilege of holding the mallet of the Master in all Lodges; but if they do not choose to receive it they place themselves at the side of the Master, taking rank of all the officers. If the Master, through ignorance of his quality, does not make him that polite offer, he must seat himself on the floor, at the column of the Entered Apprentice. When a Knight signs a Masonic paper, he must affix his rank to his signature and also seal it with his coat of arms;—

Chev.S.P.D.R.C.  *or* Kt.S.P. of R.C.

Where there is a regular chapter, they must assemble, at least, six times a year, vizt—The annual Feast, Shrove Tuesday, Tuesday after Easter, the Day of Ascension, and Saints Day; exclusive of two Grand Festivals of St. Johns, which cannot be dispensed with. In a constituted Chapter, there must be, at least, 3, till the number becomes greater; then the officers are elected as in other Lodges. The election is made the Tuesday after Easter, when they enter into their charge, and the former officers are to render an account of their proceedings for the year past.

They are obliged to be charitable to all the poor, particularly to all distressed Masons. They must visit the prisoners. If a Knight falls sick, they are obliged to visit him and pay particular attention that he wants for nothing, which they can supply him with. On the death of a Knight, he shall be decorated with his ribbon and jewel round his neck, and his funeral shall be attended by all the Knights, clothed in all their orders, if it can be done without causing reflection on the order: after which, a chapter shall be opened. The Brother who succeeds him, shall wear his jewel, covered with black crape, for three days. In the French Chapters it is usual to keep the anniversary of his death, and pronounce an eulogy on his virtues.

It is forbid, under any pretext, whatsoever, for one Brother to fight or combat with another. No Brother can absent himself from the chapter, unless in case of sickness, or other good and sufficient reasons, of which the chapter must approve. The chapter must only be lighted with wax candles, or sweet oil.

FINIS

Ordo ab Chao

The Original and Complete Rituals
of the first Supreme Council, 33°

Transcribed from newly discovered
manuscript rituals in a private collection

VOLUME TWO

Poemandres Press
Boston & New York
1995

TABLE OF CONTENTS
VOLUME TWO

Table of Contents

19th Degree of the First Series (1801) of the Southern Jurisdiction of the United States, called

✦ ✦ ✦
Grand Pontiff, or Sublime Scotch Masonry

§. Decorations of the Lodge.

he Hangings of this Lodge must be Blue spread with gold stars.

The Master of this Lodge goes by the title of Thrice Puissant. He is clothed in a white satin robe, and sits on a Throne under a Blue Canopy, behind which, in a niche, is a transparent light, sufficient to light the Lodge. The Thrice Puissant holds a scepter in his hand.

There is only one Warden, who sits opposite the Thrice Puissant in the west, and holds a golden staff in his hand. All the rest of the Brethren are clothed in white robes, and have the title of Faithful and True Brothers. They all wear a blue satin fillet round their foreheads, with 12 golden stars embroidered thereon.

§. The Draft of the Lodge.

Represents (vizt.) square city, or celestial Jerusalem, descending on clouds from Heaven, to crush the remains of the present Jerusalem, or a three headed serpent or Hydra in chains, representing the wickedness of the infidels yet remaining there. This celestial Jerusalem has 12 gates, three on each side. In the center of the city is a tree which bears 12 different kinds of fruits. The present Jerusalem underneath, seems to be turned upside down, and the celestial Jerusalem appears to crush the 3 headed serpent. On one side of the Draft you see a high mountain.

§. *To Open the Lodge.*

The Thrice Puissant strikes twelve, at equal distances, and then demands the following questions—

Q. Brother what's the o'clock?

A. The hour foretold.

M. Faithful Brethren, the whole is ALPHA, OMEGA and EMANUEL. Let us work.

Then the Warden knocks 12, as above, and says—"Faithful Brethren, the Lodge of Grand Pontiff is open."

§. *Form of the Reception.*

The Candidate must be decorated with the attributes of Knight of the East and West, a blue satin fillet with 12 gold stars, tied round his forehead, before he enters.

He is immediately introduced into the Lodge, when the Warden places him on the top of a mountain, and asks him—

"Brother, do you detest what is perfidious? Do you promise that you will break all communications, correspondence, and Friendship with those who are so?"

The Candidate answers—"I promise and swear."

Then the Warden leaves the Candidate, and comes down the mountain backwards, and goes to the Celestial city, and with a surveyors chain measures the 4 sides of it, when he goes to the Candidate again, and tells him, "Brother, that city [pointing to it] measures 12,000 furlongs each side." Then he takes the Candidate by the hand, and both come down backwards, he places him before the draft, facing the Thrice Puissant. After a minutes silence, he makes him take 3 square steps towards the chained serpent, then one step on each side of the 3 heads, he then kneels 3 times with his right knee, holding at the same time, his right hand horizontally towards the Thrice Puissant.

[This ceremony is instead of an obligation.]

The Thrice Puissant orders him to retreat 3 steps, which brings him to the bottom of the draft, where the Warden gives him the sign, token, and word— (vizt)

§. *Sign, Token & Words.*

Sign.—The Sign is, Hold your right hand horizontally, the fingers Extended, then drop 3 fingers perpendicularly downwards.

Token.—The Token is, put reciprocally, the palm of the right hand, on the fore head of the other.

Words.—The words are, one says HALLELUJAH; the other answers LET US PRAISE THE LORD. The first says again EMANUEL, the other answers, GOD GRANT.

Order.—The Order is a broad red ribbon, with 12 golden stars embroidered thereon, it is worn from the right shoulder to the left hip.

Jewel.—The Jewel is a square of Gold, on one side is engraved the word ALPHA and on the other side OMEGA.

§. *Lecture.*

Q. What are you?

A. I am a Sublime Grand Pontiff.

Q. Where have you received this degree?

A. In a place where there was neither sun nor moon to light it.

Q. Explain this to me?

A. As the Grand Pontiff never wants any artificial light, the faithful and true brothers, the Sublime Grand Pontiffs, do not want riches or titles to be admitted into the Sublime Degrees, as they prove themselves worthy of admittance by their attachment to Masonry, the faithful discharge of their several obligations, their virtue, and true and sincere friendship for their Brethren in general.

Q. What does the draft of this Lodge represent?

A. A square city of four equal sides, with three gates on each side, in the middle of which is a tree, which bears 12 different kinds of fruit. The city is suspended as on clouds, and seems to crush a 3 headed serpent.

Q. Explain this to me.

A. The square city represents Ancient Free Masonry, under the title of Grand Pontiff, which comes down from heaven to replace the Ancient Temple, which is represented by the ruins and the 3 headed serpent underneath.

Q. How comes Masonry to have fallen into ruin, since we are bound to support it, and are attached to it by our obligations, which cannot be equivocal?

A. It was so decreed in old times, which we learn from the writings of St. John, whom we know to have been the first Mason who held a Lodge of Perfection.

Q. Where does St. John say this?

A. In his revelation, where he speaks of Babylon and the celestial Jerusalem.

Q. What signifies the tree, with the 12 different fruits, which stands in the center of the square city?

A. The tree of life is placed there to make us understand, where the sweets of life are to be found; and the 12 fruits signify that we meet in every month to instruct ourselves mutually, and sustain each other against the attacks of our enemies.

Q. What is the meaning of satin fillet with the 12 golden stars, which the Candidate wore round his forehead?

A. It procures those who wear it an entrance into our Lodge, as it likewise procures the entrance of those who wear it, into the celestial Jerusalem, as St. John himself informs us.

Q. What is the meaning of the 12 Golden stars on the fillet of the Candidate, and on those of the Brethren?

A. They represent the 12 Angels, who watched at the 12 Gates of the celestial Jerusalem.

Q. What signify the blue hangings, with the golden stars thereon?

A. The blue is the symbol of Lenity, Fidelity, and sweetness, which ought to be the share of every faithful and true Brother—And the Stars represent those Masons, who have given proof of their attachment to the Statutes and rules of the order, which in the end, will make them deserving of entering into the celestial Jerusalem.

Q. What age are you?

A. I reckon no more.

Q. What remains for you to acquire?

A. The Sublime truths of the degrees above this.

Q. What is your name?

A. Faithful and True Brother.

§. *To Close.*

T.P. What is the clock?

W. Thrice Puissant, the hour accomplished.

T.P. ALPHA and OMEGA—Let us rejoice, my Brethren.

He then strikes 12, which is repeated by the Warden, and the Lodge is closed.

FINIS

20th Degree of the First Series (1802) of the Southern Jurisdiction of the United States of America, called

Master Advitam, Grand Master of all Symbolic Lodges

§. Decorations.

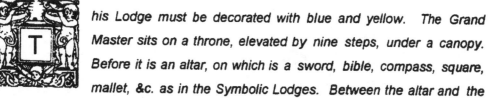

his Lodge must be decorated with blue and yellow. The Grand Master sits on a throne, elevated by nine steps, under a canopy. Before it is an altar, on which is a sword, bible, compass, square, mallet, &c. as in the Symbolic Lodges. Between the altar and the south is a candlestick with 9 branches, which is always lighted in this Lodge. There are two Wardens in the west. The Grand Master represents CYRUS ARTAXERXES, wearing his royal ornaments and a large blue and yellow ribbon crossing each other.

§. To Open.

Grand Master. — I desire to open the Lodge.

He then descends to the lowest step of the throne, and when he is assured that the Lodge is tyled, he knocks 1 and 2 with his mallet. Each Warden repeats the same, which makes 9.

G.M. — Where is your Master placed?

W. — In the east.

G.M. — Why in the east?

W. — Because the glorious sun rises in the east to illumine the world.

G.M. — "As I sit in the east, I open this Lodge," which is repeated by the Wardens.

Then all the Brethren clap with their hands 1 and 2.

§. *Form of Reception.*

The Candidate represents Zerubabel, who enters the Lodge by himself, without being introduced, decorated with the jewels and badges of the highest degrees he has taken. The Wardens take him by the hand and place him in a blue elbow chair opposite the Grand Master, who demands from him, all the words, from an Entered Apprentice up to a Grand Pontiff, & after he has satisfied the Grand Master, and is found worthy to hold a scepter, they make him travel 9 times round the Lodge, beginning in the south, and then by nine square steps he advances to the throne, and walks over two drawn swords, laid across. There must be a pot with burning charcoal close by the throne, that the Candidate may feel the heat of the fire while taking the obligation, in doing which, he lays his right hand on the Bible, which is covered by the Grand Master's right hand, and then takes the following

§. *Obligation.*

I —— do most solemnly and sincerely swear and promise under the penalties of all my former obligations, to protect the Craft and my Brethren with all my might, and not to acknowledge any one for a true Mason, who was not made in a regularly constituted and lawful Lodge. I furthermore do swear that I will strictly observe and obey all the statutes and regulations of the Lodge, and that I will never disclose or discover the secret of this degree, either directly or indirectly, except by virtue of a full power in writing, given me for that purpose by the Grand Inspector or his deputy, and then to such only as have been Masters of a regular Lodge. All this I swear under the penalties of being for ever despised and dishonored by the Craft in general.

He then kisses the Bible.

§. *Signs, Token & Words.*

1st Sign.—The 1st Sign is to make 4 squares—with your right hand and arm, the fingers clinched & the thumb elevated, clapping your hand twice on your heart, then put your left hand on your left hip, the thumb and fingers also making a square as well as the arm, at the same time putting your two heels together. forming another square.

2nd Sign.—The 2nd Sign is that of Aaron the High Priest, which me made when the tabernacle was finished; which is kneeling down with both elbows on the ground, the head inclined on the left side.

3rd Sign.—The 3rd Sign is that of Solomon when the Temple was finished, which are 5 squares, crossing both your hands on your breast, both the thumbs upward, which are 4, then, putting the heels together makes the 5th square.

Token.—The Token is to take each others elbow with the right hand, squeeze it reciprocally 4 times, slip the hand down and give the Masters Grip.

Words.—The Word is JECHSON, which signifies, "I am that I am." This is also the name of the man who found the cavern where the lion hid, who kept in his mouth the key of the ark of alliance, which was lost.

The 2nd Word is JUBELLUM, which is the name of him who fought the lion in the cavern. The lion had a gold collar round his neck, on which was engraved the word JECHSON. The rest is an enigma to you, as it is only known to the Sublime Princes of the Royal Secret; a degree which you cannot receive unless you crush the serpent of ignorance.

The 3rd Word is ZANABAZARE, which was the name of him who laid the first foundation stone of the temple, rebuilt by the Princes of Jerusalem.

Sacred Word.—The Sacred Word is RAZA BETZIJAH.

Jewel.—The Jewel is a triangle, on which is engraved the word SECRET, and is suspended by a broad blue and yellow ribbon.

§. *Lecture.*

Q. Are you a Grand Master of all Symbolic Lodges?

A. They know me at Jerusalem to be such.

Q. How shall I know that you are a Grand Master of all Symbolic Lodges?

A. By observing my zeal in rebuilding the Temple.

Q. Which way did you travel?

A. From the south to the east.

Q. How many voyages?

A. Nine.

Q. Why so many?

A. In memory of the Grand Masters who traveled to Jerusalem.

Q. Can you give me their names?

A. Their names are ESDRAS, ZERRUBABEL, HOMEN, NEHEMAIS, PHALCHI, JOSHUA, ELIAB, JOJADA, HOMAN, NEHEMIAS & MALACHIAS.

Q. What are the pass words?

A. JECHSON, JUBELLUM & ZANABAZARE.

Q. What object engaged your attention most, when you first entered into the lodge of Grand Masters?

A. The candlestick with 9 branches.

Q. Why are the 9 candles therein always kept burning in this lodge?

A. To remind us that there cannot be less than 9 Masters to form a Grand Master's lodge.

Q. What were your reasons for wishing to be admitted & received in this lodge of Grand Masters?

A. That I might receive the benefit of the 2 lights I was unacquainted with.

Q. Have you received those lights, & in what manner?

A. In receiving first the small light.

Q. Explain this.

A. When I was received by steel & fire.

Q. What signifies the steel?

A. To remind us of the steel by which our Most Respectable Chief, Hiram Abiff, lost his life, and which I am sworn to make use of whenever I can revenge that horrible murder on the traitors of Masonry.

Q. What means the fire?

A. To put us in mind that our forefathers were purified by fire.

Q. By whom were you received?

A. By Cyrus.

Q. Why by Cyrus?

A. Because it was he who ordered Zerubbabel to rebuild the temple.

Q. What did you promise & swear to perform when you received this degree?

A. I swore that I would see the laws, statutes, & regulations strictly observed in our lodge.

Q. What was your name before you received this degree?

A. Zerubbabel.

Q. What is your name now?

A. Cyrus.

Q. What means the word JECHSON?

A. "I am that I am", & it is also the name of him who found the lion's den.

Q. Why is the lodge decorated with blue and yellow?

A. To remind us that the Eternal appeared to Moses on Mount Sinai, in clouds of glory and azure, when he gave to his people the laws of infinite wisdom.

Q. Where do you find the records of our order?

A. In the archives of Killwinning, in the north of Scotland.

Q. Why did you travel from the south round to the east?

A. In allusion to the power of the Grand Architect of the universe, which extends throughout all the world.

Q. Why did you wash your hands in the 14th degree?

A. To show my innocence.

Q. Why is the history of Hiram Abiff so much spoken of?

A. To put us always in mind that he chose to sacrifice his life than reveal the secrets of Masonry.

Q. Why is the triangle, with the word secret on it, considered as the most precious jewel of Masonry?

A. Because by its justice, equality & proportion, it represents our redemption.

Q. By what mark was the place discovered where Hiram Abiff was buried by his assassins?

A. By a sprig of granate.

Q. For what reasons do the master masons in the Symbolic Lodges, speak of a sprig of cassia?

A. Because the Sublime Grand Elected descendants of the ancient patriarchs did not think proper to give the real name or truth of Masonry; therefore, they agreed to say that it was a sprig of cassia, because it had a strong smell.

Q. What are the reasons for the different knocks at the door to gain admittance?

A. To know and be assured that they have passed the different degrees, which number we must understand.

Q. For what reasons do we keep our mysteries with such circumspection and secrecy?

A. For fear there might be found amongst us some traitorous villains similar to the three Fellow Crafts who murdered our chief, Hiram Abiff.

Q. What is the reason that the Grand Masters of all lodges are received with so much honor in the Symbolic Lodges?

A. Those homages are due to their virtues as Princes of Masons, whose firmness has been shown on so many occasions, by spilling their blood in support of Masonry and the fraternity.

Q. Why do we applaud with our hands?

A. In that manner we express our happiness & satisfaction at having done a good action, & rendered justice.

Q. What reflections occur, when contemplating the conduct of Solomon?

A. That a wise man may err, & when he is sensible of his fault, correct himself by acknowledging that fault, whereby he claims the indulgence of his Brethren.

Q. Why do the Symbolic lodges take the name of St. John of Jerusalem?

A. Because in the time of the crusades, the Perfect Masons, Knights, and Princes, communicated their mysteries to the Knights of that order; whereupon it was determined to celebrate their festival annually, on St. John's day, being under the same law.

Q. Who was the first architect that conducted the works of Solomon's temple?

A. Hiram Abiff; which signifies the inspired man.

Q. Who laid the first stone?

A. Solomon cut and laid the first stone, which afterwards supported the temple.

Q. Was there any thing enclosed in that stone?

A. Yes; some characters, which were, like the name of the Grand Architect of the universe, only known to Solomon.

Q. What stone was it?

A. An agate, of a foot square.

Q. What was the form of it?

A. Cubical.

Q. At what time of the day was the stone laid?

A. Before sunrise.

Q. For what reason?

A. To show that we must begin early and work with vigilance and assiduity.

Q. What cement did he make use of?

A. A cement which was composed of the finest and purest flour, milk, oil, and wine.

Q. Is there any meaning in this composition?

A. Yes; when the Grand Architect of the Universe determined to create the world, he employed his sweetness, bounty, wisdom, and power.

Q. What is the reason why the number eighty-one is held in such esteem among Princes of Masons?

A. Because that number explains the triple alliance which the Eternal operates by the triple triangle, which was seen at the time Solomon consecrated the temple to God; and also that Hiram Abiff was 81 years of age when he was murdered.

Q. Was any thing else perceived at the consecration?

A. Perfume which not only filled the temple, but all Jerusalem.

Q. Who destroyed the temple?

A. Nebuchadnezzar.

Q. How many years after it was built?.

A. Four hundred and seventy years, six months, and ten days, after it's foundation.

Q. Who built the second temple?

A. Zerubbabel, by the grant and aid of Cyrus, King of Persia. It was finished in the reign of Darius, when he was known to be a Prince of Jerusalem. Cyrus not only gave Zerubbabel and the captive Masons their liberty, but ordered all the treasures of the old temple to be restored to them, that they might embellish the second temple, which he had ordered Zerubbabel to build.

Q. What signifies the jewel of the Right Worshipful Grand Master of all lodges being a triangle?

A. He wears it in remembrance of the presents given by monarchs and the protectors of the order, in recompense for their zeal, fervor, and constancy.

Q. What way have you traveled to become a Right Worshipful Grand Master of all Lodges, & Grand Patriarch?

A. By the four elements.

Q. Why by the four elements?

A. To put us in mind of this world, and the troubles in which we live; to cleanse ourselves from all impurities and thereby render ourselves worthy of perfect virtue.

Q. Where was the lodge of Grand Masters first held?

A. In the sacred vault, east of the temple.

Q. Where is that lodge held at present?

A. All over the world, agreeably to the orders of Solomon, when he told us to travel and to spread over the universe, to teach Masonry to those whom we should find worthy of it, but especially to those who should receive us kindly and who were virtuous men.

Q. What did Solomon give you to remember him at your departure?

A. He rewarded the merits of all the workmen, and showed to the Chief Master the cubic stone of agate, on which was engraved on a gold plate, the sacred name of God.

Q. How was the agate stone supported?

A. On a pedestal of a triangular form, surrounded by three cross pillars, which were also surrounded by a circle of brass.

Q. What signifies the three pillars?

A. Strength, wisdom, and beauty.

Q. What was in the middle of the circle?

A. The point of exactness, which teaches us the point of perfection.

Q. What else did Solomon give you?

A. The great sign of admiration and consternation, by which I am known by a Brother. He also put a ring on my finger, in remembrance of my alliance with virtue, and loaded us with kindness.

Q. Why have you a sun on the jewel of perfection?

A. To shoe that we have received the full light, and know Masonry in its perfection.

Q. Who destroyed the second temple which was finished by the Princes of Jerusalem?

A. Pompey began its destruction, and King Herodes the Great finished it.

Q. Who rebuilt it again?

A. King Herod repenting the action he had unjustly done, recalled all the Masons to Jerusalem who had fled, and directed them to rebuild the temple.

Q. Who destroyed the third temple?

A. Tito, he son of the emperor Vespasian. The Masons, who with sorrow saw the temple again destroyed, departed from Rome, after having embraced the Catholic religion, and determined never to assist in constructing another.

Q. What became of those Masons afterwards?

A. They divided themselves into several companies, and went into different parts of Europe, but the greatest part of them went to Scotland, and built a town which they called Killwinning at this time there is a lodge there, bearing the same name.

Q. What happened to them afterwards?

A. Twenty-seven thousand of the Masons in Scotland determined to assist the Christian Princes and Knights, who were at that time at Jerusalem, in a crusade for the purpose of taking the Holy Land and city from the infidels, who were then in possession of it; and they accordingly obtained leave of the Scottish monarch.

Q. What happened most remarkable to them?

A. Their bravery and good conduct gained them the esteem and respect of all the Knights of St. John of Jerusalem. The general of that order, & the principal officers, took the resolution of being admitted into the secrets of Masonry, which they accordingly received; and in return they admitted them as Scotch Masons into their order, by the name of Rose Croix, or Pelican.

Q. What became of those Masons afterwards?

A. After the crusade, they returned and spread Masonry throughout all Europe, which flourished for a long time in France and England; but the Scotch, to their great praise be it spoken, were the only people who kept up the practice of it.

Q. How came it again in vogue in France?

A. A Scotch nobleman went to France and became a resident at Bordeaux, where he established a Lodge of Perfection, from the members of the lodge in 1744; in which he was assisted by a French gentleman, who took great pleasure in all the Masonic Degrees. This still exists in a most splendid manner.

Q. What means the fire in our lodge?

A. Submission, purification of morals, and equality among Brethren.

Q. What signifies the air?

A. The purity, virtue, & truth of this degree.

Q. What does the sign of the sun mean?

A. It signifies that some of us are more enlightened than others in the mysteries of Masonry; and for that reason we are often called Knights of the Sun.

Q. How many signs have you in this degree of Grand Pontiff, which is Grand Master of all Lodges?

A. 1st — The sign of the earth, or apprentice

2nd — of water, Fellow Craft

3rd — of terror, the Master

4th — of fire

5th — of air

6th — of the point in view

7th — of the sun

8th — of astonishment

9th — of horror

10th — of stench, or strong smell

11th — of admiration

12th — of consternation.

END OF THE LECTURE

§. *To Close.*

The Grand Master says—"My Brother, enter into the cave of Siloe—work with Grand RAF ODOM—measure your steps to the sun, and then the great black eagle will cover you with his wings, to the end of what you desire, by the help of the Most Sublime Princes Grand Commanders."

He then strikes 4 & 2, makes the sign of the four squares, which is repeated by the Wardens, and the lodge is closed.—

§. *The examination of a Brother in the foregoing, degree, is as follows:*

Q. From whence came you?

A. From the sacred vault of Jerusalem.

Q. What are you come to do here?

A. I am come to see and visit your works & show you mine, that we may work together and rectify our morals, & if possible, sanctify the profane—but only by permission of a Prince Adept, or Prince of the Royal Secret, (if one is present.)

Q. What have you brought?

A. Glory, grandeur & beauty.

Q. Why do you give the name of St. John to our lodge?

A. Formerly all the lodges were under the name of Solomon's lodge, as the founder of Masonry; but since the Crusades we have agreed with the Knights Templars, or Hospitallers, to dedicate them to St. John, as he was the support of the Christians & the new laws.

Q. What do you ask more?

A. Your will & pleasure as you may find me worthy, obedient & virtuous.

21ˢᵗ Degree of the First Series (1801) of the Southern
Jurisdiction of the United States, called

Patriarch Noachite, or Chevalier Prussian.
Sometimes called The Masonic Key

t is necessary, before a Candidate is initiated into this degree, that he should previously, have received all the preceding degrees, although it is only looked upon, as the Knights Servants of K.H., or Knights of the White and Black Eagle; as it is now called for known reason. Formerly, it was sufficient to be a Master Mason of Hiram, to be initiated into this degree, which cannot be at present, for reasons which shall be given in due time.

§. Origin.

The Most Ancient Order of Noachite, now called Prussian Knights, servants of the Princes of the White and Black Eagle is translated from the Ancient German or Gaelic Language by Brother Berage, Knight of Eloquence or Grand Orator of the Chapter of Brother de St. Gillair, Grand Inspector and Knight Lieutenant Commander General of the Prussian Council of Noachites in France in the year of the Order 4658.

The Grand Master General of the order, who is styled, Knight Prince Grand Commander, is the most Illustrious Frederick of Brunswick, King of Prussia, whose ancestors have for 300 years, been the protectors of the said order, which is celebrated by the Prussian Knights, in memory of the building of the tower of babel, and the confusion of tongues which happened there. Formerly this degree was called Noachite, which is, the descendants of Noah. The Pagans

242

knew this order, under the name of Titans, who attempted to scale the heavens and dethrone Jupiter, but the present knights, acknowledge no other God but the Grand Architect of the Universe, and him only do they adore.

There is an annual celebration of the full moon in March, being the night if the confusion of Languages and disunion of the workmen at the Tower of Babel. This miracle of the Creator was awful and impressive, and was a punishment inflicted on those presumptuous Masons, for daring to seek the residence of the Divinity, except by the exercise of his religion. It is this Epoch of Gods anger and revenge which we meet to celebrate, and for this reason we assemble in a retired place, on the night of the full moon of every month, to hold our Council, by the light of the moon and stars alone.

§. *The Grand Officers of the Chapter.*

1st.—The Master of the Chapter is called Lieutenant Commander, and is decorated with a large black ribbon, in a triangular form round his neck, an Equilateral triangle hangs on his breast.

2nd.—The Senior Knight of the Chapter officiates as Senior Warden, and is a Grand Inspector, with the same Jewel, suspended by a narrow black ribbon to the third button hole of his coat.

3rd.—Another Knight acts as Junior Warden and is called Introductor, and wears the same Jewel.

4th.—Another Knight of the Chapter is called Knight of Eloquence or Grand Orator, and wears the same Jewel to the third button hole of his waistcoat.

5th.—Another Knight is called Chancellor or Grand Secretary, and wears the same jewel as the Grand Orator.

6th.—Another Knight is called Knight treasurer or Financier, and wears the same Jewel as the Grand Orator.

7th.—Another Knight is called Knight Captain of the Guards, and wears the same Jewel as the last.

All the rest of the Knights, wear the same Jewel to the third button hole of their waistcoat. The 7 officers wear their hats in the Chapter but not the rest of the Knights.

In case of scarcity of officers, three of the alone named officers can hold Chapter, viz., The Knight Lieutenant Commander, and the 2 Senior Officers Knights who officiate as Wardens.

The draft of the Chapter is the Firmament with the full moon and stars, on which the eye must be always fixed.

The place where the Chapter is held, should be so situated that the full moon and stars may enlighten it, either through the top or the windows, as it is expressly forbid that any artificial light should be used in the Chapter except and artificial Moon.

§. *To Open the Chapter.*

The Lieutenant Knight Commander opens the Chapter in the East by giving three distinct knocks. The Senior Knight in the West answers by striking one blow with a mallet on the pummel of his sword, on which the Lieutenant Knight Commander says—"To order" *then all the Knights rise, put both hands to heaven, the fingers extended, and turning their faces towards the East, where the Moon rises, and while in this position, the Lieutenant Knight Commander asks the following questions*

Q. Where is your Father?

A. Answer by looking up to Heaven.

Q. Where is your Mother?

A. Answer by looking down on the ground.

Q. Are we well prepared and in security?

A. We are.

*The Lieutenant Knight Commander then says to the Senior Knight—*Announce to the Knights that this Chapter is Illumined by the Moon, and it is time to work.

The Senior Knight announces it in the same words.

After which they let fall their hands in a circle to the bottom of the belly, and take their seats in the usual position.

§. *Reception.*

The Knights must amuse themselves by looking at the Moon and Stars, until the Candidate is announced, at the door of the Chapter.

The Candidate must be introduced bare headed in his ordinary clothing without a sword wearing an apron and gloves of white leather as used by the descendants of Hiram.

The Junior Officer, or Knight Introductor, is the friend and protector of the Candidate, he goes into the Antechamber, and conducts him to the door of the Chapter, on which he gently strikes 3 times at equal distances, when the Knight of the Guard answers by one knock and says Knight Tyler, take care to prevent the entrance of any man unless he is known to be a Knight Mason of Prussia. The Knight of the Guard, then opens the door, and on seeing the Junior Knight Introductor, he shuts it, and reports to the Senior Knight—"That the Junior Warden requests to enter the Chapter."

Who reports in the same words to the Lieutenant Knight Commander, who desires him to be admitted on his giving the Pass Word, which the Junior Knight gives to the Knight of the Guard. He then enters the chapter, and informs the Lieutenant Knight Commander—"That he has left at the door of the Chapter, a Master Descendant of Hiram, clothed in a white apron and gloves, and begs the Lieutenant Commander to receive him a Prussian Knight."

The Lieutenant Knight Commander, orders him to be admitted, in his giving at the door, the Ancient Masters pass word TUBAL CAIN.

The Candidate then enters the Chapter, by making the 3 steps of a Master— When the Lieutenant Commander addresses the Junior Knight Introductor as follows—(vizt)

L.C.—Brother Junior Warden. do you answer for the Master whom you have presented to me?

J.K.—I answer for him, as I would for myself that he is a Master Mason and a descendant of Hiram.

L.C.—If so, let him advance to the foot of the Throne, where the Lieutenant Commander demands the word of a Master Mason.

The Candidate gives it in the ancient and customary form.

The Lieutenant Commander then addresses himself to the Knights and says— "Brother Knights, I here present to you a perfect Master of Hiram, who is desirous of becoming a Prussian Knight. Do you consent that he shall be received?"

All the Knights immediately draw their swords, and, plunge them towards the Candidate, without speaking—which is the mode established of expressing their approbation.

Then the Lieutenant Commander says to the Candidate— "In the name of all the Prussian Knights, as well those who are here present, as those who are dispersed over the two Hemispheres, I consent to your request, provided you will renounce pride and ostentation during the rest of your life. Answer me— what do you say?"

C.—I consent and promise that I will from this moment divest myself of pride and ostentation, and every species of vice, which may degrade the Man or the Mason.

L.C.—Then begin by an act of Humiliation.

He is then carried by the Junior Knight to the Knight of the Guard, to the foot stool of the Throne, where he makes 3 genuflections with his left knee and then kneels on both knees. The Lieutenant Commander presents the hilt of his sword to him, which he kisses 3 times.

Then the Grand Orator, Knight of Eloquence, delivers an oration, on the proud and ostentatious attempts of the sons of Noah and the repentance and humility of Peleg the great architect of the Tower of Babel.

When the Candidate rises all the Knights, with their swords in their hands, make the sign of Master Mason, descended of Hiram, and then return their swords into their scabbards.

The Candidate again kneels and takes the following

§. *Obligation.*

L.C.—Promise and swear to me on the faith and obligation of a Master descendant of Hiram, that you will inviolably keep the secrets, which I am now about to confide in you.

Cand.—I swear and consent—*he kisses the Bible.*

L.C.—Promise and swear to me, that you never will reveal to any of the Sons of Adam the mysteries of our Order, unless you know him to be a master and a Knight of this degree—that you will be attentive, friendly, serviceable, courteous, kind & compassionate to all the Knights of this degree.

Cand.—I swear & consent—*he kisses the Bible.*

L.C.—Promise and swear to me that you will never suffer, even at the peril of your life, any person to wear the Jewel of this Order, unless he makes himself known to you to be a Knight Master Prussian.

Cand.—I swear and solemnly engage to observe the condition prescribed to me.

The Senior Knight raises him, and gives him the Sign, Word and Token.—

§. *Sign, Token & Word.*

Sign.—Put up both your hands, the fingers extended upwards, the thumbs opposite to the ears, at the same time making 3 genuflections.

Pass Word.—The Pass Word is PELEG, pronounced 3 times very slow.

Mysterious Words & Token.—The Mysterious Words and Tokens are SHEM, CHAM and JAPHETH, at the same time you make the token by taking the 2 forefingers of a Brother, between your thumb, and forefingers, and press them, saying SHEM, the other answers by pressing in the same manner CHAM, the first then presses again and says JAPHETH.

There is another Sign, Token and Word, to enter to a Chapter, which is called the Sign, Word and Token of Entrance.

He who wants to enter the Chapter shows 3 fingers, the others with the same sign, then the first takes the three fingers of the other Brother in his hand and says FREDERICK THE 3RD, the other answers by saying NOAH 3 times—this last Sign, Token and Word signifies that we are beholden to him for the precious treasure which he received from his Ancestors.

The Lieutenant Commander, then delivers to the Candidate his Jewel, which he ties to the 3rd button of his coat, with a black ribbon. He presents to him the sword, and desires him to take off the clothing of the Master Descendant of Hiram, and invests him with that of the Order, which he wears as the other Companions. The Knight Introductor instructs the Candidate to offer his gloves to the Lieutenant Commander.

§. *History.*

The Descendants of Noah, notwithstanding the covenant with God, of which the rainbow was given as a sign, that he never would destroy the sons of man again by a general Deluge, resolved to build a Tower so high that they could thereby defy the divine vengeance of the Almighty, and chose for that purpose a plain called Shinar in Asia. Ten years after they had laid the foundation of the Edifice, the Lord (says the historian) cast his eyes upon the earth, and saw the pride of the Sons of Man, and descended upon the Earth to confound the rash audacious attempts of his people and caused a confusion of Languages among the workmen, so that they were unintelligible to each other. It is from this circumstance that the Edifice was called the Tower of Babel, which signifies confusion.

Sometime after, Nimrod, who was the first who established Royalty and Distinctions among men, to avenue the right and the homage and adoration which is due to the Divinity, founded a city, and called it Babylon—that is, Ancient confusion.

It was in the night of the full Moon in March that God caused this miracle, which is the reason that the Prussian Knights or Noachites, hold their Grand Assembly every year, on the night of the full Moon in March. A Chapter for initiation or instruction is held every Month, on the night of the full Moon.

As the workmen could no longer understand each other, they separated themselves and each took a different way. Peleg, who gave the plan, and was the founder and director of the Building was the most culpable, condemned himself to a rigorous penance, and retired from the sinful spot, into the North, now called Germany, where he arrived after undergoing much labor, trouble and fatigue in crossing deserts, and dreary woods, in which he found nothing for sustenance, but the roots of the Earth, and the wild fruits of the fields. In that part of the Country which is now called Prussia, he fixed himself, and with great labor constructed several Huts to shelter himself from inclement seasons, and after some time, he built himself a small triangular Temple, in which he used to shut himself up, to implore the mercy and forgiveness of God, for the sins he had committed.

In the year 1553 in digging for salt mines which are often found in Prussia, they discovered the ruins of a triangular Edifice 15 Cubits deep, in the center of which stood a column of White marble, on its Base was engraved in Syriac Characters the whole history of the penitent Peleg. On the side of the Column, they found a Coffin of Grey Stone, in which they perceived some dust, and a black agate stone, in which was engraven the following Epitaph in Syriac Characters—

"Here lies the ashes of the great Architect of the Tower of Babel. The Lord had compassion on him, because he became humble and penitent."

Besides this stone there were several others, with characters cut in them on the one of triangular form was cut in Syriac characters which was not interpreted until the reign of his majesty Frederick the 3rd, the present King of Prussia, informing us that the world we inhabit, existed for 9000 years before the birth of Adam. The engraving on another stone informs us that our forefathers had built many Edifices under ground, to prevent the Temples of the living God from being profaned by the Infidels, and that the Temple of Enoch was the first. There were also found six other stones of white marble, with Syriac characters, which cannot be explained, until the true elected shall be united, under the banners of One Sovereign and one Law, which is that practiced by the Knights Adepts, which degree will bring you to the knowledge of it, but previously to receiving it, we must crush the foul serpent of Ignorance and prejudice in matters of religion and all the worshippers of the Living God with an eye of fraternal tenderness, however different their modes and forms of worship may be, in full hope and expectation of receiving Eternal Beatitude.

All these curious pieces of Agate, Marble, the Coffin and Column are deposited in the Archives of the King of Prussia in a secret place.

The Epitaph does not say that Peleg was the Architect of the Tower of Babel, but the inscription on the base of the column, informs us that Peleg was the son of Eber, who was the son of Salah, who was the son of Arphaxad, who was the son of Shem, who was the oldest son of Noah. Now my Brother, you are instructed in a part of our Mysteries, and have received information which you could not have obtained from any other source, and as unknown to all the profane, who have never been admitted into this degree.

I have now confided to you an important and useful information—because of indiscretion, conceal from vulgar minds a knowledge of our rich treasure, and should you be so rash and indiscreet, as to commit yourself, follow the example of the great Peleg in practicing humility, and these Lessons which are given by the Knights Philosophers, Knights Adepts of the Sun.

The Noachites are now called Prussian Knights, and are descendants of Peleg, Architect of the Tower of Babel, therefore the origin of this Order, is long before the Æra of Hiram or Solomon, as the Tower of Babel was built many centuries before the Temple of Solomon. In former ages it was not required that a Candidate should be a Master Mason of Hiram, but in the time of the Crusades, The Knights of the different orders in Europe were initiated into this degree, by the Christian princes, who were arrived to conquer the Holy Land, which was invaded by the infidels.

The Masonic descendants of Hiram, from the affection which subsisted between them and the Noachites, who were much esteemed were desirous of being initiated into this order and they were accordingly admitted Prussian Knights agreeably to the Mysteries, and from that time, a Candidate cannot be admitted unless his is at least a Perfect Mason, according to the Statutes and Regulations of the order, which are also deposited in the Archives of the King of Prussia. It is strictly prohibited by the Statutes of our order, to make use of any tables, eating or drinking, or any artificial light in this Chapter, except an artificial Moon. But the Lieutenant Knight Commander, may hold a Lodge table of Companions of Hiram, on which, nothing can be served up that had life, and the collation must consist of Roots, Fruits and Vegetables, in memory of the penitent Peleg who subsisted on Vegetables during his penance.

END OF THE HISTORY

§. *Lecture.*

Q. Brother Senior Knight, who are you?

A. If you wish to know, first let me know who you are.

Q. Do you know the Sons of Noah?

A. I know three of them.

Q. Who are they?

A. I will tell you in the manner of our spelling.

Q. Then let me hear.

A. You begin, and I will answer.

Q. S.—

A. C.—

Q. J.— What signifies these 3 letters?

A. SHEM, CHAM and JAPHETH.

Q. Give me the sign?

A. Here it is (*he makes the sign*).

Q. Give me the Pass Word?

A. PELEG—*pronounced very slow.*

Q. What name is that?

A. It is the name of the Architect, who made the plan, and conducted the building of the Tower of Babel.

Q. Who taught you the name?

A. The Lieutenant Knight Commander of the Order of Knights Prussian.

Q. In what place did he give you this name?

A. In a Chapter, which was only lighted by the Moon.

Q. Was the building of that Tower praise worthy?

A. No, because the perfecting of it was impossible.

Q. Why was it impossible?

A. Because presumption, vanity and arrogance was the foundation of it.

Q. Is it in imitation of the Sons of Noah that you keep this in memory?

A. No, on the contrary, but only for this reason, that we may have their faults before eyes.

Q. Where is deposited the Body of Peleg?

A. In a coffin made of Grey stone.

Q. Has he been rejected or disowned for his sins?

A. No, because by characters which were engraved on an agate stone, found among the dust of his body in the stone coffin, we learn that God had forgiven him, as he had repented of his sins and had become humble.

Q. In what manner was you initiated a Prussian Knight?

A. By 3 genuflections—kneeling and by kissing 3 times the hilt of the Lieutenant Knight Commanders sword.

Q. Why did you make 3 genuflections?

A. To put me in mind of practicing humility.

Q. Why do the Knights wear a triangle?

A. In memory of the Triangle, before which Peleg the penitent was accustomed to pray.

Q. Why is the Arrow in the Triangle revered?

A. It is in memory of what happened at the tower of Babel.

Q. Why a black ribbon?

A. The black shows the grief, sorrow & repentance of the workmen of the said Tower.

Q. Did they work by night as well as by day?

A. Yes, In the day by the favor of the sun, and in the night, by the Light of the Moon.

Q. Where is the Lieutenant Knight Commander placed?

A. Always opposite to the Moon.

Q. And where are the Grand Officers placed?

A. Opposite to the Lieutenant Knight Commander.

Q. Where are the other Knights placed?

A. Anywhere, to the right and left, but their eyes always fixed on the Lieutenant Knight Commander.

Q. What is the reason thereof?

A. Because a Knight Prussian, having renounced all pride and ostentation, is to substitute Humility, and therefore requires no rank in a Chapter.

Q. Have you any more particular signs?

A. Yes, and will answer them is questioned properly.

Q. Where is your Father?

A. The answer and sign is, he looks up to heaven.

Q. Where is your Mother?

A. No other answer but looking mournfully on the ground.

END OF THE LECTURE

§. *To Close.*

Q. What is the time?

A. The Moon no longer lights our Chapter.

L.C. If so, announce to all the Knights that as our Chapter is obscure, it is time to rest.

This is repeated by the 1st Knight. The Lieutenant Knight Commander then gives 3 distinct knocks.

The 1st Knight gives one knock on the hilt of his sword.

L.C. Retire my Brethren, God grant that our labor may be acceptable to him.

All the Knights answer PELEG 3 times, slow in a low voice and the Chapter is closed.

FINIS

Apron—The Apron is trimmed with yellow, with the Jewel, painted on the area in gold.

Gloves—Yellow.

Arms of the Order—First—Azure, Luna, D'Argent, Eloil d'ore.

Second—Sable triangle & Arrow ore.

Alphabet of this degree

A B C D E F G H I K L

M N O P Q R S T U Y Z

22ⁿᵈ Degree of the First Series (1801) of the Southern Jurisdiction of the United States, called

Knights of the Royal Axe or Hachet, sometimes called Grand Patriarch, by the name of Prince of Lebanus

(This meeting is called a College.)

§. To Open.

The Chief Prince says—"To order Brethren," *which is answered by the Senior and Junior Grand Wardens in the same words. After some silence is observed, the Chief Prince, holds up both his hands, the fingers and thumbs extended as wide as possible and says*—"The trees of Lebanus is grown up and fit to be cut."

—On which all the Brethren hold up both their hands in the same manner, then let them fall on their thighs in allusion that they are cut down, in order to be used for Holy purposes, vizᵗ.

1ˢᵗ.—*They were used for the Building of Noah's Ark.*

2ⁿᵈ.—*They were used for the Construction of the Ark of Alliance.*

3ʳᵈ.—*For the use of Solomon's Temple.*

The Chief Prince then says

Noah Bazaleel Sidonians	} The answers to these words are made by the Senior Warden {	Japheth Eliab Lebanus

There is no token in this Degree.

§. *Origin.*

This degree was established on the three above mentioned occasions, the cutting of cedar for Holy uses. The explanation of the Letters on the Axe or Jewel will teach you.

L, on one side of the handle is LEBANON

S, on the Top ------------------- SOLOMON

AB on the same side ------------ ABDA

D on ----------- do -------------- ADONIRAM

X on ----------- do -------------- XERXES

Z on ----------- do -------------- ZERUBABEL

A on ----------- do -------------- ANANIAS

On the other side of the Axe are the following initials—

S on the Blade ------------------- SIDONIANS

N on the top of the handle ----- NOAH

S on ----------- do -------------- SHEM

C on ----------- do -------------- CHAM

I on ----------- do -------------- JAPHETH

M on ----------- do -------------- MOSES

B on ----------- do -------------- BAZALEEL

E on ----------- do -------------- ELIAB

The said Axe or Jewel must be crowned, and should be of Gold, and must hang on the breast to a ribbon of colors of the Rainbow, it may be also worn from the right shoulder to the Left Hip.

The Sidonians were always very zealous for the Holy Enterprises, before the Deluge, the employed themselves in cutting Cedars from Mount Lebanon, for the construction of Noah Ark, under the Conduct of Japhet.

The Descendants of them, likewise cut Cedars from Mount Lebanon, that were grown up again, for the construction of the Ark of the Covenant, and their posterity, also, cut in the same forest, under the conduct of the Prince of Heroden, for the Construction of the 1st Temple of God, by the orders of Solomon. The Samaritans assisted in bringing the timbers down from the Mount, to the sea side, to be transported from thence to Joppa.

These zealous descendants have since been employed to fell the timbers of the mountain for the construction of the 2nd Temple, by the orders of Cyrus, Darius, and Xerxes, under the direction of Zerubbabel.

This celebrated Nation formed on the said mountain, Colleges or meetings, and always in their works adored the Great Architect of the Universe. They had the same signs, and their different words were taken from Different Inspectors and Conductors, as Noah and his three sons. Noah being the Chief and his sons the Conductors. It is to these Conductors and Ancient patriarchs, we owe the Knowledge of these events, in succession of time, since the Deluge. In the earliest ages of time, Colleges were established in the Mountain, for the construction of the ark of the Covenant, and in some ages after, the same Colleges were held for the construction of Solomon's Temple.

That wise King ordered a small palace to be built on Mount Lebanon, which when finished, he used to go to see what progress the workmen had made in Hewing and squaring the Cedars.

Thus by their Example, we preserve with the greatest respect, the names of those venerable patriarchs, and also the memory of the Sidonians.

The initials of the Jewel form an Abridgment of this interesting History as well as the figure of the draft.

The College is closed in the same manner as it was opened.

FINIS

23rᵈ Degree of the First Series (1804) of the Southern Jurisdiction of the United States, called

Chief of the Tabernacle

§. *Decorations of the Lodge.*

The hangings are principally white, supported by others of red and black here and there, according to the taste of the architect. At the bottom of this hall is a sanctuary, separated from the upper part by a balustrade, and by a red curtain on every side. In the sanctuary there is placed the throne over a platform, upon which you enter by seven steps. Before the throne is placed a table covered with a red cloth—upon the altar is laid the Holy Bible and a poniard. Beside the throne there is the Ark of Alliance, crowned by a Glory, in the center of which is seen God's name, (יהוה) and at the sides the Sun and the Moon. To the right of the first altar, and a little further upwards, is the altar of sacrifices. In front, to the left, is the altar of perfumes. In the west, 2 chandeliers, of 5 branches, arrayed in a pyramidal form. In the east, 1 chandelier, with 2 branches. The president is seated on the throne, and the Wardens before the altar. During receptions there is a dark apartment with an altar in the middle, over which is placed a light, and three human skulls. In front of the altar there is a human skeleton.

§. *Titles.*

The presiding officer is styled, "Great Sovereign Sacrificer." The Wardens, "High Priests"— the others, "Levites." The lodge is styled an "Hierarchy." The Chief represents Aaron; the Wardens, his sons, Eleazer and Ithamar. The

Candidate represents Hamar. He should be introduced covered, hat on, sandals on his feet, and linen small clothe on.

§. *Dress.*

The Chief, or Grand Sacrificer, wears a large red tunic, over which is placed another of yellow, shorter than the first, and without sleeves. Upon his head is a miter of gold cloth; upon the front is painted or embroidered a △יהוה, with the Ineffable name enclosed. Over this dress he puts a black sash with a silver fringe; from which hangs (by a red cockcade) a poniard. The sash is worn from left to right.

The 2 High Priests, or Wardens, have the same dress, with the exception of the △יהוה upon the miter, which they do not use.

The Levites wear white tunic, tied with a red belt, with a gold fringe. From this belt, by a black cockcade, is suspended a thurible, (censor,) which is the jewel of this degree.

Apron.—The apron is white, lined with deep scarlet, and bordered with red, blue, and purple ribbons. In the middle, it has gold chandelier of 7 branches, and on the flap a myrtle in violet color. The jewel, which is a thurible, is sometimes worn from a broad sash of yellow, purple, blue, and scarlet ribbon, from the left shoulder to the right hip.

Hour of opening—is when the descended sons of Hiram came to the sacrifices. Hour of closing—when the sacrifice is consumed, knocking 7 blows, by 6 and 1.

The Candidate knocks, and repeats the following

§. *Obligation.*

I — — do promise and swear never to reveal the secrets of this degree to any person in the world, except he has acquired all the preceding degrees, and then, not unless within the body of a Sovereign Council of this degree of Chief of the Tabernacle, regularly holding its authority from some legally established Supreme Council of the 33rd degree—nor will I be present, or aid, or assist at the communicating them, unless with the above named authority, regularly obtained. And in case I should violate this my sacred obligation, I perjure myself: I consent that the earth should be opened before my eyes, and that I should be engulfed even to my neck, and thus miserably perish. To the fulfillment of which, may God preserve me in my senses. Amen.

(N.B.—Aaron's two sons, Nadab and Abihu were so punished for their crimes. See Numbers, Ch. iii, and Levit. x.)

In token of your sincerity in this obligation you will kiss the Bible.

§. *Sign, Token & Words.*

Sign.—Advance the left foot, and with the right hand make a motion of taking the censor from the left.

Token.—Mutually take the left elbow with the right hand, arching the arms so as to form a kind of circle.

Pass Words.—One says, URIEL, the other answers, THE TABERNACLE OF REVEALED TRUTH.

Sacred Word.—JOD, HEY, VAU, HEY.

24ᵗʰ Degree of the First Series (1804) of the Southern Jurisdiction of the United States, called

🙟 🙟 🙟

Prince of the Tabernacle

⁂

§. Decorations.

his lodge consists of 2 apartments, the 1ˢᵗ of which proceeds directly into the 2ⁿᵈ, and is called the vestibule, where the brothers clothe themselves. It is ornamented with the different attributes of Free Masonry.

The 2ⁿᵈ apartment is made completely circular, by means of the suit of hangings. The decoration of this room varies agreeably to the three points of reception. In its middle, is placed a chandelier with 7 branches, and each branch with seven lights—in all 49 lights.

§. Apparel.

A blue silk tunic—the collar of which is decorated with rays of gold, representing a glory. The surplice is sprinkled with gold stars. Upon the head, a close crown, encompassed by stars and surmounted by a Delta.

The Sash—is a broad watered scarlet ribbon, worn as a collar, or as a sash from right to left.

Jewel.—The jewel of a Prince of the Tabernacle is the letter Å in gold, worn from a collar of broad crimson ribbon. This letter forms the key of the alphabet of this degree.

Apron.—The apron is white bordered with crimson. On its middle is painted, or embroidered with red, a representation of the tabernacle. The flap is sky blue.

§. *Titles.*

This assemblage is called a Hierarchy. The Chief Prince, "Most Powerful." There are 3 Wardens, styled "Powerful." The 1st placed in the south—the 2nd in the east—and the 3rd in the north. The officers of this Hierarchy represent Moses, the giver of the law—Aaron, the Chief Priest;—Bezeleel, the son of Uri.—Aholiab, the son of Ahasimach.

Candidate.—The Candidate represents Eleazar, who succeeded Aaron in the duties of the tabernacle.

§. *To Open.*

Moses—"First Powerful, are we well tyled and in perfect security & are all present, Princes of the Tabernacle?"

Aaron—"We are, Most Powerful, in perfect security; & all present, are regular Princes of the Tabernacle."

M. What is the o'clock?

A. It is the 1st hour of the 1st day of the 7, for building this Hierarchy. It is the 1st of the day of life, and the sweetness of the 7.

M. Since it is so, give notice that I am about to open this Sovereign Council of the Hierarchy.

A. Princes, the Most Powerful is about to open this Sovereign Council of the Hierarchy.

Bezaleel and Aholiab repeat. The Chief Prince gives 6 equal and 1 loud raps, and the Wardens all repeat them, one after the other, when Moses says,— "I declare this Sovereign Council duly opened."

§. *Form of Reception.*

The Candidate is first washed in water. He is then introduced and the Most Powerful reads Exodus 25th Chapter 1—40. Then he is brought to the altar by 6 equal and 1 long steps, when he kneels and takes the following

§. *Obligation.*

I —— do promise and swear that I will never reveal to any person in the world whatever, the secrets of this degree of Prince of the Tabernacle; and that I will never confer them, nor aid, or assist in conferring them on any person or persons, by my presence, or otherwise, except under; an authority regularly obtained from some Supreme Council of the 33rd Degree, which has been constitutionally established, giving full power so to do—that I will stand to, and abide by, all the laws, rules, and regulations which belong to this degree, or may regularly emanate from the Supreme Council of the 33rd Degree under which we are now acting; and in case I should violate this sacred obligation, I consent to be stoned to death, (as St. Stephen was,) and that my body be left to rot above ground deprived of burial. For the faithful performance of which, may the Almighty Architect of the Universe preserve me. Amen.

In token of your sincerity in this obligation you will kiss the book.

The Chief Prince approaches him (he still kneeling,) with a hod of oil and a trowel, and thus proceeds:—"I anoint, Eleazar, thy right ear, thy right thumb, with the holy oil, in token of thy being separated from the foibles of the world, and to set thee apart of evil doers in this tabernacle of clay, to be raised at the great and awful day of judgment, as a shining example of God's glory, in the house not made with hands eternal in the heavens."

§. *Signs, Token & Words.*

1st Sign.—Of Recognition. Raise eyes to heaven & cover them with the right hand; at the same time place the left hand on the stomach, inclining the head towards the left shoulder. Then draw the right hand diagonally to the right hip.

Grand Sign.—Form a triangle above the head, the points of the fore fingers touching each other; the other fingers closed.

Token.—Mutually clasp each other's hands, right with right and left with left, giving the

Words.—As in the last degree foregoing.

§. *History.*

The history of this degree may be found in the orders which the Almighty gave to Moses and the children of Israel, to depart from Egypt and to go to the promised land, and there build him a tabernacle (Exodus, Chapter 25.)

March.—6 equal, & 1 long steps, in all 7.

§. *Table Ceremony.*

To be observed by the Chiefs & Princes of the tabernacle. The table is round and the victuals are not placed on it, but successively presented to the brothers in turn, who are served each to his taste. In the middle of the table is a cluster or inflamed hearts (painted,) and some incense—there must be 7 lights on the table.

Manner of Toasting. 1st Toast.—The Master says—The warm mid day of our solemnities, invite our inclinations to new libations. Let us charge. Powerful Brother Junior Warden, what continuation of success do you announce?

Junior Warden.—answers according to the ritual—"Powerful Brothers Wardens, & you Powerful Brothers of the Hierarchy, let us celebrate the grandeur of the glorious destiny which associates us. Drink of the cup of one draught."

2nd Toast.—The Most Powerful, or Chief Priest says—The warm mid day of our solemnities, invite our inclinations to new libations. Let us charge. Powerful Brother Senior Warden, what is the hour?

Senior Warden.—From the ritual answers.

C.P.—How do you combine talents?
S.W.—*Answer by the ritual.*
C.P.—Where are our Brothers?
S.W.—The Sovereign Master of the Universe directs them in Lodge, & preserves them in the Hierarchy.
C.P.—Powerful Brothers of the hierarchical Lodges, I give you the health of all Free Masons, elected, or to be elected, for the unity of 7 and 3.
3rd Toast.—The Chief Prince orders to charge the censors agreeably to the ritual, & says, "Powerful Brothers, let us drink to the health of the president of

the United States, and to all in authority. May the Sovereign Grand Master of the universe fill them and us with his joy and prosperity.

§. *To Close.*

Moses.—Powerful Brother Aaron, What is the o'clock?

Aaron.—The last hour of life and of tranquillity.

Moses.—Then it is time to close this Hierarchy. To me, by the sign.

All make the sign. The Most Powerful makes the battery, the Wardens repeat, and the Most Powerful declares the Hierarchy closed.

Hieroglyphics of this degree

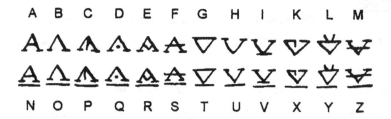

25ᵗʰ Degree of the First Series (1804) of the Southern Jurisdiction of the United States, now 26ᵗʰ Degree, called

Prince of Mercy

§. Decorations of the Lodge.

The hangings are green, supported by nine columns alternately white and red, upon each of which is an arm of a chandelier, sustaining 9 lights, forming in all 81 lights.

The canopy is green, white, and red; under which is a green colored throne. The table before the throne is covered with a cloth of the same color.

Instead of a Hiram, the Most Excellent Chief Prince uses an arrow, whose plume is on one side green, and on the other side red, the spear being white and the point gilded.

By the altar is a statue which represents "Truth," covered with the aforesaid three colors. This statue is the palladium of the order.

§. Titles.

This Chapter is styled the "Third Heaven." The Chief Prince is called "Most Excellent." Besides the two Wardens and accustomed officers, there is a "Sacrificer" and "Guard of the Palladium."

The Chief Prince represents Moses; Senior Warden, Aaron; Junior Warden, Eleazer; the Candidate, Joshua.

§. *Clothing*.

The Most Excellent Chief Prince wears a large tri-colored tunic, of green, white, and red; and on his head a crown of lace, surmounted with 9 points.

Apron.—Red, bordered with white fringe; upon its center is painted or wrought a white and green triangle. In the center is a heart, and on it the Hebraic letter ⊓. *The flap is sky blue, (sometimes green.)*

Jewel.—The jewel is an equilateral triangle of gold, and in the center a gold heart. Upon the heart is engraved the letter ⊓. *It is worn from a broad tricolored ribbon. The collar is green, white, and red.*

Age.—Eighty-one years is the age of a Prince of Mercy.

March.—Three equal steps beginning with the left foot.

Knocks.—Fifteen blows by 3, 5, and 7.

§. *Obligation*.

I — — do promise and swear, in the presence of the Grand Architect of the universe, and this respectable assembly, and by the most sacred of obligations, that I never will reveal the secrets of this sublime degree of Prince of Mercy to any person or persons whatsoever in the world, except they have received all the degrees below this in a correct manner, and so thereby I shall know him to be regularly entitled to the same. I furthermore promise and swear never to entrust this degree to any person, nor assist at any reception, unless I or they shall have been or are authorized by a particular permission or warrant for that purpose, from some Supreme Council of the 33rd degree, regularly and constitutionally established, to whose authority, laws, rules, & regulations, I now swear true faith and allegiance; and in that case I promise and swear, never to give my consent before I have been plainly informed of the life, manners and morals of the Candidate. Should I violate or transgress this, my solemn obligation, I consent to be condemned, cast out, and despised by the whole universe. And may the Supreme Architect of heaven & earth, guide, guard & protect me, to fulfill the same. Amen. Amen. Amen.

In token of your sincerity in this obligation, you will kiss the Bible.

§. *Signs, Token & Words.*

1st Sign.—Of Entrance. Place the right hand over the eyes, in the form of a Triangle, as if protecting them from the light (of the Delta).

2nd Sign.—Of Character. Form a triangle with the thumbs and fore fingers united, and place the over the belly.

3rd Sign.—Of Appeal, or Distress. Cross the 2 arms over the head, palms outward, and say, "Help me, children of the Truth!"

Due Guard.—Right hand on the hip.

Token.—Press both hands lightly on the shoulders of a Brother, saying the Pass Word.

Pass Word.—The Pass Word is GOMEL.

Common Words.—The Common Words are GIBLIM and GABAON. The 1st word signifies "Excellent Master," and the 2nd "the chamber of the 3rd heaven."

Sacred Words.—The Sacred words are JEHOVAH and JACHIN, which signify, "One God only, eternal, and Sovereign Master of all things."

§. *Lecture.*

Q. Are you a Prince of Mercy?

A. I have seen the great light, (Delta,) and our Most Excellent, as well as yourself, in the Triple Alliance of the blood of Jesus Christ of which you and I bear the mark.

Q. What is the Triple Alliance?

A. It is that which the Eternal made with Abraham by circumcision; that which he made with his people in the desert, by the intercession of Moses; and that which he made with mortals, by the death and suffering of our Savior, Jesus Christ, his dearly beloved son.

Hieroglyphics of this degree

A B C D E F G H I J K L M

N O P Q R S T U V X Y Z

26th Degree of the First Series (1804) of the Southern Jurisdiction of the United States, now 25th Degree, called

Knight of the Brazen Serpent

§. *Decorations of the Lodge.*

T he hangings are red and blue. Over the throne there is a transparency, on which there is seen a Burning Bush, & in the middle the name יהוה.

In the center of the Lodge there is a mount, elevated by 5 steps, in the form of a truncated cone.

One torch, or great taper, alone illumines the Lodge.

§. *Titles.*

The lodge is called the Court of Sinai. The Chief Knight is called, "Most Powerful Grand Master," the Wardens, "Ministers, first & second," the Orator, "Pontiff," the secretary, "Grand Inquirer," and the other Brothers, "Knights." There is also an "Examiner," & the Candidate is styled "Traveler." He must be loaded with chains to the weight of 30 lbs. at least. These heavy chains denote that this degree has reference to the deliverance of the captives.

The Lodge represents the front of Moses's tent, where he waited upon the Israelites, who came to prefer their complaints & grievances. The arch over head, sprinkled with stars, and the single light, represents the sun.

The officers represent Moses, Aaron & Joshua; the Candidate, an Israelite in chains, upon his march.

N.B.—The pleasure of bearing the yoke for our brothers, remembering that they are all our equals, & that the same arrow cannot wound us all, should determine us in receiving this degree. We should also be animated by the Divine Spirit, to avenge our country; to make our mysteries respected & to carry the law of the Most high to the 4 quarters of the universe.

§. *Clothing.*

A red collar, upon which is painted, or embroidered, the device, "virtue and valor."

Apron.—Is white, bound with black tears; upon the flap is a triangle, in a glory; in its center the Hebraic letter ח, *(signifying* חטאתי, *HATATI). Sometimes the jewel is embroidered, and on the breast of a broad watered white ribbon, worn from the right shoulder to the left hip.*

Jewel.—The Jewel is a serpent entwined upon the environs of a cross pole, in the form of a T, *about which are the Hebraic characters* חטאתי *which signify, "One who shall heal." This is the image which Moses is said to have erected in the camp of the Israelites Numbers xxi, 6&c., which possessed the virtue to heal the bites of serpents which molested them in the desert. It was afterwards preserved in the temple, with much careful attention, but as it came in process of time to be an object of idolatry with the Jews, Hezekiah, King of Judea, commanded to be taken to pieces, & full of indignation called it "NE-HUSH-TAN, old copper to be melted up," sordid stuff.*

Hour of Opening.—The Court is opened at 1 o clock, and is closed at 4 o'clock.

March—Nine serpentine steps.

Knocks.—Nine blows; 5 slow, 3 hurried, and 1 by itself.

§. *Obligation.*

I — — do solemnly promise and swear, in the presence of the Almighty God, the Grand Architect of the universe, that I will never reveal the secrets of this degree of Knight of the Brazen Serpent—nor, by my presence, aid or assist in revealing them to any person or persons whatsoever, unless the Candidate shall have taken all the preceding degrees in a regular manner—nor without a legal authority. I now swear allegiance and true faith. In case I should transgress this my solemn obligation, and thus perjure myself, I freely consent to have my heart eaten by the most venomous of serpents, and thus to perish most miserably; from which may the Almighty Creator of the universe guard and defend me.

In token of your sincerity you will kiss the Bible.

§. *Sign, Token & Words.*

Sign.—Extending the arms to the side of the body, as a cross.

Token.—Place yourself on the right of a Brother. Take his left wrist with your left hand. He takes your right wrist with his right hand.

Pass Word.—I.N.R.I., as given the Rose Croix.

Covered Word.—JOHN RALPH, the founder of this degree.

Sacred Word.—MOSES.

§. *History.*

The history of this degree is drawn from the Bible, Numbers, xxi, when God, to punish the Israelites for their wickedness, sent into their country serpents, which should devour them. They came to Moses with their grievances and confessed their faults. Moses invoked the Almighty for them, and God ordered him to fasten a fiery serpent upon a pole, that all the Israelites who might have been bitten, should turn and look upon it, and be made whole. The signification of the jewel is this; when Moses made a brazen serpent, and placed it upon a pole, as God had ordered him, and it came to pass that every one bitten, looking upon it and pronouncing the word, HATATI was immediately made whole.

27th Degree of the First Series (1804) of the Southern Jurisdiction of the United States, called
☙ ☙ ☙
Grand Commander of the Temple
⚜

§. Decorations of the Lodge.

T he hangings are red, ornamented with black columns; upon each of which there is an arm (or branch) holding a light.

The canopy and throne are red, sprinkled with black tears.

In the center of the Lodge there is chandelier of 27 lights, in 3 rows, thus arranged—12 on the 1st row, 9 on the 2nd, & 6 on the 3rd. There are also 27 lights on a round table around which are seated all of the Commanders.

§. Titles.

This Lodge is styled a Court. The Grand Commander, "All Powerful," and is placed in the east. The Wardens are styled "Most Sovereign," and are in the west.

§. Clothing.

The All Powerful is clothed in a white tunic, and over it a Knight's mantle, of red, lined with ermine skin. Upon his head he wears a crown of lace.

Jewel.—The Jewel is golden triangle, upon which engraved the word ינרי (I.N.R.I.,) in Hebraic characters, and is suspended from a white ribbon, bordered with red.

Apron—Flesh colored, lined and edged with black. On the flap there is a Teutonic cross, encircled by a crown of laurel. Beneath it, upon the flap, there is a key.

The gloves are white, lined and bordered with black.

Knocks.—Twenty-seven blows with the flat of your sword, by 12, then by 12 & 3. The Candidate passes 3 times round the room.

Hours of opening.—10 o'clock.

Hours of closing.—4 o'clock.

§. *Obligation.*

I —— in the presence of the one Almighty and only true God, the Grand Architect of the universe, and of this Venerable Court of Grand Commanders of the Temple, do, of my own free will and accord, most solemnly and sincerely vow, promise, and swear, never to reveal the secrets of this degree which I am now receiving, to any person or persons below me, except in a court lawfully holden, with a warrant or authority from some regularly established Supreme Council of the 33rd Degree, empowering me, and them with me, to work in this sublime Degree. I furthermore promise and swear, that I never will confer, nor assist in conferring his degree, upon any person who has not, in a legal and regular manner, taken all the foregoing degrees of Free Masonry. I furthermore promise and swear, that I will pay due regard and submission to the Supreme Council, under whose authority we are now acting; and that I will always govern myself by their laws, rules, and regulations, so far as the same shall come to my knowledge; and will do all in my power to support them, for the good of the craft and the advantage of Free Masonry, agreeable to the constitutions of the order. To all this I solemnly swear, under the penalty of having the severe wrath of Almighty God inflicted on me; and may He have mercy on my soul in the day of judgment, agreeably to my performance of this sacred obligation. Amen. Amen. Amen.

In token of this you will kiss the Bible.

§. *Signs, Token & Words.*

Sign.—Of acknowledgment. Make the sign of the cross upon a Brother's forehead, with the thumb, the fingers closed. In answer, he kisses your forehead. This is only done in open Court. Elsewhere, instead of kissing the forehead, the answer is to place the first fingers of the right hand over the mouth, closing the fingers, and turning the palm outwards.

Due Guard.—In open Court, place the right hand upon the round table, and with the thumb form a square. Elsewhere, place it in like manner on the left breast instead of the table.

Token.—Strike gently the left shoulder of a Brother 3 times with the right hand. In answer, he with his right hand gently squeezes your right hand 3 times.

Grand Word.—I.N.R.I., alternating the letters.

Pass Word.—SOLOMON.

28th Degree of the First Series (1802) of the Southern Jurisdiction of the United States of America, called

Grand Knight of the Sun, or Prince Adept

§. Preliminaries.

n this degree, the Master of the Council is Adam, and the Brethren, Knights. There are no Wardens, but only an introductory Master who alone performs the duty of Master of Ceremonies, and whose name in the Council is Truth.

There are 7 officers who are called Cherubims—their names are

1st	ZAPHRIEL	5th	URIEL
2nd	ZABRIEL	6th	MICAEL
3rd	CAMAEL	and the	
4th	RAPHAEL	7th	GABRIEL

These seven officers wear no Aprons. There should be twelve other Brethren who are called sylphs, these are taken from those lately admitted. The number of these cannot be augmented in a regular Council, except on the death of a Brother, when a Knight of the East, who has received all the preceding degrees be initiated.

The twelve Sylphs are clothed, they have a small blue silk bonnet, bound with yellow ribbon, and apron of brown skin, without being cut round with the scissors; it must be tied with strings of the same skin—they wear the ribbon & Jewel of the Grand Master.

The Knights wear an Apron of white, in the middle a golden sun, surrounded with rays, on the flap a triangle in a glory, in the middle of which is the letter I, which is the first letter of the name of the divinity. The apron lined with pink, and bordered with pink and yellow.

The Sylphs attend the Council in rotation with Docility and Decorum. Should any prove refractory they are expelled from the Council for ever.

All the Knights are obliged to assist at this Council with all their knowledge in Masonry, whether of the true or false, in order that one may be instructed in true as well as in false in Masonry, to guard them from the snares penetrating and crafty.

The council should be lighted by one light only, because there is but one luminary, which enlightens the world, which is the sun, and one luminary which enlightens the mind of Men, who have had the happiness to emerge from the darkness of ignorance & prejudice, and fills them with Celestial Truth.

The Candle by which the Council lighted should be placed behind a large glass Globe filled with water, with a reflecting mirror behind that it may shine more brilliantly.

The Order is a golden sun, suspended to a golden chain worn round the neck—and a broad white water tabby'd ribbon, with an eye embroidered in gold worn as a collar above the chain & jewel of the sun.

Adam wears a golden scepter with a globe at the end of it. This scepter indicates, that he is constituted King of the World & the common Father of Mankind.

At table the same ceremonies are observed as in the Lodge of Grand Master Ecossais. The duties of the Brethren are the same as those of the Knights of the East. The rules are similar to the general rules of the Ecossais Masters.

§. *To Open.*

Adam. — What time is it on earth?

Truth. — Among the profane it is night, but in this Council, the Sun is at its meridian height.

Adam. — Let us profit my dear Brethren by the kindness of this supreme planet, who by enlightening and conducting us into the way of truth, teacheth us that the Law which the Eternal hath engraven on our hearts is the only Law by which to arrive at a knowledge of pure truth.

The Master gives the Sign, which the others return.

§. *Reception.*

The Candidate appears at the door alone, having a black bandage over his eyes; he goes groping about & feeling for some time before he arrives at the door of the Sanctuary; having found it he knocks six times with the flat or palm of his Hand.

Brother Truth opens the door a little, and asks him what he desires?

The Candidate answers being prompted by one of the Sylphs:—

A. To be brought out of darkness that I may see the true light, and know the truth.

Q. What do you desire farther?

A. To be divested of the reality of man, to eradicate from within me all Prejudice, the offspring of error into which men have fallen by a thirst after all riches and by pride.

Q. Let the Candidate be introduced into the Center of Happiness.

Brother Truth opens the door, takes him by the hand and conducts him to the middle of the Sanctuary, where the Draft of the Council is drawn, covered with a Black Carpet.

Adam. —Do you persist my Brother, in wishing to arrive at the summit of truth?

Cand. —I still persist.

Then Adam says—Brother Truth, as the Brother persists, approach with him to the Sanctuary, that he may take a solemn and awful obligation and bind himself to us for ever.

The Candidate then falls on his knees when Adam takes his hands between his own, which are on the Bible, when the Candidate takes the following

§. *Obligation.*

I — — do most solemnly & sincerely swear and promise in the presence of the Omnipotent Author of the Created World, whose sacred name was first made known to Moses, on Mount Sinai, in the vision of the burning bush, and in the presence of the Knights here assembled, that I never will reveal either directly or indirectly, the secrets or mysteries of this degree to any person on earth, except to those, to whom they shall justly and lawfully belong. That I will not for trifling causes change my religion, only from a full conviction of conscience. I will not despise any man on account of his religion—that I will not suffer any blasphemy to be uttered in my presence against the Holy Bible, and that I will defend it with my sword and blood, and I do furthermore sear that I will pay due obedience & submission to the Sublime Princes of the Royal Secret and Supreme Council of Inspectors General of the 33rd, and govern myself by their recommendation, and I do furthermore swear, that I will not consent to admit any person into this degree unless I am perfectly convinced of his good character and believe him to be an honorable acquisition to our body. All this I swear, under the penalty of all my former obligations with this addition—that the grass may grow before my door, that I may never be believed in any expression I utter, but be considered as one void of truth and veracity. So God maintain me in justice & equity. Amen. Amen. Amen.

Adam addresses the Candidate—My Son, since you have by your labors in the Royal Art arrived at the point of deserving a knowledge of Truth, she must be shewn to you in her native colors. Consult yourself at this moment—see if you are sufficiently willing to obey her in every thing which she shall enjoin. If you are now, such as I wish you to be, I am, persuaded she is already in your heart, and that you must feel some sensations, which were before unknown to you. If that is the case, you may hope that she will not long delay to manifest herself to you. But take care that you do not come to defile her sanctuary by a silly spirit of curiosity and beware of augmenting the number of the profane who have so long ill treated her, as even to oblige her to conceal herself and no longer to appear on earth, but under a thick veil, from which her feet are scarcely discovered. She will always conceal her glory, and will not suffer her face to be uncovered, except to true Free Masons, that is to say, to the true extirpators of superstition and falsehood. I hope my dear Brother, that you will become one of her intimate favorites: The trials through which you have passed, sufficiently assure me of what I ought to expect from your zeal; therefore that nothing may be hid from you, I direct Brother truth to instruct you in what you ought to know, to arrive at the center of Happiness.

After Adam is done speaking they uncover the eyes of the Candidate, and show him the draft of the Council, without explaining any part.

Brother Truth then addresses him—My Dear Brother, Through me, Holy Truth now speaks to you. Before she would manifest herself to you, she has required of your certain proofs with which she is now satisfied. On your entering into the order of Masonry, she showed you several things which, without her aid would still have been enigmatical to you, materials from which you would have derived no salutary advantage. But, as you have been so happy as to have arrived at this Brilliant Mansion, learn then, that the three first working tool with which you became acquainted, being the BIBLE, SQUARE

AND COMPASS have a signification which you have not hitherto been able to comprehend.

BY THE BIBLE you are to understand, that you are to be guided by no other law than that, which governed Adam at the Time of his creation and which the Eternal engraved on his heart. That you are to make no distinction in religious sects, and as Masons, it is indispensably our desire to acknowledge and adore that great and Beneficent Being, which has the Heavens for his couch, and the Earth for his footstool. All that God has created is good, and in him there can be nothing wrong. He hath made every thing right, even as with a COMPASS we form a circle, of which all the points of the circumference are at an equal distance from the central point: God then is the central power of all things, all other things form component parts of our Circle. By the SQUARE you are also taught to believe that this same God hath made all things in due proportion. Thus, as it would be impossible to make anything round by forming it with a square, the proportion of which is to form as figure with four sides and right angles. Even so the Eternal in creating the World by his own power, could have had but one intention, and have acted accordingly, that is to say, in one manner only, and that perfectly right. You were also shown a LEVEL A PLUMB AND AN UNHEWN STONE.

BY THE LEVEL you will learn to be upright and square, not suffer yourself to be led away by the crowd of the ignorant and blind, to be firm and inflexible in supporting the rights of the natural Law, and the pure and unsophisticated knowledge of Holy truth. BY THE PLUMB and UNHEWN STONE you are to understand man in his rough, uninitiated state, polished by reason and brought to perfection by the assistance of our Masters. You have seen a plate for designing. This represents to you a man occupied in the act of thinking and who employs his reason in nothing but what is just and reasonable. Compared also to an unhewn stone, which signifies that all our actions, should be uniformly directed to the Sovereign God.

BY THE TWO COLUMNS we are to endeavor to become ornaments of our Order, that is of enlightened Brethren to serve as Beacons to them. These columns also are like the pillars of Hercules. These pillars were said to fix the boundaries of the world. Our columns signify that Masonry is the boundary or limit of the Human understanding. You have seen that bright BLAZING STAR in the Middle Chamber where the Master Masons were paid, which afterwards served as the Holy place, in which the Ark was shut up. This emblem points out to you, that you ought to apply yourself, to the making of you pure and proper, to admit Truth, that is, that you may be fixed as in a Tabernacle, as there it is that she will recompense you with her most precious gifts. You also saw another STAR.

It signifies that a true Mason by perfecting himself in the paths of virtue, will resemble a brilliant star, which gives light amidst the thickest darkness: that is, he will become useful to those who listen to him and who are disposed to profit by his instructions. You have also obtained a knowledge of the Masons of Hiram, and of the words & signs which were substituted in room of those, which were believed to have been extorted, but which, the assassins were not able to obtain the least knowledge of, as was afterwards clearly ascertained. Let this example be an useful lesson to you to be on your guard! Be assured that it is very difficult to escape the snare which are daily laid to entrap you by Ignorance and Envy. Let it remind you that the Most virtuous men, are frequently deceived, but that in such unfortunate cases we ought to be as firm as was our respected Master Hiram, who preferred being massacred to yielding to their importunities. Wherefore, when Truth shall once be heard in the inmost recesses of your heart, you ought not to hesitate, on your part which you have to take, you should be ready to die to maintain those rights by which the Sovereign good is obtained, and never expose yourself to the discovery of your secrets in your conversations with the profane: Be circumspect even with those who are most initiated in our mysteries. Do not discover yourself, to any persons whomsoever, until you are perfectly well acquainted with the character & manner of such Brethren, as may appear to you prepared to be admitted into the sacred sanctuary where Holy Truth utters her divine oracles. The search for our Master Hiram and the words which were changed signify that the ignorant rabble are attached only to words void of sense, & to them superfluous, founded on error and gross falsehood, and ground their creed and faith on such mysteries as those of the ancient Egyptians, and on a tradition which has been changed from one age to another.

You have passed through the degree of Perfect Master, you have there seen a GRAVE, a CORPSE, a CORD to draw it our, and place it in the sepulcher, found in the shape of a pyramid, at the top of which was a triangle to contain the sacred name of the Eternal. By the GRAVE & CORPSE, you are to understand mankind in the state which you were, before you had the happiness of being initiated into our Order. The CORD to draw our the Corpse, is the Bond which draws us from the bosom of Ignorance, that we may arrive at the Celestial abode, where Truth resides and represents also the true Mason who rises by degrees to the highest Heaven, there to be absorbed by the holy and unchangeable name of the Supreme Being.

In the Degree of MAÎTRE ANGLAIS (English Master) or MAÎTRE PARISIEN (Parisian Master) you saw a blazing star, a large candlestick with seven branches, and altar, purifying vases, & a large brazen sea: By this degree you are to learn, that we must be cleansed from bitterness of sin, before we can pass to other degrees we must feel ourselves capable of having brilliant light of reason emitted by Truth, of which this star is an emblem. The candlestick of seven branches designates the essential number of the Royal Art, in which seven Brethren, may imitate on of the profane who desires to emerge from darkness, and impart to him seven gifts of the spirit, which will be fully shewn to you when you shall have been cleansed and purified in the brazen sea. In the degree of MAÎTRE IRLANDES DU PRÉVÔT ET JUGE (Irish Master of the Provost & Judge) you saw a small box suspended, a Key, a pair of scales and a lighted urn. This degree teaches you the manner in which you ought to combat your passions & that you should be with respect to them as a Provost and a severe Judge: by the box you are instructed in the grand observance of keeping the secret which you have lodges in your heart and to cover it with a dark veil, that is to say, so to act as that the profane may never obtain the least knowledge of it. By the KEY you are taught that you have already been instructed in part of the mysteries and that by conducting yourself towards your Brethren sincerely with fervor and zeal, you will soon arrive at a knowledge of the general good of the society. The SCALES AND THE LIGHTED URN represent to you that you are not to rest satisfied with the sublime knowledge which you have obtained, but that you should also by your means and your actions leave after you on the minds of your Brethren, and even of the profane, a high idea of your virtues, and see that your knowledge and reputation shall enlighten and perfume as far as does materially, the Urn filled with lighted perfumes.

In the degree of D'ECOSSAIS DE PARIS (Scotch of Paris) you have seen many things, which were merely a repetition of what you had already gone through: however, you there met with three J.J.J. enclosed in a Triangle, the planet Mercury, the 3rd Chamber called Gabaon, the Ladder made in the shape of a screw [winding ladder] the figure of Solomon, and that of J&B. By the 3 J you learn the sacred names of the attributes of the Eternal, the seven winding steps represent the different degrees through which you must pass to arrive at the height of Glory represented by the Mount Gabaon, on which sacrifices were offered to the Most High. Being arrived on this mount you are to make a sacrifice of your passions and do nothing but what is prescribed by our laws. The planet mercury, the fabulous God of robbers, is an emblem of distrust, serving to caution you to show such of your Brethren, who totally forgetful of their duty, associate with wicked men, and who most frequently seem not to recollect our sacred mysteries, in other words to avoid those who by their worldly habits indicate to us, that they are ready to disown their engagements. The arch near which you are now arrived, teaches you that being admitted into the Holy of Holies, that you ought to resolve rather to perish like our Grand Master Hiram, who was there interred, than to betray the Mysteries of the order. The figure of Solomon, the founder of the Order, is presented to you as a pattern to follow. John the Baptist teaches you to become an apostle of the order, that is, that you should perform secret missions among men who you may think qualified to enter into the path of Truth, that they may arrive at a full knowledge of her.

In the Grade of FAVORI (Favorite Degree) you saw the two Kings embracing, their regret at the loss of one of their Brethren, a golden blade, the guards, a man seized and about to suffer death for having listened in. The conversation between the two Kings represents the connection between our laws and the Law of Nature, which perfectly accord with each other. The regret & the tears of the two Kings are figurative of the regret which you feel when any of your Brethren go astray from the paths of virtue. He who was listening, discovered, seized and led to punishment is an emblem of those who have been initiated into our sacred mysteries from motives of curiosity, and having been discovered are fore ever banished from our sanctuaries, and if they should be such villains as to be indiscreet we have a right by every means, even the most secret, to take vengeance on them for their perfidy. Let us pray to the Eternal to preserve our order from such misfortunes.

In the degree of Master Elect, you must have remarked that from among all the favorites in the Chamber of Solomon, there were but nine, who were elected to avenge the death of our respectable Master Hiram. This will give you an idea of what passes in our Lodge. Many of the profane have the happiness of entering into our sanctuary, but few are so happy as to arrive at a knowledge of the sublime Truth.

28th Degree of the 2nd series (1825) of the Supreme Councils
of the 33rd for the United States, Northern & Southern.
Copied from ancient M.S.S. by Br. Giles F. Yates
& presented to said Councils for adoption—called,

Knight Adept of the Eagle, or Sun

This Council must be illuminated by only one single light, and is enlightened by one Divine Light. Because there is one single light that shines among men, who have the happiness of going from the darkness of ignorance and of the vulgar prejudices, to follow the only light that leads to the celestial truth.

The light that is in our Council, is composed of a glass globe filled with water and a light placed behind it, and therefore renders the light more clear. The glass of reflection, the globe, when it is lighted, is placed in the South.

The Grand Master or Thrice Puissant, is named "Father Adam," who is placed in the east, vested in a robe of pale yellow like the morning. He has his hat on, and in his right hand a scepter, on the top of which is a globe of gold; the handle or extremity of the scepter also gilt.

The reason that Adam carries the globe above the scepter in this Council is, because he was constituted Sovereign Master of the World, and created Sovereign Father of all men.

He carries a Sun suspended by a chain of gold around his neck, and on the reverse of this jewel of gold is a globe. When this degree is given, no jewel or apron is worn.

There is only one Warden, whose name is Brother Truth, he sits in the west opposite Father Adam and entitled with the same ornaments as Father Adam—

he wears besides a large white watered ribbon, as a collar, with an eye of gold embroidered or painted thereon, above the gold chain sun.

The number of other officers are 7, and are called by the name of Cherubims (vizt.) ZAPHRIEL, ZABRIEL, CAMAEL, URIEL, MICHAEL, ZAPHAEL & GABRIEL. These ought to be decorated in the same manner as the Thrice Puissant Father Adam. If there are more than that number of the Knights of the Sun, they go by the name of Sylphs, and are the preparers of the Council and assistants in all the ceremonies or operations of the Lodge. They are entitled to the same jewel, but have a ribbon of a fiery color tied to the third buttonhole of their coats.

§. *To Open the Grand Council.*

Father Adam says—Brother Truth what time is it on earth?

A. Mighty Father, it is midnight among the profane or Cowans, but the sun is in its meridian in this Lodge.

Father Adam—My dear children, profit by the favor of this austere luminary, at present showing its light to us, which will conduct us in the path of virtue and to follow that law which is eternally to be engraved on our hearts, and the only law by which we cannot fail to come to the knowledge of pure truth.

He then makes a sign by putting his right hand on his left breast, on which all the Brethren put up the first finger of the right hand above their heads, the other fingers clinched, shewing by that there is but one God, who is the beginning of all truth.

Then Father Adam says—This Lodge is opened.

When Father Adam says—to order Brethren, they all put their right hands on their hearts, and he puts up his first finger and so VISA VERSA.

§. *Form of Reception.*

After the Council is opened, the Candidate is introduced into an antechamber where there are a number of Sylphs, each with a bellows, blowing a large pot of fire, which the Candidate sees, but they take no notice of him. After he is left in this situation two or three minutes, the most ancient of the Sylphs goes to the Candidate and covers his face with black crape. He must be without a sword, and is told that he must find the door of the Sanctuary, and when found, to knock on it 6 times with an open hand. After he finds the door and knocks, Brother Truth goes to the door, and having opened it a little, asks the Candidate the following questions, which he answers by the help of the Sylphs.

Q. What do you desire?

A. I desire to go out of darkness to see the true light, and to know the true light in all its purity.

Q. What do you desire more?

A. To divest myself of original sin, and destroy the juvenile prejudices of error, which all men are liable to, namely, the desires of all worldly attachments and pride.

On which Brother Truth comes to Father Adam, and relates what the Candidate has told him, when Father Adam gives orders to introduce the Candidate to the true happiness. Then Brother Truth opens the door, and takes the Candidate by the hand, and conducts him to the middle of the Lodge or Sanctuary, which is also covered by a black cloth, when Father Adam addresses him:—

"My son, seeing by your labor in the royal art, you are now come to the desire of knowledge of the pure and holy truth, we shall lay it open to you without any disguise or covering. But before we do this, consult your heart and see in this moment if you feel yourself disposed to obey her, (namely truth) in all things which she commands. If you are disposed, I am sure she is ready in your heart, and you must feel an emotion that was unknown to you before.

This being the case, you must hope that she will not be long to manifest herself to you. But have a care not to defile the Sanctuary by a spirit of curiosity, and take care not to increase the number of the vulgar and profane, that have for a long a time ill-treated her, until Truth was obliged to depart the earth and now can hardly trace any of her footsteps. But she always appears in her greatest glory without disguise, to the true, good and honest Free Masons, that is to say, to the zealous extirpators of superstition and lies. I hope, my dear Brother, you will be one of her intimate favorites. The proofs that you have given, assure me of every thing I have to expect of your zeal, for as nothing now can be more a secret between us, I shall order Brother Truth, that he will instruct you what you are to do in order to come to true happiness."

After this discourse of Father Adam, the Candidate is unvailed and shown the form of the Lodge or Council, without explaining any part thereof. Brother Truth then proceeds (vizt.)—

"My dear Brother, by mouth, holy truth speaketh to you, but before she can manifest herself to you, she requires of you proofs in which she is satisfied in your entrance in the Masonic order. She has appeared to you in many things, which you could not have apprehended or comprehended without her assistance; but now you have the happiness to arrive at the brilliant day, nothing can be a secret to you. Learn, then, the moral use that is made of the 3 first parts of the furniture—vizt: Bible, Compass and Square.

Bible.—By the Bible, you are to understand, that it is the only law you ought to follow. It is that which Adam received at his creation, and which the Almighty engraved in his heart. This law is called NATURAL LAW, and shews positively that there is but one God, and to adore him only without any subdivision or interpolation.

Compass.—The Compass gives you the faculty of judging for yourself, that whatever God has created, is well, and he is the sovereign author of every thing. Existing in himself, nothing is either good or evil, because we understand by this expression, an action done which is excellent in itself, is

294

relative and submits to the human understanding, judgment to know the value and price of such action, and that God, with whom everything is possible, communicates nothing of his will, but such as his great goodness pleases; and everything in the universe is governed as he has decreed it, with justice, being able to compare it with the attributes of the Divinity. I equally say that in himself there is no evil, because he has made every thing with exactness, and that every thing exists according to his will, consequently as it ought to be. The distance between good and evil with the Divinity, cannot be more justly and clearly compared than by a circle formed with a compass from the points being reunited there is formed an entire circumference; and when any point in particular equally approaches or equally separates from its point, it is only a faint resemblance of the distance between good and evil, which we compare by the points of a compass forming a circle, which circle when completed, is GOD.

Square.—By the Square we discover that God who made every thing equal, in the same manner as you are not able to dig a body in a quarry complete, or perfect; thus the wish of the Eternal in creating the world by a liberal act of his own well foresaw every matter that could possibly happen in consequence thereof; that is to say, that every thing therein contained at the same time of the creation was good.

Level—You have also seen a Level, a Plumb, and a rough Stone. By the level you are to learn to be upright and sincere, and not to suffer yourself to be drawn away by the multitude of the blind and ignorant people; to be always firm and steady to sustain the right of the natural law, and the pure and real knowledge of that truth which it teacheth.

Perpendicular and rough stone.—By these you ought to understand the prejudiced man made polished by reason, and put censure away by the excellence of our Master.

Trestle board.—You have seen the trestle board, to draw plans on. This represents the man whose whole occupation is the art of thinking, and employs his reason to that which is just and reasonable.

Cubic stone.—You have seen the cubic stone, the moral of which, and the sense you ought to draw from it, is to rule your actions, that they might be equally brought to the sovereign good.

Pillars.—The two pillars teach you that all Masons ought to attach themselves firmly to become an ornament to the order, as well as to its support—as the pillars of Hercules formerly determined the end of the ancient world.

Blazing Star.—You have seen the blazing star, the moral sense of which is, a true Mason perfecting himself in the way of truth that he may become like a blazing star which shineth equally during the thickest darkness; that is to say, it is useful to those that it shineth upon, and who are ready and desirous of profiting by its light.

The first instructions have conducted you to the knowledge of Hiram Abiff, and the inquiries that were made in finding him out. You have been informed of the words, signs, and tokens which were substituted to those we feared would have been surprised, but of which they afterwards learnt, that the treacherous villains had not been able to receive any knowledge of, and this ought to be an example and salutary advice to you, to be always on your guard, and well persuaded that it is difficult to escape the snares that ignorance, joined to conceited opinion, lay every day against us, and thereby to overcome us; and the most virtuous men are liable to fall, because their candor renders them unsuspecting: but in this case you ought to be firm, as our Respectable Father, Hiram, who chose rather to be massacred than to give up what he had obtained. This will teach you that as soon as truth shall be fixed in your heart, you ought never to consider the resolution you should take, you must live and die to obtain the light, by which we acquire the sovereign good; we must never expose ourselves to the conversation of Cowans, and must be circumspect even with those with whom we are the most intimate, and not to deliver up ourselves to any, excepting those whose character and behavior have proved them brothers, who are worthy to come and appear in the sacred sanctuary, where holy truth delivers her oracles.

You have passed the Secret & Perfect Master, the 4th & 5th degrees of Masonry; you have been decorated with an ivory key, a symbol of your distinction; you have received the pronunciation of the Ineffable name of the Great Architect of the universe, and have been placed at the first balustrade of the Sanctuary; you have had rank among the Levites, after you knew the word ZIZON, which signifies a balustrade of the Levites, where all those are placed as well as yourself, to expect the knowledge of the sublime mysteries.

Coffin and Rope.—In the Degree of Perfect Master, they have shown you a grave, a coffin, and a "whith rope," to raise and deposit the body in a sepulcher, made in the form of a pyramid, in the top of which is a triangle, and within which was the sacred name of the Eternal, and on the pavement were the two columns of Jachin and Boaz laid across.

Ivory Key.—By the ivory key you are to understand that you cannot open your heart with safety, but at proper times. By the corpse and grave is represented the state of man, before he had known the happiness of our order.

Rope.—The rope to which the coffin is tied, in order to raise it, is the symbol of raising a unit, as you have been raised from the grave of ignorance to the celestial place where truth resides.

Pyramid.—The Pyramid represents the true Mason who raises himself by degrees, till he reaches heaven, to adore the sacred and unalterable name of the Eternal Supreme.

Intimate Secretary.—This new degree leads you near to Solomon and honor, and after you redoubled your zeal you gained new honors and favors, having nearly lost your life by curiosity; which attachment to Masonry gave you the good qualities of your heart, and which found you grace and led you to the Intendant of the Buildings, and where you saw a blazing star, a large candlestick with seven branches, with altars, vases, and purification, and a great brazen sea.

Blazing star.—By the expression of purification, you are to understand that you are to be cleansed from impiety and prejudice, before you can acquire more of the sublime knowledge in passing the other degrees to be able to support the brilliant light of reason, enlightened by truth, of which the blazing star is the figure.

Candlestick and seven branches.—By the candlestick with 7 branches, you are to remember the mysterious number of the 7 Masters who were named to succeed one, and from that time it was resolved that seven Knights of Masonry, united together, were able to initiate into Masonry, and show them the 7 gifts of the Eternal, which we shall give you a perfect knowledge of, when you have been purified in the brazen sea.

Brazen Sea.—You have passed from the Secret and Perfect Master to the Intimate Secretary, Provost and Judge, and the Intendant of the Buildings. In these degrees, they have showed you an ebony box, a key suspended, a balance, and an inflamed urn.

Ebony box.—The ebony box shows you with what scrupulous attention you are to keep the secrets that have been confided to you, and which you are to reserve in the closet of your heart, of which the box an emblem. And were you to reflect on the black color of said box, it would teach you to cover your secrets with a thick vail, in such a manner that the profane Cowans cannot possibly have any knowledge there of.

Key.—The key demonstrates that you have already obtained a key to our knowledge and a part of our mysteries, and if you behave with equity, fervor and zeal to your brothers, you will arrive shortly to the knowledge and meaning of our society, and this indicates the reason of the balance.

Inflamed urn.—By the inflamed urn you are to understand that as far as you come to the knowledge of the Royal and Sublime Art, you must, by your behavior, leave behind you, in the minds of your Brethren and the vulgar, a high idea of your virtue, equal to the perfume of the burning urn.

Two kings.—In the degree of Intimate Secretary you have seen and heard two kings, who were entering into their new alliance and reciprocal promise, and of the perfection of their grand enterprise. They spoke of the death of Hiram Abiff, our Excellent Master & you saw guards and a man overseen, and ready to be put to death for his curiosity of peeping. You also heard of the prospect of a plan called the vault, to deposit the precious treasure of Masonry, when the time should be fulfilled, and you afterwards became a Brother. The conversation of the two kings, is the figure and report that our laws must hold with the natural law, which forms a perfect agreement with the conveniences, and promises to those who shall have the happiness to be contracted to you in the same manner and perfect alliance, they will afterwards come to the center of true knowledge.

Tears.—The tears and regret of the two kings are the emblem of the regret you ought to have when you perceive a Brother depart from the road of virtue.

The man peeping.—By the man you saw peeping, and who was discovered, and seized, and conducted to death, is an emblem of those who come to be initiated into our sacred mysteries through a motive of curiosity; and if so indiscreet as to divulge their obligations, we are bound to cause their death, and take vengeance on the treason by the destruction of the traitor. Let us pray the Eternal to preserve our order from such an evil you have hereof seen an example in the 9th degree, to which you are come, by your fervor, zeal, and constancy.

In that degree you have remarked, that from all the favorites that were at that time in the apartments of Solomon, only nine were elected to avenge the death of Hiram Abiff; this makes good that a great many are often called, but few chosen. To explain this enigma:—a great many of the profane have the happiness to divest themselves of that name to see and obtain the entrance in our sanctuary, but very few are constant, zealous, and fervent to merit the happiness of coming to the height and knowledge of the sublime truth.

If you ask me what are the requisite qualities that a Mason must be possessed of to come to the center of truth, I answer you, that you must crush the head of the serpent of ignorance. You must shake off the yoke of infant prejudice, concerning the mysteries of the reigning religion, which worship has been imaginary, and only founded on the spirit of pride, which envies to command and be distinguished, and to be at the head of the vulgar, in affecting an exterior purity, which characterizes a false piety, joined to a desire of

299

acquiring that which is not its own, and is always the subject of this exterior pride, and unalterable source of mans disorders, which being joined to gluttonness, is the daughter of hypocrisy, and employs every matter to satisfy carnal desires, and raises to these predominant passions, altars, upon which she maintains without ceasing, the light of iniquity, and sacrifices continually offerings to luxury, voluptuousness, hatred, envy, and perjury.

Behold, my Brother, what you must fight against and destroy, before you can come to the knowledge of the true good and sovereign happiness.—Behold this monster which you must conquer—a serpent which we detest as an idol that is adored by the idiot and vulgar, under the name of Religion.

Solomon, King Hiram, and St. John the Baptist.—In the Degrees of Elected of 15, Illustrious Knights, Grand Master Architects, and the Royal Arch, you have seen many things which are only a repetition of what you have already examined. You will always find in those degrees, initial letters enclosed in different triangles, or Deltas. You have also seen the planet Mercury, the chamber called GABAON, or the Third Heaven, the winding staircase—the ark of alliance—the tomb of Hiram Abiff facing the ark and the urn—the precious treasure found by the assiduous travelers—the three zealous Brethren Masons—the punishment of the haughty Master Mason, in being buried under the ancient ruins of Enoch—and finally you have seen the figures of Solomon, and Hiram, King of Tyre, and St. John the Baptist.

By the 3. J.J.J. you know the three sacred names of the Eternal, and mount Gabaon, where you came to by 7 degrees which compose the winding staircase.

The 7 stars represent the seven principal and different degrees to which you must come to attain the height of glory represented by the mount, where they formerly sacrificed to the Most High. When you arrive to that, you are to subdue yourself in your passions, in not doing any thing that it is not prescribed in our laws.

By the planet Mercury, you are taught continually to mistrust, shun, and run away from those, who, by a false practice maintain commerce with people of a vicious life, who seem to despise the most sacred mysteries; that is, to depart from those, who by the vulgar fear, or have a bad understanding, and are ready to deny the solemn obligations that they have contracted among us. When you come to the foot of our arch, you are to apprehend that you come to the Sanctum Sanctorum. You are not to return, but rather to persist in sustaining the glory of our order, and the truth of our laws, principles, and mysteries in like manner as our Respectable Father, Hiram Abiff, who deserved to have been buried there for his constancy and fidelity. We have also, another example in the firmness of Galaad, the son of Sophina, chief of the Levites, under Surnam, the High Priest, as mentioned in the history of perfection. Learn in this moment, my dear Brother, what you are to understand by the figures of Solomon, Hiram, King of Tyre, and St. John the Baptist. The two first, exert you, by their zeal in the royal art, to follow the sublime road of which Solomon was the institutor, and Hiram, King of Tyre, the supporter; a title legitimately due to that King, who not only protected the order, but contributed with all his might to the construction of the temple which Solomon built to the honor of the Almighty.

The 3rd, or St. John the Baptist, teaches you to preach marvelous of this order, which is as much as to say, you are to make secret missions among men, which you believe to be in a state of entering the road of truth, that they may be able one day to see her virtues and visage uncovered. Hiram Abiff, was the symbol of truth, on earth. Jubelum Akirop was accused by the serpent of ignorance, which to this day raises altars in the hearts of the profane and fearful. This profaneness, backed by a fanatic zeal, becomes an instrument to the religious reign, which struck the first stroke in the heart of our dear Father, Hiram Abiff; which is as much as to say, undermined the foundation of the celestial temple, which the Eternal himself had ordered to be raised to the sublime truth and his glory.

The first stage of the world has been witness to what I have advanced. The simple, natural law rendered to our first fathers the most uninterrupted happiness; they were in these times more virtuous, but so soon as the monster of pride started up in the air, and disclosed herself to those unhappy mortals, she promised to them every seat of happiness, and seduced them by her soft and bewitching speeches; vizt, That they must render to the Eternal Creator of all things, an adoration with more testimony and more extensive, than they had hitherto done, &c. This Hydra with an hundred heads, at that time misled, and continues to this day to mislead men, who are so weak as to submit to her empire; and it will subsist, until the moment that the true elected shall appear and destroy her entirely.

The Degree of Sublime Elected, that you have passed, gives you the knowledge of those things which conducts you to the true and solid good. The grand circle represents the immensity of the Eternal Supreme, who, has neither beginning nor end.

The triangle, or Delta, figured here is the mysterious figure of the Eternal. The three letters which you see signify as follows:—G, at the top of the triangle, "Grandeur of Masons"—the S, "submission to the same order" and the U, "Union," that ought to reign among the Brethren; which all together make but one body, or equal figure in all its parts.

This is the triangle called equilateral. The great letter G, placed in the center of the triangle, signifies, "Great Architect of the Universe," who is God; and in this ineffable name is found all the divine attributes. This letter being placed in the center of the triangle, is for us to understand that every true Mason must have it profoundly in his heart.

There is another triangle repeated, wherein is enclosed three letters of which you have had the explanation in the 6th degree. This triangle designs the connection of the Brethren in virtue. The solemn promise they have made to love each other; to help, succor, and keep inviolably secret their mysteries of the perfection proposed, in all their enterprises. It is said in that degree, that You have entered the third Heaven; that means that you have entered the place where pure truth resides, since she abandoned the earth to monsters who persecuted her.

The end of the Degree of Perfection, is a preparation to come clearly to the knowledge of true happiness in becoming a true Mason, enlightened by the celestial luminary of truth, in renouncing voluntarily, all adorations, but those that are made to one God, the Creator of heaven and earth, great, good, and merciful.

The Knights of the East, the Princes of Jerusalem, and Knights of the East and West, are known to us, in our days, to be Masonry renewed, and all of them lead us to the same end of the celestial truth, which is to say finished.

The Knights of the White and Black Eagle, and the Sublime Princes of the Royal Secret, and Grand Commander, are the Chiefs of the great enterprise of the order in general."

Then Father Adam says to the Candidate—"My dear son, what you have heard from the mouth of Truth, is an abridgment of all the consequences of all the degrees you have gone through, in order to come to the knowledge of the holy truth, contracted in your last engagements. Do you persist in your demand of coming to the holy Brother, and is that what you desire, with a clear heart, answer me?"

The Candidate answers—"I persist."

Then Father Adam says—"Brother Truth, as the truth persists, approach with him to the sanctuary, in order that he may take a solemn obligation, to follow our laws, principles, and morals, and to attach himself to us forever."

Then the Candidate falls on his knees and Father Adam takes his hands between his own, and the Candidate repeats the following obligation three times (vizt)

303

§. *Obligation.*

I — — promise in the face of God, and between the hands of my Sovereign, and in presence of all the Brethren now present, never to take arms against my King, directly or indirectly, in any conspiracy against him.

I promise never to reveal any of the degrees of the Knight of the Sun, which is now on the point of being entrusted to me, to any person or persons whatsoever, without being duly qualified to receive the same; and never to give my consent to any one to be admitted into our mysteries, only after the most scrupulous circumspection, and full knowledge of his life and conversation; and who has given at all times full proof of his zeal and fervent attachment for the order, & submission at all times to the Tribunal of the Sovereign Princes of the Royal Secret.

I promise never to confer the degree of the Knights of the Sun, without having a permission in writing from the Grand Council of Princes of the Royal Secret, or from the Grand Inspector or his deputy, known by their titles and authority.

I promise and swear to redouble my zeal for all my Brethren, Knights, and princes, that are present or absent, and if I fail in this my obligation, I consent for all my Brethren, when they are convinced of my infidelity, to seize me, and thrust my tongue through with a red hot iron; to pluck out both my eyes, and to deprive me of smelling and hearing; to cut off both of my hands, and expose me in that condition in the field, to be devoured by the voracious animals; and if none can be found, I wish the lightning of heaven might execute on me the same vengeance.—O God, maintain me in right and equity.

Amen. Amen. Amen.

After the obligation, Father Adam raises the Candidate; and gives him one kiss on his forehead, being the seat of the soul. He then decorates him with the collar, and jewel of the order, and gives him the following sign, token, and word.

304

§. *Sign, Token & Words.*

Sign.—The sign is, to clap your right hand on the left breast, which the other answers by putting up the 1st finger of the right hand (the others clinched) to the height above the head—this shews there is but one God, which is the true source of great truth. Consequently there can be but one and true religion, and the same which Adam received from God.

Pass Words.—The first says STIBIUM, which signifies PRIMA MATERIA, or the principal co-operator of all things—the other answers ALBRA-EST, which signifies a King full of glory and without blot.

Covered Word.—Is ADONAI, a sacred word, which signifies Sovereign Creator of all things.

The sign to know a Knight of the Sun—You ask him to give you his hand, which he will put together to put between yours, you kiss his forehead, and say ALPHA, which the other answers by saying OMEGA.

Then the Candidate goes round, and gives the Sign, Token and Word to every one, which brings him back to Father Adam, when sits down with the rest of the Brethren, when Brother Truth gives the following explanation of the Philosophical Lodge.

Sun.—The sun represents the unity of the Eternal Supreme, the only grand work of philosophy.

3 S.S.S.—The 3 S.S.S. signifies the STELLATO, SEDET, SOLO, or the residence of the Sovereign Master of all things.

3 candlesticks.—The 3 candlesticks show us the 3 degrees of fire.

4 triangles.—The 4 triangles represent the 4 elements.

7 planets.—The 7 planets design the 7 colors that appear in their original state, from whence we have so many different artificial ones.

7 Cherubims.—The 7 Cherubims represent the 7 metals, vizt gold, silver, copper, iron, lead, tin, & quicksilver.

Conception in the Moon.—The conception or woman, rising in the moon, demonstrates the purity that matter subsists of, in order to remain in its pure state unmixed with any other body, from which must come a new King, and a revolution or fullness of time, filled with glory, whose name is ALBRA-EST.

Holy Spirit.—The Holy Spirit, under the symbol of a dove, is the image of the Universal Spirit, that gives light to all in the three states of nature; and on the animal, vegetable, and mineral.

Entrance of the temple.—The entrance of the temple is represented to you by a body, because the grand work of nature is complete as gold, portable and fixed.

Globe.—The globe represents the matter in the original state—that is to say, complete.

Caduceus.—The caduceus represents the double mercury that you must extract from the matter; that is to say, the mercury fixed, and from thence is extracted gold and silver.

Stibium.—The word STIBIUM signifies the antimony, from whence, by the philosophical fire, is taken an alkali which we empty in our grand work. End of the philosophical explanation.

Then Father Adam explains the Moral Lodge.

Sun.—The sun represents the divinity of the Eternal; for as there is but one sun to light and invigorate the earth, so there is but one God, to whom we ought to pay our greatest adoration.

3 S.S.S.—The 3 S.S.S. shews you that science, adorned with wisdom, creates a holy man.

3 candlesticks.—The 3 candlesticks are the image of the life of man, considered in youth, manhood, and old age, and happy are those that have been enlightened in these ages, by the light of truth.

4 triangles.—The 4 triangles show us the four principal duties that create our tranquil life; vizt Fraternal love among men in general, and particularly among Brethren, and in the same degree with us. 2dly In not having anything but for the use and advantage of a Brother. 3dly Doubting of every matter that cannot be demonstrated to you clearly, by which an attempt might be insinuated as mysterious in matters of religion, and hereby lead you away from the holy truth. 4thly Never do any thing to another that you would not have done unto you. The last precept, well understood and followed on all occasionally is the true happiness of philosophy.

7 planets.—The 7 planets represent the seven principal passions of man.

7 Cherubims.—The 7 Cherubims are the images of the delights of the life, namely, by seeing, hearing, tasting, smelling, feeling, tranquillity, and health.

Conception.—The conception in the moon shows the purity of matter, and that nothing can be impure to the eyes of the Supreme.

Holy Spirit.—The Spirit is the figure of our soul, which is only the breath of the Eternal, and which cannot be soiled by the works of the body.

Temple.—The temple represents our body, which we are obliged to preserve by our natural feelings.

Figure of a man.—The figure in the entrance of the temple, which bears a lamb in his arms teaches us to be attentive to our wants, as a shepherd takes care of his sheep; to be charitable, and never to let slip the present opportunity of doing good, to labor honestly, and to live in this day as if it were our last.

Columns of Jachin and Boaz.—The columns of J. and B. are the symbols of the strength of our souls in bearing equally, misfortunes, as well as success in life.

7 steps of the temple.—The 7 steps of the temple are the figures of the seven degrees, which we must pass, before we arrive to the knowledge of the true God.

Globe.—The globe represents the world which we inhabit.

Lux ex Tenebris.—The device of LUX EX TENEBRIS teacheth that when man is enlightened by reason, he is able to penetrate the darkness and obscurity, which ignorance and superstition spread abroad.

River.—The river across the globe represents the utility of the passions, that are as necessary to a man, in the course of his life, as water is requisite to the earth, in order to replenish the plants thereof.

Cross surrounded.—The cross surrounded by two serpents, signifies that we must watch the vulgar prejudices, to be very prudent in giving any of our knowledge and secrets in matters, especially in religion.

End of the Moral Explanation.

EXPLANATION OF THE PHYSICAL COUNCIL IN MANNER OF LECTURE

Q. Are you a Knight of the Sun?

A. I have mounted the 7 principal steps of Masonry. I have penetrated into the bowels of the earth, and among the ancient ruins of Enoch, found the most grand and precious treasure of the Masons. I have seen, contemplated and admired the great, mysterious, and formidable name engraved on the △ .
I have broken the pillar of beauty, and thrown down the two columns that supported it.

Q. Pray tell me what is that mysterious and formidable name?

A. I cannot unfold the sacred characters in this manner, but substitute in its place the word אדני.

Q. What do you understand by throwing down the columns that sustained the pillar of beauty?

A. Two reasons:—1st. When the temple was destroyed by Nabuzaradan, general of the army of Nebuchadnezzar, I was one that helped to defend the Delta, on which was engraved the ineffable name; and I broke down the column of beauty, in order that it should not be profaned by the infidels. 2nd. As I have deserved, by my travel and labor, the beauty of the great Adonai the mysteries of Masonry, in passing the seven principal degrees.

Q. What signifies the 7 planets?

A. They are the lights of the celestial globe and their influence, by which every matter exists on the surface of the earth or globe.

Q. From what is the terrestrial globe formed?

A. From the matter which is formed by the concord of the four elements, designed by the 4 triangles, that are in regard to them, as the four greater planets.

Q. What are the names of the seven planets?

A. Sun, Moon, Mars, Jupiter, Venus, Mercury, and Saturn.

Q. Which are the 4 elements?

A. Air, Fire, Earth, and Water.

Q. What influence have the seven planets on the four elements?

A. Three general matters of which all bodies are composed: life, spirit, and spirit; otherwise, salt, sulfur, and mercury.

Q. What is life or salt?

A. The life given by the Eternal Supreme, or the planets, the agents of nature.

Q. What is the spirit or sulfur?

A. A fired matter subject to several productions.

Q. What is the body or mercury?

A. Matter conducted or refined to its form by the union of salt and sulfur, or the agreement of the three governors of nature.

Q. What are those three governors of nature?

A. Animal, vegetable, and mineral.

Q. What is the animal?

A. We understand in this life, all that is divine and amiable.

Q. Which of the elements serve for his productions?

A. All 4 among which nevertheless, air and fire are predominant—it is these that render the animal the perfection of the three governments, which man is elevated to breath of the Divine Spirit, when he receives his soul.

Q. What is the vegetable?

A. All that seems attached to the earth reigns on the surface.

Q. Of what is it composed?

A. Of a generative fire, formed into a body, whilst it remains in the earth, and is purified by its moisture and becomes vegetable, and receives life by air and water; whereby the four elements, though different, co-operate jointly and separately.

Q. What is the mineral?

A. All that is generated and secreted in the earth.

Q. What do we understand by this name?

A. That which we call metals and demi-metals and minerals.

Q. What is it that composes the minerals?

A. The air penetrating by the celestial influence, into the earth, meets with a body, which by its softness, fixes, congeals, and renders the mineral matter more or less perfect.

Q. Which are the perfect metals?

A. Gold and silver.

Q. Which are the imperfect metals?

A. Brass, lead, tin, iron, and quicksilver.

Q. How come we by the knowledge of these things?

A. By frequent observations and the experiments made in natural philosophy, which have decided to a certainty, that nature gives a perfection to all things, if she has time to complete her operations.

Q. Can art bring metal to perfection so fully as nature?

A. Yes; but in order to do this, you must have an exact knowledge of nature.

Q. What will assist you to bring forth this knowledge?

A. A matter brought to perfection, this has been sought for under the name of the philosopher's stone.

Q. What does the globe represent?

A. An information of philosophers, for the benefit of the art in this work.

Q. What signifies the words LUX EX TENEBRIS?

A. That is the depth of darkness you ought to retire from, in order to gain the true light.

Q. What signifies the cross on the globe?

A. The cross is the emblem of the true elected.

Q. What represents the 3 candlesticks?

A. The 3 degrees of 5, which the artist must have knowledge to give, in order to procure the matters from which it proceeds.

Q. What signifies the word STIBIUM?

A. It signifies antimony, or the first matter of all things.

Q. What signifies the seven degrees?

A. The different effectual degrees of Masonry which you must pass to come to the Sublime Degree of Knights of the Sun.

Q. What signifies the diverse attributes in those degrees ?

A. 1st—The Bible or God's law, which we ought to follow.

2nd—The Compass, teaches us to do nothing unjust.

3rd—The Square, conducts us equal to the same end.

4th—The Level, demonstrates to us all that is just and equitable.

5th—The Perpendicular, to be upright and subdue the vail of prejudice.

6th—The Trestle-board, is the image of our reason, where the functions are combined to effect, compare, and think.

7th—The Rough Stone, is the resemblance of our vices, which we ought to reform.

8th—The Cubic Stone, is our passions, that we ought to surmount.

9th—The columns, signify strength in all things.

10th—The Blazing Star, teaches that our hearts ought to be as a clear sun, among those that are troubled with the things of this life.

11th—The Key, teaches to have a watchful eye over those who are contrary to reason.

12th—The Box, teaches to keep our secrets inviolably.

13th—The Urn, learns us that we ought to be as delicious perfumes.

14th—The Brazen Sea, that we ought to purify ourselves, and destroy vice.

15th—The Circles on the Triangles, demonstrate the immensity of the divinity under the symbol of truth.

16th — The Poniard, teacheth the step of the elected, many are called, but few are chosen to the sublime knowledge of pure truth.

17th — The word ALBRA-EST, signifies a King full of glory, and without blot.

18th — The word ADONAI, signifies the Sovereign Creator of all things.

19th — The 7 Cherubims, are the symbols of the delights of life, known by seeing, hearing, tasting, feeling, smelling, tranquillity, and thought.

Q. What represents the Sun?

A. It is an emblem of Divinity, which we ought to regard as the image of God. This immense body represents the infinity of God's wonderful will, as the only source of light and good. The heat of the sun produces the rule of the seasons, recruits nature, takes darkness from the winter, in order that the deliciousness of spring might succeed.

End of the Physical Lecture.

ANOTHER LECTURE IN GENERAL

Q. From whence came you?

A. From the center of the earth.

Q. How have you come from thence?

A. By reflection and the study of nature.

Q. Who has taught you this?

A. Men in general who are blind, and lead others in their blindness.

Q. What do you understand by this blindness?

A. I do not understand it to be privy to their mysteries; but I understand under the name of blindness, those who cease to be ardent after they have been privy to the light of the spirit of reason.

Q. Who are those?

A. Those who, through the prejudices of superstition and fanaticism, render their services to ignorance.

Q. What do you understand by fanaticism?

A. The zeal of all particular sects, which are spread over the earth, who commit crimes, by making offering to fraud and falsehood.

Q. And do you desire to rise from this darkness?

A. My desire is to come to the celestial truth, and to travel by the light of the sun.

Q. What represents that body?

A. It is the figure only of one God, to whom we ought to pay our adoration. The sun being the emblem of God, we ought to regard it as the image of the Divinity; for that immense, body represents wonderfully, the infinity of God. He invigorates and produces the seasons, and replenishes nature, by taking the horrors from winter, and produces the delights of spring.

Q. What does the triangle, with the sun in the center, represent?

A. It represents the immensity of the Supreme.

Q. What signifies the 3 S.S.S.?

_A_. SANCTITAS, SCIENTIA, & SAPIENTA, that science accompanied with wisdom, makes men holy.

_Q_. What signifies the three candlesticks?

_A_. It represents the courses of life, considered in youth, manhood, and old age.

_Q_. Has it any other meaning?

_A_. The triple light that shines among us, in order to take men out of darkness and ignorance into which they are plunged, and to bring them to virtue, truth and happiness, a symbol of our perfection.

_Q_. What signify the 4 triangles, that are in the great circles?

_A_. They are the emblems of the four principal views of the life of tranquillity, vizt Fraternal love to all mankind in general, more particularly for our Brethren, who are more attached to us, and who, with honor, have seen the wretchedness of the vulgar.

2nd—To be cautious among us of things, and not to demonstrate them clearly, to any who are not proper to receive them; and to be likewise cautious, in giving credit to any matter, however artfully it may be disguised, without a self conviction in the heart.

3nd—To cast from us every matter which we perceive we may ever repent of doing, taking care of this moral precept, "To do to every one of your fellow creatures, no more than you would choose to be done to" &

4th—We ought always to confide in our Creator's bounty, and to pray without ceasing, that all our necessities might be relieved, as it seems best to him for our advantage; to wait for his blessings patiently in this life; to be persuaded of his sublime decrees, that whatever might fall, contrary to our wishes, will be attended with good consequences; to take his chastisements patiently, and be assured that the end of every thing has been done by him for the best, and will certainly lead us to eternal happiness hereafter.

_Q_. Teach us the signification of the 7 planets which are enclosed in a triangle, that forms the rays of the exterior circles, and enclosed in the grand triangle.

A. The 7 planets according to philosophy, represent the seven principal passions of the life of man. Those passions are very useful when they are used in moderation, for which the Almighty gave them to us, but grow fatal and destroy the body when let loose, and therefore it is our particular duty to subdue them.

Q. Explain the 7 passions to us?

A. 1st—The propagation of species.

2nd—Ambition of acquiring riches.

3rd—Ambition to acquire glory in the arts and sciences among men in general.

4th—Superiority in civil life.

5th—Joys and pleasures of society.

6th—Amusements and gaieties of life.

7th—Religion.

Q. Which is the greatest sin of all that man can commit, and render him odious to God and man?

A. Suicide and homicide.

Q. What signify the 7 cherubim, whose names are written in the circle, called the 1st Heaven?

A. They represent the corporeal delights of this life, which the Eternal gave to man, when he created him, and are, seeing, hearing, smelling, tasting, feeling, tranquillity and thought.

Q. What signifies the figure in the moon, which we regard as the figure or image of conception?

A. The purity of nature, which procures the holiness of the body; and that there is nothing imperfect in the eyes of the Supreme.

Q. What signifies the figures of the columns?

A. They are the emblem of our souls, which is the breath of life, proceeding from the All Puissant, which ought not be soiled by the works of the body, but to be firm as columns.

Q. What does the figure in the porch, which carries a lamb in his arms, represent?

A. The porch ornamented with the columns of JACHIN and BOAZ. and surmounted with the grand J, represents our body, over which we ought to have a particular care, in watching our conversation, and also to watch our needs, as the shepherd his flock.

Q. What signify the two letters J and B, at the porch?

A. They signify our entrance in the order of Masonry; also the firmness of the soul, which we ought to possess from the hour of our initiation; these we ought to merit, before we can come to the sublime degree of knowing Holy truth, and we ought to preserve them, and be firm in whatever situation we may be in, not knowing whether it may return to our good or evil in the passage of this life.

Q. What signifies the large J in the triangle, on the crown of the portico?

A. That large J, being the initial of the mysterious name of the Great Architect of the Universe, whose greatness we should always have in our minds, and that our labors ought to be employed to please him; which we should always have in our view, as the sure and only source of our actions.

Q. What signify the seven steps, that leads to the entry of the porch?

A. They mark the 7 degrees in Masonry, which are the principle we ought to arrive to, in order to come to the knowledge of holy truth.

Q. What does the terrestrial globe represent?

A. The world which we inhabit, and wherein Masonry is its principal ornament.

Q. What is the explanation of the great word Adonai?

A. It is the word which God gave to Adam, for him to pray by; a word which our common father never pronounced without trembling.

Q. What signifies LUX EX TENEBRIS?

A. A man made clear by the light of reason, penetrating this obscurity of ignorance and superstition.

Q. What signifies the river across the globe?

A. It represents the utility of our passions, which are necessary to man in the course of his life, as water is necessary to render the earth fertile.

Q. What signifies the cross, surrounded by two serpents, on the top of the globe?

A. It represents to us not to repeat the vulgar prejudices; to be prudent, and to know the bottom of the heart. In matters of religion to be always prepared not to be of the sentiments with sots, idiots and lovers of the mysteries of religion; to avoid such, and not holding any conversation with them.

Q. What signifies the book, with the word BIBLIA written on it?

A. As the Bible is differently interpreted, by the different sects who divide the different parts of the earth: Thus the true sons of light, or children of truth, ought to doubt of every thing at present, as mysteries or metaphysics: Thus all the decisions of theology and philosophy, teach not to admit that, which is not demonstrated as clearly, as that 2 and 2 makes 4; and on the whole to adore God, and him only; to love him better than yourself; and always to have a confidence on the bounties and promises of our Creator. Amen. Amen. Amen.

§. *To Close.*

Q. (Father Adam)—Brother Truth, what progress have men made on earth, to come to true happiness?

A. (Brother Truth)—Men have always fallen on the vulgar prejudices, which are nothing but falsehood; very few have struggled, and less have knocked at the door of this holy place, to attain the full light of real truth, which we all ought to acquire.

Then says Father Adam—"My dear children, depart and go among men, endeavor to inspire them with a desire of knowing holy truth, the pure source of all perfection."

Father Adam then puts his right hand on his left breast; when all the Brethren raise the first finger of the right hand, and then the Council of the Knights of the Sun is closed by seven knocks.

29th Degree of the First Series (1802) of the Southern
Jurisdiction of the United States, now
30th of the new series, called
🜨 🜨 🜨
K—H, Knight of White & Black Eagle
☿

hapter of the Grand Inspector of Lodges, Grand Elected Knight of
Kadosh, or the White and Black Eagle.

The Chief is the Thrice Illustrious Frederick, King of Prussia,
under the title of Thrice Illustrious Knight, Grand Commander.

§. *Opening of the Chapter of Consistory.*

The Chapter of the Grand Elected must be composed of five Brothers, every
one vested in this degree. They must be all dressed in black, with white gloves.
The order, a broad black ribbon, worn from the left shoulder to the right hip; to
which hangs the attribute of the order, being a Red Cross; the same as the
Teutonic Knights used to wear, in the middle of two swords, a cross like a St.
Andrews. No aprons are worn.

In this Chapter there are no decorations, nor any emblem, as the curtain is
entirely drawn. There is nothing figured on the ground but the mysterious ladder,
which must be covered until the Candidate, has taken his obligation.

Note.—You are never to admit a person to this eminent degree, unless you
have full proof of his fidelity. Of the five Brothers who compose this Chapter, two
must be with the Candidate in another apartment, until he is introduced, the other
three remain in the Chapter to assist in the reception.

N.B.—In a distant place, a Knight of Kadosh cannot imitate another Brother
in this eminent degree, unless he has a power or patent from an Inspector

319

General or a Deputy Grand Inspector, under his hand and seal; and when a reception is made, the Grand Commander remains alone in the Chapter with the Candidate, and must be so situated that the Candidate cannot see him, as he is not to know who initiated him.

§. *Form of Opening the Chapter.*

Q. Illustrious Knight, are you elected?

A. Thrice Illustrious Knight, Grand Commander, I am.

Q. How came you to be elected?

A. Fortune decided for me.

Q. What proof can you give me of your reception?

A. A cavern has been witness of it.

Q. What did you do in the cavern?

A. I executed my commission.

Q. Have you penetrated further?

A. Yes, Thrice Illustrious Grand Commander.

Q. How shall I believe you?

A. My name is Knight of Kadosh, or White and Black Eagle—you understand me?

Q. What's the o'clock?

A. The hour of silence.

Q. As it is so, give me the sign, to convince me of your knowledge—*on which they all draw their swords, when the Grand Commander knocks one, very hard, on the table before him, and says:* Illustrious Knights, the Chapter is open.

*One of the Knights with the Candidate out of door, hearing the great knock, goes to the door of the chapter and knocks one; one of them within goes to the door and asks—*what he wants?

He replies, that a servant Knight demands to come to the degree of Grand Elected, as he has all the degrees and qualifications of Masonry which are necessary—which being reported to the Thrice Illustrious Commander, who says— Illustrious Knights, can we admit this Free Mason among us, without running any risk of indiscretion from him?

The other two Knights then answer, We swear and promise for him. *Then the Thrice Illustrious Grand Commander approaches, and they all three take each other by the hand, and take the following obligation to each other, first giving a great knock—* We promise and swear, by the living God, always supreme, to revenge the death of our ancestor, and which of us that should in any manner commit the most light indiscretion, touching the secret of our order, shall suffer death, and shall have his body buried under this throne of this Illustrious Assembly. So God protect us in our design, and maintain us in equity and right. Amen.

§. *Form of Reception.*

A short time after the two Knights with the Candidate have heard the loud rap of the Grand Commander, to open the Chapter, they both take their hands, and after one of them has been at the door, and when they think the Grand Commander has finished the necessary business, they introduce the Candidate, and leave him in the hands of the Grand Commander, and all four retire to guard the door of the entrance, and every other door of the adjacent rooms, (if any)— the reason of their leaving the Chapter is, that no person ever assisted at the reception of a Knight Templar.

When the Candidate enters the Chapter, he prostrates his face to the ground, when the Grand Commander, behind the curtain, reminds him of the principal points of Masonry, from its beginning, to the epoch of the assassination of Hiram Abiff; Solomon's desire of punishing the traitors, in the most exemplary manner; the method he took in disposing the Masters who went in search of the three villains in order to execute his vengeance. He repeats to him the zeal, constancy and fervency of Joabert, Stokin and Jubelum, who, after the most painful search, (by Solomon's order) had the happiness of finding among the ruins of Enoch's temple in the Ninth Arch, the precious treasure of the Perfect Masons. He continues to remind him of the firmness of the Grand Elect, and Perfect Masons, at the time of the temple's destruction, when they passed through the enemy at all risks, till they obtained an entrance into the sacred vault, to find the pillar of beauty, that they might by effacing the ineffable word, hinder its being exposed to the profane. He then reminds him of the seventy-two years captivity, and the clemency of Cyrus, king of Persia, who, by the request of Zerubbabel, not only gave the Israelites their freedom, but ordered that all the treasure of the temple (taken by Nebuchadnezzar) should be restored to them, in order to decorate the new temple, which he ordered them to build to the infinite God, and at the same time created them Knights. Then he repeats the clemency of Darius to Zerubbabel (when at the head of the embassy from Jerusalem to Babylon) with their complaints against the Samaritans, who refused to contribute to the sacrifices of the new temple, according to the proclamation of his

322

predecessor, Cyrus, in favor of the Knights of the East; when they received Darius's letters to all the governors of Samaria, &c., and how the ambassadors were received on their return to Jerusalem; and elected princes by the people. He then reminds him, that after this, the second temple being destroyed, how the Most zealous Masons united under chiefs, and worked to the reformation of manners, and elevated in their hearts some spiritual edifice, and rendered themselves worthy by their works. They were more particularly esteemed and distinguished in the time of Manchin, who was the most remarkable among them. A great many others embraced Christianity, and communicated their secrets to those Christians, whom they found had the good qualities of it, living in common and forming themselves as one family, which shows how the brilliant order of Masons sustained themselves until the sixth age, and how it fell into a state of lethargy.

Notwithstanding which, there have been always found some faithful Masons; which is clearly proved by the brilliant manner in which the order of Masonry was received in the year of 1118, when eleven Grand Elect and Perfect Masons, the most zealous, presented themselves to Garinous, prince of Jerusalem, Patriarch and Knight Mason, and pronounced their promises between his, hands. They taught him the succession of the time, and progress to the time that, the princes went to conquer the holy land.—The alliance and obligations that were formed between those princes, was, that they would spill the last drop of their blood, in order to establish in Jerusalem, the worship of the Most High.

He informs him that the peace which took place after these wars hindered them from accomplishing their design, and, therefore, have continued in theory what they had sworn to do practically, never admitting in their order only those who have given proofs of friendship, constancy and discretion.

In fine, the Illustrious Grand Commander makes a general history in genealogy, of the Masonic order, its progress, its decline, and the manner how it was sustained, till the epoch of the crusades, and until the historical circumstances, that have given occasion to the degree which the Candidate expects; a degree that will give him a perfect knowledge of the precedent *degrees, and the manner how Masonry has come to us; after which, the Candidate takes the following obligation, his right hand on the Bible, his left hand under the curtain between the hands of the Grand Commander.*

§. *Obligation.*

I promise and swear, never to reveal the secrets of the Grand Elected Knights of Kadosh, or White and Black Eagle, to any person. I swear to take revenge on the traitors of Masonry; and never to receive in this degree, none but a Brother who has come to the degrees of Prince of Jerusalem and Knight of the Sun, and then only by an authority given to me by a Grand Commander or Deputy Inspector, under his hand and seal. I promise to be ready at all times to conquer the Holy Land, when I shall be summoned to appear, to pay due obedience at all times, to the Princes of the Royal Secret; and if I fail in this my obligation, I desire that all the penalties of my former obligations may be inflicted on me. Amen."

He kisses the Bible and rises. Then the Grand Commander proceeds and says—My dear Brother, he who has bestowed this degree on you, which you have now aspired to, and who is described in this place, as Grand Commander, and Grand Inspector of all Lodges, and Grand Elected, is sensible of the importance of the secret already confided in you; it is therefore necessary to recommend a circumspection, and also to observe to those who take the name of Knights of the White and Black Eagle, and Kadosh, to be always attentive, and not to give the least suspicion relative to our mysteries, order, progress, and end of Masonry. The imprudence and indiscretion of many Brothers, has given a knowledge to the world of many of our emblems, by which Masonry has greatly suffered, and will be repaired with difficulty. Their indiscretion has caused the loss and retreat of many Puissant Brothers, who would have been an ornament and support of our Lodges. Such indiscretion in this degree, my dear Brother, would be without any recovery, as there are no more emblems, when every matter shall be disclosed and discovered to you, that will give room for some events, of which you will see the consequences, when you shall have heard all my instructions.

The words which our Brothers place at the end of their obligations, (vizt) Amen, which signifies because there is no more; that shall be no more; if this shall be again. This ought no longer to be a secret to you, who are going to have an explanation of the origin of Masonry, and what has occasioned the society. Truth penetrates the cloud and the shade, which we can leave, to come to the knowledge of what we were before in quality of Knights of Kadosh, White and Black Eagle, and what we are as Symbolic Masons, and what we can be by the destruction of our enemies.

LET US PRAY

O most Eternal, Beneficial and all gracious, Great Architect of the Universe; we from the secret depths of our hearts, offer thee a living sacrifice. We beseech thee to inspire our enemies with a just sense of the evil they have done us, and from their having a conviction of their wrongs, they might atone for their manifold injuries, which doth not belong to us thy servants to redress ourselves, but by their eyes being opened we might be reconciled, and by a hearty union take possession of those blessed lands where the original Temple was first established, where we might be gathered into one band, there to celebrate thy holy praises once more on the holy mount, in whose bowels was deposited thy ever glorious, respectable, ever blessed, and awful name. Amen.

Then the covering is taken from the draft of floor, and he continues—"Learn that the slightest indiscretion, will infallibly undermine us and throw us into an horrible abyss, where we should see buried the order of Masonry, the remains of an Illustrious and Glorious Order. By its heroism in favor of the unfortunate, how great it has been in the time when its power, authority and riches were arrived to the highest pitch, when the distinguished birth of those who were members of it, celebrated its glory. It was not less so in its tragic end, when by the noble firmness of these Knights who appeared in the middle of irons frames and torments. What can we think of the prophecy of James DeMolay, and which was verified a little after—What respect ought we not to have for the courageous zeal of those who have kept the precious remains of an order which the blackest treason, envy, and the most atrocious malignity has not been able to extinguish? What hatred ought not we to have, to those usurpers who occupy the wealth and dignity of this order? They cannot be, regarded but only as a powerful enemy, the ashes of which ought to renew that unfortunate period, when the members of the Knights shall be increased, so that they shall be able, under the auspices and conduct of a Grand and Powerful Commander, to retake the possession of all the wealth and dignity which did belong to them formerly, and is now held by those who have no other title, this day, but injustice and malignity.

This is not said, my dear Brother, to intimidate those who have, as well as yourself, aspired to this degree which we are going to confer on you this day, or to inspire them with an ardor or indiscreet zeal, for they ought every one to wait the time in silence, to become essential; and if the trust is the more authentic mark of sincere friendship, they ought to wish to augment the number of the Knights, and fear to confer this degree, with too much confidence, on an ordinary friend, lest his discretion should not be assured as your own.

You remember, my dear Brother, the obligation you have taken between my hands, at the beginning of the ceremony—and to render you the justice you deserve, I have too good an opinion of you to fear the least indiscretion in you, concerning the first notions I have given you of this last degree of Masonry.

If in this discourse you have made any remark that would keep you from pronouncing the obligation or vow we are obliged to take from you, before we can give you greater knowledge of the degree of Grand Elected Knights of Kadosh, consult yourself and see if you are disposed to penetrate further, and fulfill exactly all the points of the obligation you are going to pronounce with me, in order to link you to us forever.

326

There is a pause for a minute.

N.B.—If the Candidate is afraid to engage in or hesitates to pronounce the further obligations, the Illustrious Grand Commander, without going further, sends him out, and closes the Chapter. In regard to the notions which the Candidate might have already, the obligation which he has already taken, will assure us of his discretion. If, on the contrary, he persists in going further, and will take the obligation, the Grand Commander continues the ceremony in the following manner:—The Candidate kneels at the feet of the Grand Commander, puts his right hand on the Bible, and his left between the hands of the Grand Commander, when in this posture, the Grand Commander says—"You swear and promise to me, on that you hold most dear and sacred,

1st.—To practice the works of corporeal mercy, to live and die in your religion, and never declare to any man who received you, or assisted at your reception in this sublime degree?

The Candidate answers—I promise and swear.

Then the Grand Commander says—Say with me, 'Tsed halaad, *which he repeats.*

2dly.—You promise and swear to have candor in all your actions, in consequence never to receive in this degree, any Brother who is not your most intimate friend, and then by the consent of two Grand Elected Inspectors, if to be met with, or by a patent given you for that purpose?

The Candidate answers, I promise and swear.

He then repeats—Scharlabac.

3dly.—You promise and swear at all times to possess a sweetness of mind, as much as you are capable, to love and cherish your Brothers as yourself, to help them in their necessities, to visit and assist them when they are sick, and never draw arms against them on any pretense whatsoever?

Ans. —I promise and swear.

Say with me, MOTECK.

4thly.—You promise and swear to regulate your discourse by truth, and to keep in great circumspection and regard the degree of the White and Black Eagle or Kadosh?

He answers—I promise and swear.

Say with me, EMUNAH.

5thly.—You promise and swear that you will travel for the advancement of heaven, and to follow at all times, and in all points, every matter that you are ordered and prescribed, by the Illustrious Knights and Grand Commander, to whose orders you swear submission and obedience, on all occasions without any restrictions?

He answers—I promise and swear.

Say with me, HAMACH SCIATA.

6thly.—You promise and swear to me, to have patience in adversity, and you swear never to receive a Brother in this degree, on any pretext whatsoever, whose will is not free, as religious monks and all those who have made vows without restriction to superior?

He answers—I promise and swear.

Say with me, SABAÈL.

7thly.—You promise in the end, and swear to keep inviolably secret, what I am going to confide to you—to sacrifice the traitors of Masonry, and to look upon the Knights of Malta, as our enemies—to renounce for ever to be in that order, and regard them as the unjust usurpers of the rights, titles and dignities of the Knights Templars, in whose possession you hope to enter with the help of the Almighty?

He answers—I promise and swear.

Then say with me, CHOMEL, BINAH, TABINA.

After the Candidate has pronounced the last word, the Grand Commander relieves him and says—By the seven conditions, and by the power that is transmitted to me, which I have acquired by my discretion, my untired travels, zeal, fervor and constancy, I receive you Grand Inspector of all Lodges, Grand Elect Knight Templar, and take rank among the Knights of Kadosh, or White and Black Eagle which we bear the name of I desire you not to forget it. It is indispensable for you, my Brother, to mount the mysterious ladder, which you see there, it will serve to instruct you in the mysteries of our order and it is absolutely necessary that you should have a true knowledge of it.

Draft of the Mysterious Ladder of K—H.

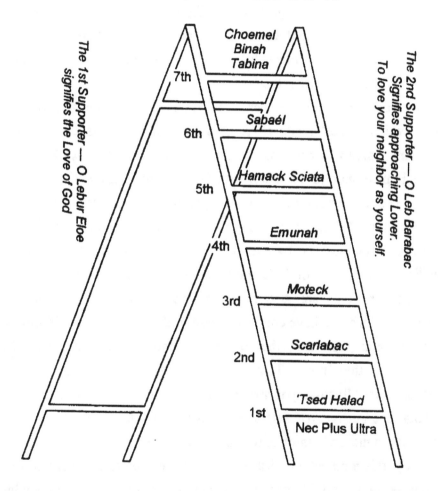

The Candidate then ascends the ladder, and pronounces at each step he rises, the name belonging to it, and when he is on the seventh or highest step,

329

and has pronounced the three last words, the ladder is lowered backwards, and the Candidate passes over it, because he cannot go back, as he would in such a case be obliged to go back against which he has taken his obligation, not to retire by the same way he came—the interests and views of the order, which is the reason that the ladder is lowered and he passes over it. He then reads the words at the bottom of the ladder, NEC PLUS ULTRA.

Then the Grand Commander embraces the Candidate, and says to him—My dear Brother, I am going to give you the Sign, Token, and Word, with the Pass Word of the Grand Elected and Grand Inspectors, after I have given you the explanation of the mysterious ladder which you have ascended and passed over, without knowing the reason thereof.

This ladder, my dear Brother, is the most essential and analogous to the history which I shall recite to you. Like a ladder it is composed of two supporters, which will give you a just idea of the strength which Philip the Fair, king of France, had, in his union with Pope Clement the 6th. The reunion of the second supporters, by the seven steps, gives you a just idea of the seven conditions that Philip, the fair, imposed on the archbishop, Bertrand Got, to make him Pope, and the two supporters being united by the seven steps or conditions, are the base of the union between the King and this Pope elect.

The seven steps are also a resemblance of the seven points of your obligation, which you have contracted, and in the same manner Philip the Fair, made Bertrand, Got take; that by the seventh article, he swore the final destruction of the Knights Templars; and in the same manner, of the seven points of your obligation, you swear to bear an implacable hatred to the Knights of Malta, and engage yourself to endeavor their total destruction, in order to reclaim the rights and dignities which they possess.

Lastly, this moment, my dear Brother, is the time to instruct you in full, in the degree of Grand Elected, and which gives us a true knowledge how Masonry came to us. Attend to that painful history—you will easily make the application yourself the more you are instructed.

§. *History.*

After the death of Benedict the 11th, who died July 13th, 1304, the cardinals met for the election of a new Pope, and formed themselves in two factions, French and Italians. Philip the Fair, king of France, had then several views which could be accomplished without the assistance of the Pope, to be elected; and as his party in the conclave fomented these divisions to favor Philip's design (who taking advantage of these circumstances) sent for Bertrand Got, then archbishop of Bordeaux (son of Bertrand, Lord of Villandran, in the same diocese) and in the conference which he had with him at a pleasant country seat, near St. John of Angely, when he informed him of his design, and the division of the conclave, which put it in his power to elect a Pope, and that he (Philip) was disposed to favor him, provided he would swear to perform seven articles, the seventh of which was, to be even a secret to him (the new Pope) until the time for the execution of it should be ripe. Accordingly he revealed the six first articles which are foreign to our purpose, but the seventh, for the exact performance of which, they both took the sacrament to each other's promise. The king having found a man to his purpose to be agent for his revenge, caused him to be elected Pope and promoted to St. Peter's chair. In the year 1305, under the name of Cement 6th, this Pope after his election established his see at the city of Lyons, where his first care was to execute the six first conditions which Philip had imposed on him. The time of declaring the seventh being arrived, Philip did not delay in declaring to the Pope, that by his oath he was to join him, to entirely destroy and exterminate the Knights Templars, to the extent of Christianity. Here is what attracted the hatred of Philip the fair, and what made him take the barbarous resolution against them all.

Some time before the death of Benoit the 11th there was a sedition in Paris, occasioned by Philip, who had coined some money, which was light, mixed with base metal, on which the populace were mutinous, who plundered and demolished the house of Stephen Barbet, master of the mint. They went afterwards to the king's dwelling, and committed a great deal of indecency, so that every matter conspired an insurrection.

The Knights Templars (against whom envy had raised many powerful enemies) were suspected to have been at the bottom of these outrages, although without any foundation, and their ruin was determined by the king, for which purpose he sought the means of obtaining assistance, when the most favorable opportunity offered itself by the death of Benoit the 11th. In order to put in his stead a Pope, on certain conditions, that should be imposed on him.

Nothing was now wanting but a pretense (for when force and authority are in hand, every matter becomes easy) for which purpose they prevailed on two abandoned men with money (whose names were Gerard Labé and Benoit Mehui). They proposed to them to get admission among the Knights Templars, and when admitted into their mysteries, to accuse the whole order of the greatest crimes, which these two villains executed exactly. They desired to be received into the order, which was an easy matter, as they had an honest exterior, titles, and apparent qualities, besides a supposed credit at court.

Every one was in their favor, and they were received. But it was not long before the Templars repented heartily of having lighted the fire brand, which was the cause of the deplorable and tragic scene, in which most all of the Templars were involved in one common destruction; for those two wretches, soon after their admission, accused the whole order of the most dreadful and most execrable crimes, demanding to be separated from them, for the unheard of terrible things which were suggested. The treason is good but the traitor is detestable. Thus did they suffer the same lot that was intended for the Templars, for they by their treachery received the most dreadful torments, and were not suffered to live. They had been the instruments, or the cause of vengeance to the Templars, by their false accusations.

Upon their reports, the King, (who had lately an interview with the Pope at Potier) took the surest measures to arrest all the Templars in his dominions in one day. This was done on the 13th of October 1307, two years after the accusation of these two villains was made. They seized on all their papers, titles, and treasures, and most of their wealth, over which were placed overseers.

King Charles of Naples, in like manner, ordered all the Templars in his province to be arrested. Those taken in France were locked up in the Castle of Mehun, to wait for their trials.

The Pope, at the same time, sent for their Grand Master, James DeMolay, a native of Burgundy (who was then at war on the Island of Cyprus) who, as soon as he received the orders of the Pope, came to Paris with his Knights of the order, among which was one Guy, Brother of the dauphin, Devienois, Hughes DePeraldés, and Theodore Bazille DeMonancourt. They were all arrested and made to suffer the most dreadful torments, in order to draw from them a confession of the crimes they were accused of, though without effect, as they bore bravely every torment, rather than accuse themselves of things of which they were innocent. So that on no other proof than that of two infamous suborners, their trials were concluded (it being impossible to obtain the least evidence against them, as never any person assisted at the making of a Templar). They executed and burnt alive fifty-seven on one day; on the next fifty-nine, and so on, until they had completed almost their total destruction. They pardoned none, not even those that served them in accusing the whole order, for as Templars they were included in the general sentence and burnt alive with the others.

Let the end of these unhappy wretches serve as a lesson to us, that we are not in future to be seduced by fine promises, and initiate any but those who have given us, by a long train of service, proofs of the most solid worthiness, lest we might by their indiscretion, be dragged again with all the Knights of Kadosh, or White and Black Eagle, in a common fate.

The Grand Master and the three above mentioned Brethren, were nevertheless not comprehended in the first execution. The Pope (for reasons which no historian has mentioned) kept the judgment to himself. Most all of the Templars at the time of this prosecution, (which lasted till the year 1314) were arrested in all Christian states, but were not all put to death.

Philip the Fair, was continually hurrying the Pope to make an end of James De Molay, the Grand Master of his companions (after having groaned nearly seven years in prison, overloaded with irons) which was at last executed, when they were burnt alive, the 11th of March 1314, in the isle of Paris, which moved to pity and tears, the numerous spectators who were present. They were steady, heroic, constant, and made the most solemn vows of their innocence, which was afterwards apparent, supported by an event extremely memorable. James De Molay, the Grand Master, seeing himself on the scaffold ready to end his life in the flames (after having lingered in irons for several years) and which was now a relief to him, to end his life in any manner rather than undergo a longer lingering in prison in this uncertain world, with great composure turned himself and directed to God the following prayer (vizt)—

"Oh, Almighty and Everlasting God, who knows the innocence of the victims, who have been sacrificed for several years, permit us to reflect on the reproach and infamous torments which you permitted Jesus Christ to be covered with at his death, to redeem us from the slavery of our sins, to give an example to the innocent, in teaching them, by his mildness to suffer without murmuring, the persecution and torments, which injustice and blindness prepare for them. Forgive, O God, the false accusations and imputations, which have caused the destruction of the whole order, of which your Divine Providence has established me chief; and if you are pleased to accept the prayer which we now humbly offer you, permit, O God, that one day these people may know the innocence of those who have endeavored to live in thy holy fear and love.—We wait your bounty and compassion the reward of the torments and death we suffer, which we offer to you in order to enjoy your divine presence in everlasting happiness."

Then addressing himself to the people, he said—"Good people, who see us ready to perish in the flames, you will be able to judge of our innocence, for I now summon Pope Clement the V in forty days, and Philip the Fair, in twelve months, to appear before the awful and tremendous throne of the ever living God, to render an account of the blood they have wickedly shed"—after which they were hurried to execution, fearing the rescue of the populace. The prediction of James de Molay was accomplished, as Pope Clement the V died the 19th of April, the same year, at Rocquemour on the Rhone, and Philip the Fair, within Twelve months at Fontainbleau.

The news of the persecution of the Knights Templars, had already reached the Knights which were left in Cyprus, and in the absence of their Grand Master had been overpowered by the Turks, when they lost Acre, with several other places in that island, and were obliged to retire to the isle of Rhodes and the adjacent islands.

The prosecutions against them in open council at Vienna, the 19th of October 1311, when the order was banished, their estates confiscated and left at the Pope's disposal, who in the year 1312, gave a part to the Knights of St. John of Jerusalem, who at this day possess the greatest part of their estates. This adversion makes to this day, a part of the obligations of the Grand Elect and Knights Templars.

As the number of them who escaped was very small, it rendered that adversion more powerful; they sought to increase their order by admitting persons in whom they believed, and thought worthy of keeping the most important secret. Such they found among the good and virtuous Masons, whom Solomon had distinguished and favored, after the construction of the temple. The candor and intrepidity which appeared among them in the greatest dangers; their wisdom, union, charity, love, impartiality, firmness, discretion and zeal, all led them to believe they could do no better than unite themselves to them. Their fathers, protectors, and supporters, sought the favor to be admitted into their society, and initiated into their mysteries.

Those who were newly initiated into their mysteries were informed by the Masons, who they were, the barbarous events which they had escaped, and the resolution they had taken, secretly to increase their numbers, in order to reclaim their rights. to re-establish their order and take possession again of their estates.

The Templars offered their Brethren Masons their assistance, in taking their revenge, and as a common cause to accept the tribute from them, of the most just gratitude and thankfulness.

The Grand Elected Knights, and Princes Masons approved their designs, accepted their offers, and agreed among themselves, instead of the character of their order, which was a cross, to use the Word, Sign and Token of Masons, and by the conformity of several analogies (events in their history) persuaded them that the different signs of Masons would put them entirely under cover, against the maliciousness of such as Gerard Labé, and Benoit Mehuy, should endeavor to be admitted into the order, and that they should not entrust the true secret to any but those whom they had tried, and of whom they had the utmost confidence. After having made them pass through the different degrees which we know in Masonry, the birth of which was take from the construction of Solomon's temple, until its destruction; characterized by the most remarkable events, entirely analogous to the destruction of the Knights Templars, whom, as Elects of Masonry, crieth only to revenge the death of their Illustrious Grand Master and retake their possession.

My dear Brother, from the degree of Master Mason that you have received, and from your having learned to shed tears at the tomb of Hiram Abiff, have you not been disposed to take vengeance? Did they not show you the traitor, Jubelum Akirop in the most dreadful colors? Would it be exaggerating to compare the conduct of Philip the Fair, with his? and to compare the two infamous informers, Gerard Labé, and Benoit Mehuy, to the two villains who joined Akirop, to murder Hiram Abiff? Do they not kindle in your heart the game revenge which those Fellow Crafts deserved, and was executed on them?

The trials you have gone through to learn the historical facts of the ancient Bible; do they not serve to make an impression on your heart and enable you to make a just application of the death of Hiram Abiff, in comparing it with that of James de Molay? By the degree of Nine Elected, when your heart was disposed to revenge, you have been prepared to the implacable hatred that you have sworn to the Knights of Malta, on whom you ought to revenge the death of James de Molay—as a Grand Elected, you have acquired, by your proved discretion in Symbolic Masonry, the light which leaves nothing more for you to desire, than your submission to the Degree of the Sublime Princes of the Royal Secret, our Chief and Grand Elected of the Order, who has bestowed on you this singular favor.

This is, my Most Illustrious Brother, how, and by whom, Masonry is derived and has been transmitted to us. You ought to see what it is to enter to our lawful rights, which leads us to associate with men whom merit, bravery, and good manners give titles to; which only birthrights grant to the ancestors of the Templars. You are now a Knight, and on a level with them—you have the same hazards to run, as much from the side of envy as persecution, which you may escape by keeping carefully your obligation, and secreting from the vulgar, your estate and what you are.

Having attained to this degree of light, which you merit, and the knowledge we have of your manners, we are persuaded that our confidence towards you will be sufficient to make you apprehend, how important it is to you, not to be the cause of our repenting your initiation. We know you too well to have the least doubt of you. We therefore, do not hesitate to enlighten you into the true interests of the order, and that by your uniting yourself to us, with a sincere submission, will acquire that perfection your zeal deserves.

You are now in the rank of those who shall be elected to the grand work. When once your name is in the urn of your election, the delicious perfumes of your actions will bring you to the true happiness you desire, which I wish you. Amen. Amen. Amen.

After this discourse the Grand Commander knocks one great blow on the table, in order to call the four Knights to enter into the Chapter, who were out. After which the Grand Commander finishes the reception, and gives the new Knight the Sign, Token and Word. He arms him and decorates him with the attributes, and communicates the name he must take in future, which is uncommon to all others, and is Knight Kadosh, or Knight of the White and Black Eagle, instead of Knight Templar.

Jewel.—The Jewel is a red cross, as before described, but in the room of that, now it is a black spread eagle, with two heads suspended to a broad order of fiery, bloody color, worn from the left shoulder to the right hip. The eagle, as if going to fly, with a naked sword in his claws.

§. *Sign, Token & Words.*

Sign.—The Sign is sitting, your right hand on the heart, the fingers extended; then let the hand fall on your right knee, fingers open.

Token.—The Token is the same as the Nine Elected.

Pass Words.—The Pass Word, NECUM or NIKATS, otherwise MANCHEN.

Grand Words.—The one says MI CHAMOCHA BAELIM יהוה, יהוה, יהוה. The Answer is BAGULKAL, PHARASKAL, then they embrace and both say ADONAI.

The Brother who desires to be better acquainted with the foregoing interesting history of the Knights Templars, may consult the following authors, (viz[t]*)—*

Villaneus's History.

History of all Orders, by Mathai, (in Paris).

History of Malta, by Vertot.

Essay on Paris, by St. Foix.

Then follows the doctrine of the Kadosh, now called Knights of the White and Black Eagle, in manner of a

§. *Lecture.*

Q. Are you a Grand Elected?

A. I am, Thrice Illustrious Knight.

Q. Who received you in this degree.

A. A worthy Deputy Grand Inspector, by the consent of two others.

Q. What was done with you?

A. He created me a Knight.

Q. How can I believe you?

A. My name, which I bear, will convince you.

Q. What is your name?

A. Kadosh, or Knight of the Black Eagle.

Q. Was any thing else done to you?

A. The Deputy Inspector adorned me with the habit, ribbon, and jewel of the order.

Q. Where have you received the prize of your election?

A. I have received it in a very deep grotto, and in the silence of the night.

Q. What do you apply to?

A. I work with all my might and strength to raise an edifice, worthy my Brother.

Q. What progress have you made?

A. I have conquered the knowledge of the mysterious ladder.

Q. What composes that ladder?

A. Two supporters and steps.

Q. What are the names of the two supporters?

A. O LEBUR ELOE and O LEB BARABAC.

Q. What design have these two supporters?

A. The first is the love of God, and the second the love of our neighbor.

Q. What are the seven steps of the mysterious ladder?

A. The virtues which I must practice, conformable to my obligations.

Q. Name them to me?

A. 1st. — TSED HALAD, practice or works of Mercy.

2nd. — SCARLABAC, candor of our actions.

3rd. — MOTECK, sweetness of character, which all Brethren must follow.

4th. — EMUNAH, truth in discourse.

5th. — HAMACK SCIATA, advancement to the practice of Heaven.

6th. — SABAÉL, patience in adversity.

7th. — CHOEMEL, BINAH, TABINA, prudence, which we ought to keep in every secret confided to us.

Q. What is your ordinary Pass Word?

A. MANCHEN, the name of the Grand Master, most renowned among the solitaries, known by the name of Kadosh, or White and Black Eagle.

Q. What signifies that name?

A. Solitary or separate.

Q. What was the answer of the solitaries, when they were asked to what they pretended?

A. AVERECHA RECOLGIT ADONAI KLAMED TELLESATE SOPHY, which signifies, "I bless at all times and will praise him with my mouth."

Q. Do they never say any thing else?

A. Yes, they say, BEGAHERAD STIBIUM HEMUY, which is, I will assist the poor, and always sustain them with all my might and power.

Q. How comes the cross surmounted with the eagle and sword?

A. For me to remember that I must employ it in the fullness of time, under the banner of the black eagle, to support the order.

Q. Where did you work?

A. In a place of security, to re-establish secretly the edifice ruined by the traitors.

Q. What success do you expect from it?

A. The reign of virtue, the accord of Brothers, and the possessions of our forefathers, and everlasting happiness.

Q. Have you shed tears?

A. I have.

Q. Have you wore mourning?

A. Yes, and I still wear it.

Q. Why do you wear it?

A. Because virtue is disposed, and crime will continue unpunished as long as vice reigns, and innocence will be oppressed.

Q. Who is it that will punish vice and reward virtue?

A. The Great Architect of the Universe alone.

Q. How?

A. To favor our designs and desires. *N.B.—Here every Brother says three times,* "God favor our design."

Q. Have you any other name than Kadosh, or Knight of the White and Black Eagle?

A. Yes, I have that of ADAMA to teach me, that from the most low I must go to the most high.

Q. Give me the sign of knowledge against surprise?

A. Here it is. *He gives it in the following manner. He puts his right hand on the heart of a Brother, in the same manner as with the poniard in the degree of Nine Elected, and then gives the token of the same degree. Then both strike on right knee.*

Q. How came you to carry your hand extended on your Heart?

A. That my trust is in God.

Q. How came you after that to extend your hand?

A. To show to my Brother, that he is welcome to all in my power, and to encourage him to revenge.

Q. How came you to let your hand fall on your right knee?

A. To show we must bend our knees to adore God. Amen.

End of Lecture

§. *To Close.*

    Q. What's the o'clock?

    A. The break of day demonstrates.

    Q. If the break of day demonstrates, let us depart for revenge.

After which the Grand Commander puts his hand on his heart; then lets it fall on his right knee, which is answered by all; then the Grand Commander embraces each, and each other all around, when the Chapter is closed.

29th Degree of the Second Series (1804) of the Southern Jurisdiction of the United States, called

Grand Master Ecosé, or Scottish Elder Master, and Knight of St. Andrew

§. Admission.

Blue Masters Lodge is opened, the Candidate, who has been proposed, is then vouched and balloted for—after which the Lodge is closed.

§. Form of the Lodge.

The Grand Master is styled "High Exalted." He is seated in the east, at the head of a table which is covered with green cloth. Over his head is suspended a Blazing Star, with the letter G in the center of it. On his right is seated the Grand Secretary and Grand Treasurer; on his left, the grand Orator and Grand Master of Ceremonies. The two Grand Wardens are seated in the West, and all the Knights are seated round the table. This Lodge must be illuminated by seven large lights; two in the east, two in the west, one in the north, and one in the center of the Table.

§. *To Open.*

The Grand Master from the chair addresses the Brethren in the following manner (vizt)—Most honorable Knights and Brethren, I have resolved to open this, our high exalted Lodge, in the name of the Almighty Grand Architect of the Universe. That we may propose, consider and undertake one thing for the good of mankind in general, and this our honorable Order in particular, therefore, my dear Brethren and exalted Scottish Knights, arm yourselves with four towards the Scottish Chair, to enable this our assembly, strictly to consider with me every thing, that we may never resolve or undertake anything for which we should have cause to repent. Assist me in opening the Lodge.

Q. What is the duty of the Grand Senior Warden in opening the Scottish Lodge?

The Senior Warden rises and—

A. To see that this Grand Lodge is perfectly secured and that it may so remain.

Then the High Exalted orders the grand Senior Warden to do his duty in every point, which he does by going out and examining if all things is in perfect security. When he returns he stands behind the chair, with his sword drawn in his hand, and makes his report to the Grand Master. Then the Grand Master asks the Junior Grand Warden (who rises and draws his sword)

Q. How many is the number of our exalted Scottish Lodge?
A. Four.
Q. How many makes four and three?
A. Seven complete.
Q. What is the reason that Masons are attached to the number seven?
A. Because it is the most perfect number, as by it we make our calculations.
Q. How does the wind blow?

A. From the four quarters of the globe.

Then the Grand Master addresses himself to the Grand Secretary, who rises and draws his sword.

Q. Is every thing prepared and in readiness for the opening of the Grand Scottish Lodge?

A. Yes, Most exalted Grand Master, every thing requisite for this Grand and Sublime business is in readiness.

Q. What weather is it?

A. A most glittering star light sky.

Q. What is the clock?

A. It is high midnight.

Then the Grand Master says—My Grand Scottish Masters, exalted Knights and Brethren, I declare this Lodge to be opened and every Brother will conduct himself accordingly.

Then the Grand Senior Warden says—Noble Knights and Brothers, let us not forget the duty we owe to out Most exalted Grand Master.

The Knights all rise, drawing their swords and holding them in their left hands, taking off their hats with their right hands, they salute the Grand Master (all at one motion by taking it from the master of Ceremonies) by lowering the points of their swords, bowing their heads very low. They then put on their hats, sheathe their swords, and give the Common Scottish Sign, when each takes his seat.

§. *Reception.*

The Grand Master of Ceremonies goes out and orders the Candidate to be washed, his shoes taken off, and blindfolds him. He then gives four knocks on the door, which is opened by the Junior Grand Warden, who at the entering of the Candidate, throws a gold colored rope with four knots in it, round his neck.

N.B.—The knots must be tied in such a manner that with one pull they may be easily loosened. And during the opening of the Lodge, the Candidate should lay on the ground or floor.

After the Candidate has entered with the preceding ceremony, he is placed between J and B.

Then the Most Exalted speaks as follows—

G.M.— My Brother, do you desire to become a Grand Scottish Master?

Cand. —I do most cordially.

G.M.—I must inform you that your desire is of a very high nature, are you perfect in the common Blue Master's degrees?

Cand. —Yes, I am.

G.M.—Then give the Signs, Token and Words the Grand Senior Warden.

Cand. —(*He gives them.*)

G.M.—Dear Brother, since you have proved your knowledge and duties in the Blue Master's degrees, to our satisfaction, I will now instruct you in the mysteries and duties of the Scottish Masters, provided you have confidence to go through the same.

An Elder Scottish Master is a high Priestly Order, my Brother, and highly different from the Blue Master. A Master of the three lower degrees, wherein until now you was only taught to venerate the Godhead, under the name of the Most Great, Most Wise and Almighty Architect of the Universe—But an Elder Scottish Master must pay a more deep and feeling veneration to the Almighty God. That due veneration we are taught by the teacher and declarer of our Holy Order, when he says, "The true worshipers will worship him in spirit and in truth." Farther he says, "And they shall be unto me my people, and I will be unto them their God." The first veneration is common to all men and Brethren, as directed by common sense, but the latter belongs to those who dedicate their hearts for the dwelling of the Most High and Merciful God, the Grand Architect of the Universe. Will you, my Brother, adhere to your former loose mode of worship, or, are you resolved to begin your veneration in Spirit and Truth? and henceforward to be instructed and directed in the system, practiced by the Grand Scottish Masters?

Cand. — Yes I will, most cordially.

G.M. — Have you, during the time you were in the Blue Master's degrees, duly and faithfully observed the following articles? —

1st. — Have you paid due veneration to the Most Wise and Mighty Architect of heave and Earth?

Cand. — Yes, I always have.

2ndly. — Have you improved yourself by flying from vice and practicing virtue?

Cand. — Yes, I have.

G.M. — Did you study the industrious labors and the useful precepts of the wise?

Cand. — I did most carefully.

G.M. — Did you always live peaceably among the Masters, and did you at all times defend their right from the rebellious craft?

Cand. — I did to the utmost of my power.

G.M. — Well, my dear Brother, I am happy to find you worthy of being received among the Elder Masters, but I must first ask, have you resolution and fortitude enough to go through the holy work of the Masters? For this work is more exalted, and greatly differs from the works, you have hitherto been used to. you have only used the Square and Compass for mathematical geometry, and for drafts for architects, but in the Scottish Masonry, the Square and Compass is differently employed. you have only used it on single and outward buildings, and made but an imperfect draft of the world. But by the Scottish work, you will bring forth the most shining and brilliant materials, sufficient for drafting the world, complete. Will you most sacredly and solemnly swear and promise to keep the mysteries of the Scottish Masonry, which will be communicated to you, in everlasting silence, not directly or indirectly disclose or communicate them, or any pat thereof to the Brethren of the Blue Order, or to any in the world who is not entitled to it?

Cand. —I do most willingly consent to all the preceding injunctions, and do most solemnly promise to observe them.

Then the Grand Master orders the Junior Warden to lead the Candidate out of the Porch into the Outer Court of the Temple, from thence into the Sanctuary and then into the Sanctum Sanctorum, and from thence to conduct him to the three Golden Basins.

The Junior Warden leads him four times round the Lodge, and as often as the Candidate comes before the altar, the Grand Master from the chair gives the four Scottish knocks, and gives the Common Sign, which is repeated by the Brethren.

Then the Grand Master says— O! how great and glorious is the presence of the Almighty God, who gloriously shines from between the Cherubims!

After the second four knocks, he says— We adore the great and Mighty Jehovah, who exists from eternity; glorified be his great and mighty name for ever and ever.

At the third four knocks, he says— How adorable and astonishing are the rays of that glorious Light, which sends forth its bright and brilliant beams from the Holy Ark of Alliance and Covenant.

At the fourth and four last knocks, he says—Let us, with the deepest veneration and duty adore the fountain of that glorious spirit which is the Most Merciful and Beneficent Ruler of the Universe and all the creatures it contains.

After this the Candidate is led to the altar where he kneels on both knees and takes the following

§. *Obligation.*

I — — of my own free will and accord, do most solemnly swear, in this most sacred and Holy Temple in the presence of the most brilliant and glorious rays, infused by the Most Puissant, Most Terrible, and Most merciful Almighty God and Grand Architect of the Universe, and before this right Worshipful exalted Chapter assembled of Grand Scottish Masters, and valiant Knights of St. Andrew, that I will always hail, for ever conceal and never will reveal, any part or parts of the mysteries of the Scottish Masonry which I am to receive now, or shall be instructed therein any time hereafter, to any of the Brethren of the Blue order of St. John's Lodge, and still less to any profane, or to any person in the world beside. I do furthermore swear that I never will give this degree and order of Scottish Master and it mysteries to a Brother singly by myself, unless duly and properly authorized so to do, and the person to whom the same shall be given must be duly qualified for it, by having regularly and lawfully passed through all the preceding degrees of Sublime Masonry, and at least having served, regularly, as Master in the Chair, in a regular constituted Lodge of the order of St. Johns. All this I sincerely and solemnly promise with a steady resolution to keep, and in failure thereof, I invoke, that all the causes may be fastened on my soul that I may be an everlasting example of a cursed wretch to all mankind, in future ages. I promise to redouble my zeal and friendship towards my Brethren, more particularly towards my Brother Scottish Masters. That I will heartily and sincerely love them, that I will assist them with my Council, support them with my power, even if it should be attended with a probability of the loss of my property, honor or life, as far as lays in my power, and consistent with my own and families preservation. So God maintain me in Equity and Justice, to persevere in the same with steadfastness. Amen. Amen. Amen.

After taking the obligation, the Candidate is carried back to the west, and is placed between the two Grand Wardens, when the High Exalted Grand Master addresses him as follows—

G.M. — My dear Brother, do you desire to see the Great and Glorious light of the Temple?

Cand. — Yes, I am most desirous.

Upon which, the Junior Warden unfolds the bandage from his eyes, when he beholds the glory of Solomon's Temple, particularly the rays of the blazing star, which is suspended over the head of the Grand Master.

G.M. — Do you see, my dear Brother, the Glorious Light, which so brilliantly shines from between the Cherubims of the Ark of the Mercy Seat?

Cand. — I see with joy the most glorious light.

Upon which the Grand Master advances to the Candidate, with his sword drawn in his hand. The Brethren also draw theirs.

The Grand Master then says — My Brother, this [*pointing his sword at him*] and all the swords of the Scottish Knights shall deprive you of your life, in any part of the Globe, should you be so unconscionable a wretch, as to disclose or discover the least of the mysteries of the order of Scottish Knights, but I can assure you, as long as you continue constant and true to your promise and obligations, that all the valiant Knights, will protect you, and save you from impending dangers, even at the risk of their honor, property and lives.

I give you joy in this exalted station, and the honorable degree you have arrived at. May the great Jehovah assist you to persevere in the solemn and sacred engagements into which you have entered, that you may be able to fulfill them in every point.

After which, the new Brother is taught to make the four Scottish steps, vizt, from west to south, from thence to east, and then to north, and from thence to west again, which is afterwards fully explained in the draft.

The Grand Master of Ceremonies gives him the following Signs, Token and Words—

§. *Signs, Token & Words.*

1ˢᵗ Sign.—This is called the Common Scottish Sign, and is made by carrying the right hand half clinched, to your left thigh, as if going to draw a sword or dagger, then draw up your hand to your throat, as if you would rip open your belly.

2ⁿᵈ Sign.—Is called the Grand Scottish Sign. bring your hands across your forehead in the form of a St. Andrew's cross, the right hand uppermost, the fingers extended and forming a square with your thumbs, then bring them under your chin, at the same time clinching your fingers, which represents a death's head and cross bones.

Token.—Put your right hand to the other's neck, the left hand to each others arm pit, and do as if you would raise each other.

Pass Word.—GABAON, signifying a river or spring.

Sacred Word.—JEHOVAH, the Grand and Ineffable name of the Grand Architect of the Universe.

A Knight of St. Andrew, to make himself known to another, takes his sword or dagger, in his left hand, in such a manner, as if he was going to give a back strike, crossing at the same time his right hand over it, in form of a St. Andrew's cross, the fingers clinched, holding it upwards, as if he was holding a working tool.

The first part of the Grand Scottish Sign alludes to the Priests in the temple, who always put their hands to their foreheads, their fingers and thumbs extended as is to keep off the rays, whenever they gave the Benediction. This ceremony is still used in the Synagogue.

Then the Grand Master invests him with the Apron, and at the same time explains to him the mystery and meaning of the green color, vizᵗ, that a Scottish Master in all his works and undertakings must put his trust in Almighty God, that only from him success can be hoped. He arms him with a naked sword, which he puts into his left hand, and a trowel in his right, in such a position, that they form a St. Andrews cross, holding the sword, as if he was going to give a back stroke or thrust—signifying by that sign, that the Knight of St. Andrew having carried on the war against the Saracens, with their swords in their hands, they at the same time forwarded and protected the workmen, having the working tools in one hand, and the sword in the other.

The Grand Master then girths the sword to his side, and he is placed between the two Grand Wardens, while the Grand master gives him the explanation of the draft before him—

It is well known to you, my dear Brother, that the Porch with its Courts, the Sanctuary and Sanctum Sanctorum, was open to the High Priest, who officiated in Solomon's temple, and since you are now admitted a Grand Scottish Master and are of course in the highest orders, you have free access into the Porch, Out Courts and Sanctuary, and even into the Sanctum Sanctorum, as a Secret place for your works. You see also the whole before your eyes. Consider then the consecrated Out Court and the two pillars, but they are now shortened and broken. The signification thereof you shall know. Now behold the sanctuary and the Sanctum Sanctorum of Solomon's Temple, in which was placed the Ark of Alliance and Covenant, wherein were the two tables, containing the Ten Commandments, and the Rod of Aaron, which had blossomed, laid on the outside before it. On each side of the Ark of Alliance (which was the Mercy Seat) stood a Cherubim, with their wings extending over it. Between these Cherubims the Godhead discovered himself to the High priest in a stream of fire, under a thick cloud, and delivered his oracles from thence.

The Ark you see painted before you serves a Knight of St. Andrew, as an emblem to adore the Invisible and Eternal Jehovah, and at the same time signifies that a Knight of St. Andrew should have the Law of the Eternal God always deeply impressed in his heart, and never to contemplate, undertake, or do anything contrary to those laws and precepts.

You must now, my dear Brother, as a Grand Scottish Master, under the Great and Holy name of Jehovah, adore the Godhead in sincerity and truth, and such adoration and spiritual veneration must surpass the common adoration of Adonai. The Brazing Sea and Flaming Star are emblems you meet here, but were not found in the Temple—but they are hieroglyphic emblems of the Scottish Works. The seven dots you see here, does not signify the sevenfold arrangements of our order, as it does in the lower degrees of the Blue Order of St. John—but they signify, physically, the seven different metals, and when you see the seven planets, besides other star marked, it signifies the other mineral matters, as well as the seven planets. From this you may conclude, that the secret knowledge of the Grand Scottish Master points to the mixing and changing of the different materials, and to enable you to understand the subject, you must be informed that, every thing in this world, is formed from three substances, which are intimately and substantially mixed together, and from which is derived the four elements.

The three substantial elements are ⊖ Salt, ♀ Sulfur and ⌒△ Spirit. The first causes firmness, the second the softness, and the third mixture, the spiritual and vaporous particles. From the remarks of the three mixtures is to be understood, the three Golden Basins. In the first is engraved M, in the second G, and in the third, nothing.

These initial letters, in the two first Basins signify in the Hebrew language, the M for MELACH which signifies Salt, and G for GOPHRITH, which signifies sulfur; for the vaporous spirit, there is no letter to express it—therefore there is no letter in the third Basin.

These three Basins, were found, in the time of the Crusades or Holy Wars, by four Elder Masters from Scotland, in the ruins of the Temple, in a square hollow corner stone, and in memory of those four Elder Masters from Scotland, all the Elder Masters are called Scottish Masters to this day.

The aforesaid three substantial matters, by which you can facilitate the changing of metals, must be done, through the five points or rules of the Scottish Mastership. The first Master point shows us the Brazen Sea, wherein

353

must be some sea water. Out of this water, the Scottish Masters extract the first matter which is Salt ⊖ , which must afterwards undergo a sevenfold preparation. This sevenfold preparation, by which we must understand the seven steps of Solomon's Temple, and the Brazen Sea, the first point or rule of the Scottish Master, as an emblem. The second substantial matter, namely the ♀ , must be out of the purest gold, to which must be added, some purified ⊖ and mixed according to Art. This mixture must be put in a vessel in the shape of a ship, in which it must remain, like the Ark of Noah, 150 days, and then be brought into the first degree of damp heat, that it may not rot. This is the second point or rule of the Scottish Masters, therefore you must for the second time set your foot on the Ark of Noah. The third work consists in adding to the above materials, the ethereal spirit through the mother water of ⊖ as well as the ⊖ itself, which must be daily added. The utmost care must be taken not to add too much, or you will destroy its tenacity, nor too little, or you will prevent it. This third point or rule of the Scottish Masters, is emblematical of the building of the Tower of babel where confusion and destruction reigned from the improper and injudicious admixture of the materials, therefore my Brother, you must for the third time, put your foot on this Tower, as this is the third point and work of the Scottish Masters. Now follows a fourth work, which is represented by this Cubical Stone, which is equally square and fits on all sides. As soon as the work is completed by the addition of the foregoing materials, it must be placed in the degree of fire, wherein it must received that degree of strength, which may be judged necessary. Therefore you must, my Brother, for the fourth time put your foot thereon. Then follows the fifth and last work, which is discovered to us by the Flaming Star. After the work is brought to a proportional substance, it must be placed in the fourth and strongest degree of heat, wherein it must remain three times twenty-seven hours, until it is red hot, by which means it becomes a bright and shining Tincture, and becomes fit, to change the lighter metals. Since the Flaming Star shows us the fifth and last point of the Scottish Master, so you must, my Brother, for the fifth and last time, put your foot on it, by which you complete the four Scottish Masters steps.

These five different installments you have performed only in ceremony, but you should also go through these five master points and rules, practically—and with one part, one thousand parts exchanged and ennoble them. So you may truly say, that you are a thousand years old, which we can as yet, no otherwise communicate to you them by ceremony.

This great and noble Art, has in the time of Solomon, and afterwards until the time of the Crusades, remained among the Brotherhood, and more particularly reigned in Jerusalem. After our enlightened and most respectable Grand Master Hiram Abiff was murdered, by three vicious and villainous Fellow Crafts, the Art was entirely forgotten. This unhappy event is represented by the two overthrown and broken pillars of which the posture of the bases and the columns is still erect, but part of the columns, capitals, chapiters and architrave are still missing, which gives us to understand, that, not only the foundation of the Divine Art, is already laid, but they have also been raised to a considerable height, but the true measure and proper height is still wanting. From all this, my Brother, you should draw the following observations. Whatever Art or work your inclination leads you to, if you want to be an expert Scottish working Master, you must be attentive to study, true physical knowledge, learn the principles and practice of chemistry, that you may be more expert and handy, in the use of the Square and the Compass, which you likewise see in the draft, and lastly you will perceive a sorrowful emblem of the tragical history of our respectable Grand Master Hiram Abiff at your entrance. The rope round your neck, which you wore for the honor and the immortal memory of our enlightened and noble Grand Master, but I will soon recompense and reward you, by decorating your neck with a more brilliant Jewel. You must further observe, the grave of our respectable Grand Master is in the Holy and Consecrated part of the Temple and in the secret parts of the Scottish Master, Knights of St. Andrew. Lastly, I must inform you that the Scottish Masters, in consequence of the great zeal and valor which they showed during the Crusades, were associated with the Scottish Knights of St. Andrew. They were honored with the Thistle, and were created Knights of this most honorable and ancient order of Knighthood, with all its formalities, which honor of Knighthood I shall invest you with, as a reward for your valor, virtue, fervor and constancy.

The newly initiated Brother kneels down on a perfect square ⌐⌐. *The Grand Master draws his sword, in form of a St. Andrews cross over his back and says as follows—*

N.B.—During the ceremony two naked swords in the form of a St. Andrew's cross are held on his back.

§. *Form of Knighting.*

1st.—I create you Knight of the Holy Order of the great Jehovah.

2ndly.—I create you a Knight by the title of Sir — — in the name of our noble Grand Master — —.

3rdly.—I create you a Knight of the honorable and noble Order of St. Andrew.

4thly.—I create you a Knight in the name of Grand Worshipful Scottish Elder Lodge, and in the name of the whole Order of Knighthood, over the surface of the two Hemispheres.

N.B.—At every Knighthood he confers on him, the Grand Master strikes him with his sword on his forehead, in the form of a St. Andrew's Cross, and all the Brethren stand round him with their swords drawn.

The Grand Master raises him, and kisses him four times, after which he invests him with the Order and Jewel, and says—

I decorate you, my dear Brother, with the order of Hope and Perfection.

Then follows the consecration. The Grand Master puts both his hands on the new created Knight's head and says—

The Lord bless thee and keep thee.

The Lord make his face to shine upon thee and be gracious unto thee.

The Lord lift up his countenance upon thee and give thee peace. Amen.

N.B.—This benediction must be made in a solemn tone of voice, such is used in Synagogues on festivals by the Cohen or Priest descendants of Aaron.

After which the new initiated Brother makes himself known to all the Knights by giving them the Signs, Token and Words.

The Grand Orator then delivers the following

§. *Oration.*

To us, my Brethren, as Grand Scottish Masters, the whole Temple is open, and by our exertions the whole work therefore is completed. By this you see the great pre-eminence we have to the Masters of the Blue order of St. John's lodge, to the Sanctuary or Middle part of the Temple. The three divisions of the Temple which you see here, vizt., the Out Court, the Sanctuary, and the Sanctum Sanctorum, signifies the three principles of our Holy Order, which directs to the knowledge of Morality, and teaches the practice of those virtues which should be pursued by mankind. Therefore the seven steps which lead up to the Outer Court of the temple, is the emblem of the sevenfold light, we are in need of, before we can arrive at the height of knowledge. Next to this we come to the Mosaic pavement which puts us in mind, that mankind are in their nature unpolished and imperfect and take to themselves so many different figures, as their disappointments, sorrow, and drive them from place to place.

Over two pillars J and B, which signify strength and establishment, our shortened and disfigured, because they have lost their capitals by the death of our most respectable Grand Master Hiram Abiff.

357

The table which is divided by three lines in the length, to learn and understand the signification thereof, we must begin at the right, where we find the Tower of Babel. It is well known to us that it was a foolish undertaking by men, who were ridiculously fearful of the Almighty God. This serves to remind us, that we should never feel ourselves with too high and exalted notions of our own consequence but that we must, in all our undertakings and works, use the greatest foresight and consideration, at the same time, the very careful and circumspect that we do not act against the will and Holy Ordinances of the Great and Mighty Jehovah, that we may not, like inconsiderate people, meet in our works, our destruction and our graves.

The beauty of our Order suffered also a severe shock by the tragical end of our respectable Grand master, Hiram Abiff, which is constantly remembered and lamented by every true Brother. who humbly pray to the Great and Mighty Jehovah to reestablish the order in honor and safety.

Let us now turn to the left, where you perceive the shortened pillar B which leads us to the Ark of Noah. This signifies the wonderful escape, and the establishment of our Order, under a thousand dangers and difficulties, which is not unlike the memorable adventures, dangers and sufferings, of our Holy forefathers.

The Cubic Stone, signifies the perfection of our Order, as the Cube is the most regular body, whose sides are equal. So is the structure of our Order, if you consider its regularity, unanimity and its sacred connections, which are like the regularity and perfection of the Cube.

Father we see in the draft of the Temple, the most noble and elegant structure that we ever was raised, which the Almighty God, had himself ordered, and honored it in the most particular manner, with his glorious presence as a testimony of his favors, of which we have the representation in our assemblies.

The Sun signifies the form and glory of the Temple, the fame whereof, was spread through all nations.

The Pillar ⊏, which signifies the establishment of our Order, has likewise suffered very much, but it is yet very large and still makes a very splendid appearance, it stands under the sun in a direct line, the most notable and complete of the heavenly bodies. Observe the middle road, the steps of which, lead is over the Mosaic pavement between the B, strength; and J, establishment, of the order to the Brazen Sea, where we must purify ourselves, and wash off all pollutions.

The Flaming Star is the emblem of the Holy and Glorious SHECHINAI before we dare approach the seat of the most exalted wisdom.

The Ark of Alliance, wherein the tables of the laws were formerly deposited, serve to remind us, that our heart, are now the depository thereof, and where the laws must be forever engraved.

This holy wisdom remained among the Brethren of the Order, even in the most sorrowful periods. This we remark on the middle road, where, not the least track, diminution or darkness or any remembrance of those sorrows are to be seen.

God loved the order and protected them openly, at the time, when every thing conspired to its destruction—he suffered it to fall, that he might raise it with greater glory.

§. *Lecture.*

Q. Are you a Grand Scottish Master?

A. I am, the whole worshipful Brotherhood acknowledge me as such, and I am perfectly acquainted with the letters M and G.

Q. Where was you received a Scottish Master?

A. In the Sanctum Sanctorum under the Cassia.

Q. How did you come there?

A. Through the Porch, Out Court and Sanctuary.

Q. After you was received and brought to light what did you see?

A. A Brazen Sea.

Q. Of what use was that Brazen Sea?

A. That the Scottish Master may wash and purify themselves, in the same manner as the priests and Levites, who were obliged to wash themselves before they could enter the Temple.

Q. What did you see more?

A. Three golden basins, in the first was the letter M, in the second the letter G, and in the third there was not letter. These three basins were found by the Scottish Elder Masters in the ruins of the Temple, in the time of the Crusades.

Q. Did you see nothing else?

A. Yes, I saw the Ark of Alliance, wherein was deposited the tables of the Laws.

Q. What doth all this signify?

A. That the Scottish Masters must keep the laws of God in their hearts, that they may have a Covenant with God.

Q. Have you seen anything else?

A. I have seen the Flaming Star.

Q. What signifies the Flaming Star?

A. The holy presence of Almighty God.

Q. What Brethren have you seen in the temple?

A. The Apprentice and Fellow Craft in the Out Court. The Masters in the Sanctuary and the Elder Masters in the Sanctum Sanctorum.

Q. Is that all you have seen there?

A. No, I have seen other things, which I and all the Grand Scottish Masters keep in our hearts.

Q. How old are you?

A. A thousand years.

Q. How many pillars has a Scottish Lodge?

A. Four, two broken and shortened, and two which are overset and thrown down.

Q. What do they signify?

A. That the Temple lays in ruins.

Q. What's the clock?

A. It is break of day.

§. *To Close*

The Grand Master to the Senior Warden—Most honorable Knight and Brother, as we are going to leave off for the present, this our holy work, which we carry on through the assistance of Almighty God, the Grand Architect of the Universe, and are resolved to close this Grand Scottish Lodge, I must ask you if our holy labors were carried on in such a manner as to procure us at all times, praise and honor?

S.W.—High exalted Grand Master and honorable Knight of St. Andrew, this right worshipful assembled Lodge of valiant Knights and Brethren, do in honor, most submissively thank you for your high and commendable zeal, work and foresight, which you have so handsomely shown and taught to this holy assembly. Your native greatness of soul, comprehensive mind and Brotherly love, has filled our hearts with the greatest veneration, which makes us for ever bound to you in ties of gratitude. We now, more than ever, find the truth of your observations by your practices. We desire moreover, most exalted Knight and Grand Master, that you may never leave off assisting us with your good councils and examples and provide for our future works, that we may be enabled readily to transmit to our successors. the true foundation of our labors, and the practice of our works that we may rejoice.

The Junior Grand Warden speaks—The wonderful secrets, the Scottish Knights and Brothers have discovered, in clearing the ruins of the Temple at Jerusalem, makes it highly necessary for us to discover the true use thereof, and that we may always make a happy use thereof. The Knights and Masters of this exalted Scottish Lodge, request the most exalted Grand Master, that our labors and assiduity may be assisted with his great wisdom and foresight, that we may make further beneficial discoveries, and through wisdom, strength and beauty, never fail in our happy undertaking of hallowed Masonry.

The Knight Grand Secretary speaks— We most heartily thank our most high exalted Grand Master for holding this Lodge. We are all unanimously resolved to regulate ourselves, agreeable to his will. But now, my Brethren, we must remember our duty towards our high exalted Grand Master, by 4 times 4 with all Knightly honors, due to his exalted station. My Brethren and exalted Knights, assist me therein.

All the Knights rise up and clapping with their hands 4 times 4, they then take off their hats with their left hands, and draw their swords with their right, raising them up before their foreheads, and after holding them up a short time in that position, they lower the points to the ground (in tempo), in one motion taking their time from the Grand Master of Ceremonies, they then make a low bow, and remain standing.

The Grand Master then draws his sword and returns the compliment, and then speaks as follows—

Me dear Brethren and exalted Knights, I am happy to find that you are not deficient in your duty, it is not to me those honor are due, it is to the Mighty Grand Architect of the Universe, whose precepts and holy laws we practice in our holy assemblies; to HIM alone, all homage is due. Let the fear of his mighty name always be before your eyes, his laws engraved on your hearts, and endeavor as much as possible to imitate his goodness. Be forgiving and merciful to your enemies, benevolent and bountiful to your friends and fellow creatures, do to every one, as you would be done by, by which you will propagate his Holy name. Blessed be his great and mighty name, for ever and ever. Amen.

Retire my Brethren in peace and friendship and practice those virtues you are here taught. This Lodge is closed.

The Brethren then put on their hats, sheath their swords and applaud by 4 times 4, and give the common Scottish Sign.

Apron.—The Apron is white lined with green. On the flap must be embroidered or painted a death head and cross bones over a Cubic Stone, and in the middle of the Apron, a blazing Star, with the letter G in the middle thereof.

Order.—The Order is a broad green watered ribbon, worn from the left shoulder to the right hip, to which is suspended the

Jewel.—which is, a St. Andrews Cross of gold or silver gilt, and enameled, the thistle between the points.

§. *Other Signs, &c., of this Degree.*

When this degree is given by the Germans, the Candidate is styled GABAON, (which, to us, is a Pass Word) and comes for the rebuilding the Temple, as did Zerubbabel. He must discover the Sacred Word on a golden plate, as in the Royal Arch, &c., not the golden basins, &c., &c.

Sign.—The sign is made by raising the right hand in the form of a square to the forehead, above the eyes, the thumb near the right ear (as in the Royal Arch.)

Token.—The Token is given in two parts. First place the left hand on the sword, to signify that the labor has been accomplished, then grip the other's right hand.

Word.—The Word is JEHOVAH.

Word of a Scottish Master.—Is NOTUMA.

The Knocks are four—Two quick & two slow.

GRAND SCOTCH OF ST. ANDREW OF SCOTLAND,
or PATRIARCH OF THE CRUSADES, KNIGHT OF THE SUN
& GRAND MASTER OF LIGHT (1806)

Form of the Lodge.—The Lodge is painted in red, and supported by white columns. The seats of the Master and two Wardens are red, trimmed in gold, those of the Knights are blue.

At each end of the Lodge is a St. Andrew's Cross—in front of each are four lights, in a row, making sixteen in all. The Lodge is illumined by eighty-one lights, nine by nine.

Hour of opening.—Noon.

Hour of closing.—The beginning of night.

Titles.—The Lodge is styled "Grand Lodge," the Master, "Patriarch" and the Scottish, "Respectable Masters."

Clothing.—A red robe.

Order.—The order is crimson, with a rose, of green and red, at the point whereof hangs the

Jewel.—A compass set on three triangles, each within the other. Below the Jewel is a reversed square, with a poniard in the angle.

The Jewel of St. Andrew's Cross is surmounted by a crown, and in the center of the cross is a pineapple or a J, within a triangle, within a ring. From this ring hangs a key between the two branches of the cross, and in the four ends of the cross are the initials of the four sacred words, B∴J∴M∴N∴

Steps.—Make a Jerusalem cross by the three steps of an Apprentice, the three steps of a Fellow Craft, and the three steps of a Master.

Knocks.—Nine, by 2, 3 and 4.

Age.—The cube of nine, or eighty-one.

SIGNS, TOKENS, &c.
(which were formerly those of Grand Master of all Lodges)

First Sign.—Of earth. Draw the back of the four fingers of the right hand across the forehead, inclining the head a little.

First Token.—Mutually and in succession, take the first, second and third joints of a Brother's forefinger of his right hand, each spelling, by alteration of letters, the word BOAZ.

Second Sign.—Of water. Place the right hand upon the heart, then, extend it as high as the breast, letting it fall to the right side, as if saluting.

Second Token.—Mutually and in succession, take the first, second and third joints of a Brother's middle finger of his right hand, each spelling, by alteration of letters, the word JACHIN.

Third Sign.—Of surprise and terror. Turn the head to the left, towards the earth, and raise the hands, clasped, a little to the right.

Fourth Sign.—Of fire. Interlace the fingers, and cover the eyes with the palms outward.

Answer, or Sign of Air.—Extend the right arm as high as the shoulder.

Third Token.—Take the forefinger of the Brother's right hand by the first joint, the first saying MAH, the other, HA, and the first, BON.

Fifth Sign.—Of admiration. Raise the eyes to heaven, and the hands in the air, with the left arm a little lower than the right, as when a priest says, "Dominus vobiscum"—the heel of the left foot being raised a little, the left knee forming a square with the right.

Sixth Sign.—Of the Sun. Place the thumb of the right hand over the right eye, extend the forefinger, forming a square, as if viewing a distant object, and say, I MEASURE THE SUN.

Seventh Sign.—Common Sign. Cross the two hands upward on the breast, forming a St. Andrew's cross.

General Token.—Take the knuckle of the Brother's forefinger of his right hand, the first saying, NE, the other, KA. Then take the knuckle of his little finger, the first saying, MAH, the other giving in full, the word, NEKAMAH.

Sacred Word.—is NEKAMAH.

Pass Words.—ARDAREL, angel of Fire.

CHASMARAN, angel of Air.

TALLIUD, angel of Water.

PHURLAC, angel of Earth.

30ᵗʰ, 31ˢᵗ and 32ⁿᵈ Degrees of the First Series (1802) of the
Southern Jurisdiction of the United States of America, now
32nd, called

Sovereign, or Sublime Prince
of the Royal Secret

he assembly of Princes is termed a "Consistory."

Officers.—The first officer represents Frederick II king of Prussia—he is styled "Sovereign of Sovereigns," "Grand Prince," "Illustrious Commander in Chief." The two next officers are styled "Lieutenant Commanders." The fourth officer is the "Minister of State," who acts as the orator. The fifth officer is the "Grand Chancellor," then the "Grand Secretary," the "Grand Treasurer," the "Grand Captain of the Guards," a "Standard Bearer," a "Grand Master Architect," and two "Tylers."

Place of Meeting.—This is to be a building at least two stories in height, situated on elevated ground, in the open country. Three apartments on the second floor are necessary in this degree. In the first of these the guards are stationed. The second is used as a preparation room. The third is occupied by the members of the Consistory. This last apartment is hung with black sprinkled with tears, death's heads, cross bones, and skeletons. The throne is in the east, elevated by seven steps. On the throne is the chair of state, lined with black satin, flamed with red. Before the chair is a table covered with black satin, strewed with tears. On this cloth, in front, is a death's head and cross bones— over the death's head, is the letter J, and under the cross bones is the letter M. On the table is placed a naked sword, a buckler, a scepter, a balance, and a book containing the statutes of the order. In the west is placed another table covered with crimson, bordered with black, and strewed with tears—on the front of this cloth are the letters N∴K∴—M∴K∴ in gold.

§. *Dress and Stations of Officers.*

The Sovereign of Sovereigns is dressed in royal robes, and seated in the chair of state.

The Lieutenant Commanders dressed like the modern princes of Europe, and seated at the table in the west; their swords are crossed on the table.

The Minister of State is placed at the Sovereign's right hand.

The Grand Chancellor stands on the left hand of the Sovereign.

Next to the Minister of State is placed the Grand Secretary.

Next to the Grand Chancellor is placed the Grand Treasurer.

Below the last named officers are placed on one side the Standard Bearer, the Grand Master Architect, and the Captain of the Guards.

Below these officers are placed six members dressed in red, without aprons, wearing the jewel of the order, suspended on the breast by a black ribbon.

§. *Collar of the Order, & Jewel.*

The collar is black, and edged with silver. On its point is embroidered in red a Teutonic cross. In the middle of the cross is a double headed-eagle in silver. The collar is lined with scarlet, on which is embroidered a black Teutonic cross. Around the waist is girded a black sash, embroidered with silver. The cross is embroidered on that part of the girdle which is in front.

Jewel.—The jewel is a golden Teutonic cross.

§. *Qualifications of Candidate.*

The Candidate who receives this degree must be faithfully examined in that of Kadosh, previous to admission. The Master of Ceremonies will acquaint him with the Pass Word—which he is to give to the Lieutenant Commander. The Master of Ceremonies will then lead him to the Sovereign of Sovereigns.

§. *Opening and closing.*

The Sovereign of Sovereigns say—SALIX.

The Lieutenants reply—NONI.

They then together say—TENGU.

All give the sign.

The Sovereign of Sovereigns says—Let us imitate our Grand Master Jacques DeMolay, Hiram Abiff, who to the last placed all his hopes in the Great Architect of the Universe; and pronounced the following words just as he passed from this transient life into eternal bliss:—SPES MEA IN DEO EST.

§. *Description of the Draft Representing the Camp*

On the carpet is drawn an enneagon, in which is inscribed a pentagon, within this is an equilateral triangle, and in the triangle a circle.

Between the heptagon and pentagon, upon the sides of the latter, are placed the standards of the five Standard Bearers, and the pavilions inscribed by the letters T∴E∴N∴G∴U∴

The emblems on the standard T are the Ark of the Covenant, an olive tree, and a lighted candlestick, on each side. The ground color of this standard is purple. On the Ark is written the motto LAUS DEO.

The standard E bears a golden lion, holding in his mouth a golden key, bearing around his neck a golden collar, on which is engraved S.Q.S. The ground is azure—the motto is AD MAJOREM DEI GLORIAM.

On the standard N is an inflamed heart, in red, with two wings, surrounded by a laurel crown. The ground is white.

The flag G bears a double headed eagle, crowned, holding a sword in his right claw, and in his left a bloody heart. The ground is sea green.

The flag U has an ox, sable, on a golden ground. On the sides of the enneagon are nine tents, and on its angles nine pendants, each belonging to its appropriate tent. The pendants are distinguished by numerals, and the tents by the letters ∴I∴N∴O∴N∴X∴I∴L∴A∴S, disposed from right to left. These tents signify the different grades of Masonry, thus:—

Tents	Names of Tents	Color of Pendants	Represents
S.	Malachi	White, spotted with red	Knights of Rose ✠ Knights of E and W Princes of Jerusalem
A.	Zerubbabel	Light Green	Knights of the East
L.	Nehemiah	Red	Grand, Elect, Perfect and Sublime
I.	Hoben, or Johaben	Black and red	Royal Arch, or Sublime Elect, and Elect of Fifteen
X.	Peleg	Black	Elect of Nine, Illustrious Elected, or Grand Mr. Architect
N.	Joiada	Red and Black in lozenges	Provost and Judge
O.	Aholiab, or Eliab	Red and Green	Intendant of the Building, and Intimate Secretary
N.	Joshua	Green	Perfect Master
I.	Ezra, or Esdras	Blue	Symbolic Masons

The equilateral triangle in the middle represents the center of the army, and shows where the Knights of Malta are to be placed who have been admitted to our mysteries, and have proved themselves faithful guardians. They are to be joined with the Knights of K—H. The corps in the center is to be commanded by five Princes, who command jointly or in rotation according to their degrees, and receive their orders immediately from the Sovereign of Sovereigns. These five Princes must place their standards in the five angles of the pentagon, as above described. These Princes, who are Standard Bearers, have the following names, (vizt.)

Standard   Names

T.---------------------BEZALEEL
E.---------------------AHOLIAB, or ELIAB
N.---------------------MANCHEN
G.---------------------GARIMONT
U.---------------------AMARIAH, or EMERK

The heptagon points out the Encampment destined for the Princes of Libanus, Jerusalem, &c. and these are to receive their orders from the five Princes. The enneagon shows the general order of Masons of all degrees.

Instructions for the reunion of the Brethren, Knights, Princes, and Commanders, of the Royal Secret or Kadosh, which really signifies "Holy Brethren of all degrees separated."

Frederick III, king of Prussia, Grand Master and Commander in Chief, Sovereign of Sovereigns, with an army composed of the Knights, Princes of the White and Black Eagle, including Prussian, English, and French—likewise joined by the Knights Adepts of the Sun, Princes of Libanus or the Royal Axe, the Knights of the Rose Croix de Heroden, Knights of the East and West, the Princes of Jerusalem, Knights of the East or Sword, the Grand Elect Perfect and Sublime Masons, the Knights of the Royal Arch, Sublime Knights Elected, &c. &c.

The hour for the departure or march of the army is the fifth after the setting of the sun, and is to be made known by the firing of five great guns in the following order ●-●●●●—that is, with an interval between the first and second. The first rendezvous is to be the port of Naples—from Naples to the port of Rhodes—from Rhodes to Cyprus and Malta, whence the whole naval force of all nations is to assemble. The second rendezvous is to be at Cyprus and at Joppa. The third rendezvous is to be at Jerusalem, where they will be joined by our faithful guardians.

The watchwords for every day of the week are as follows, and they are not to be changed by express order from the King of Prussia:—

Names of the Protectors	Answer	Names of the Prophets
Sunday------------Cyrus	do	Ezekiel
Monday-----------Darius	do	Daniel
Tuesday-----------Xerxes	do	Habakkuk
Wednesday--------Alexander	do	Zephaniah
Thursday----------Philadelphus	do	Haggai
Friday-------------Herod	do	Zechariah
Saturday-----------Hezekiah	do	Malachi

§. *Signs & Words.*

Sign.—Place the right hand on the heart, extend it with the palm down, letting it fall to the right side.

Sacred Words.—One says, SALIX, to which the other replies NONI, both repeat the word TENGU.

Pass Words.—PHUAL KOL, which signifies "separated." PHARASH KOL, which signifies "reunited." NEKAM MAKA, which signifies "to avenge." Each then letters the word SHADDAI, which signifies "Omnipotent."

§. *Charge.*

My dear Brother—The Saracens having taken possession of the Holy Land, those who were engaged in the Crusades not being able to repel them, agreed with Godfrey De Bouillon, the conductor and chief of the Crusaders, to veil the mysteries of religion under emblems by which they would be able to maintain the devotion of the soldier, and protect themselves from the incursion of- those who were their enemies, after the example of the scriptures, the style of which is figurative.

Those zealous Brethren chose Solomon's temple for their model. This building has strong allusions to the Christian church. Since that period they have been known by the name of Master Architect, and they have employed themselves in improving the law of that admirable Master. From hence it appears that the mysteries of the Craft are the mysteries of religion. Those Brethren were careful not to entrust this important secret to any whose discretion they had not proved. For this reason they invented different degrees to try those who entered among them, and only gave them symbolic secrets, without explanation, to prevent treachery and to make themselves known only to each other. For this purpose it was resolved to use different signs, words, and tokens, in every degree, by which they would be secured against Cowans and Saracens.

The different degrees were fixed first to the number of seven by the example of the Grand Architect of the universe, who built all things in six days and rested on the seventh. This is distinguished by the seven points of reception in the Master's degree.

Enoch employed six days to construct the arches, and on his seventh, having deposited the secret treasure in the lowest arch, was translated to the abodes of the blessed. Solomon employed six years in constructing his temple, and celebrated its dedication on the seventh, with all the solemnity worthy of the divinity himself. This sacred edifice we choose to make the basis of figurative Masonry. In the first degree are the three symbols to be applied.

1st.—The first day of the creation, which was only chaos, is figured by the Candidate's coming out of the black chamber, neither naked nor clothed, deprived of light, which the Master gave him, and his suffering the painful trial at his reception and his obligation. The Candidate sees nothing before he is brought to light, and his powers of imagination relative to what he is to go through are suspended, which alludes to the figure of the creation of that vast, luminous body, confused among the other parts of creation, before it was extracted from the darkness and fixed by the Almighty Fiat.

2ndly.—The Candidate approaches the footstool of the Master, and there renounces all cowans; he promises to subdue his passions, by which means he is united in virtue, and by the regularity of his life, demonstrates what he proposes. This is figured to him by the steps that he takes in approaching the altar; the symbolic meaning of which is the separation of the firmament from the earth and water on the second day of creation.

3rdly.—The Master gave the Candidate his first Masonic light, explained the first figures, gave him the Sign, Word and Token which distinguishes a Mason, by means of which he is known by his Brethren on any occasion, and in the midst of all who are not Mason, from whom virtue has separated him. These are the three symbols of the first degree, which distinguish the Apprentice from the other degrees. The second degree has to figures applicable thereto, which, joined to the three first, makes five, which distinguishes the Fellow Craft.

4thly.—The fourth day the Grand Architect produced fruits on the earth, which was separated from water, and figured by the reception of the Brother to the second degree; that is, separated from the Apprentice, that he might learn the use of the Square, Level and Plumb, by which he renders himself able and works to improve his knowledge of the society, which is the fruits of his reception.

5thly.—The Grand Architect adorned his work on the fifth day, by filling the earth with animals, the waters with fish, and the air with birds, which is figurative of the Fellow Crafts employing themselves to polish and cut stones, by the beauty of the Shining Star. To the third degree are two symbols, which, joined to the five former, makes seven, which is the Master Mason's.

6thly.—In Master's degree you were taught to pass from the Square to the Compass, which shows you are to pass from one virtue to another, until you have obtained the whole. The death of Hiram Abiff, at your reception, teaches you what you ought to do, what you have been, what you are, and where you will go; which is compared to the sixth day, when god created man from the dust, gave him life, put into him a soul, and prescribed laws for his government.

7thly.—We lead most Masons to these degrees, where they rest under the shade of the sprig of cassia, which the Master of Masters, who passed seven days in tranquillity, dedicated to divine use, until the world is dissolved.

You were taught in the first and second degrees to labor by the example of the Masons, who built Solomon's temple, in order to improve and raise in our hearts an edifice, proper to offer homage to the Grand Architect of the Universe, and of which we ought to be the living Temple, which ought to be only ornamented with virtue. We are taught to polish stones, which teaches is to correct our manners, to regulate ourselves by the Compass, to square our actions, which will conduct us to good works, which every virtuous man should seek. We have the two pillars, Jachin and Boaz, as symbols of virtue and prudence, which prove to us that man is made for society where he ought to display his virtues and be an ornament of humanity. The three pillars (which support the Temple) demonstrate that every Brother induced by virtue becomes, of need, a supporter of the Craft.

In the Master's degree is represented the assassination of Hiram by false Brethren. This ought to put us in mind of the fate of Adam; occasioned by perverseness in his disobeying his great and awful Creator..

The symbolic mystery of the death of Hiram Abiff represents to us that of. the Messiah; for the: three blows which were given to Hiram Abiff at the three gates of the Temple, allude to the three points of condemnation against Christ, at the High Priest Caiphas, Herod, and Pilate. It was from the last that he was led to that most violent and excruciating death.

The said three blows with the Square, Gauge, and Gavel, are symbols of the blow on the cheek, the flagellation, and the crown of thorns. The Brethren assembled around the tomb of Hiram is a representation of the disciples lamenting the death of Christ on the cross. The Master's word, which is said to be lost, since the death of Hiram Abiff, is the same that Christ pronounced on the cross, and which the Jews did not comprehend, ELI, ELI, LAMA SABACHTHANI, "my God, my God, why hast thou forsaken me, have pity on and forgive my enemies"—instead of which words are substituted, M.B.N. (Mac-be-nac) which, in Arabian, signifies, "The son of the widow is dead."

The false Brethren represent Judas Iscariot, who sold Christ. The red color worn by the Grand Elect Perfect and Sublime Masons, calls to remembrance the blood of Christ. The sprig of cassia is the figure of the cross, because of this wood was the cross made.

The captivity of the Grand Elect and Sublime Masons, shows us the persecution of the Christian religion under the Roman emperors, and its liberty under Constantine the Great. It also calls to our remembrance the persecution of the Templars, and the situation of Jacques DeMolay, who, lying in irons nearly seven years, at the end of which our worthy Grand Master was burnt alive with his four companions, on the 11th of March, 1314, creating pity and tears in the people, who saw him die with firmness and heroic constancy, sealing his innocence with his blood.

My dear Brother, in passing to the degree of Perfect Master, in which you shed tears at the tomb of Hiram Abiff, and in some other degrees, has not your heart been led to revenge? Has not the crime of Jubelum Akirop been represented in the most hideous light? Would it be unjust to compare the conduct of Philip the Fair to his, and the infamous accusers of the Templars, to the two ruffians who were accomplices with Akirop? Do they not kindle in your heart an equal aversion? The different stages you have traveled, and the time you have taken in learning these historical events, no doubt, will lead you to make the proper applications; and by the degree of Master Elect and Kadosh, you are properly disposed to fulfill all your engagements, and to bear an implacable hatred to the Knights of Malta, and to avenge the death of Jacques De Molay.

Your extensive acquaintance with symbolic Masonry, which you have attained by your discretion, leaves you nothing more to desire here. You see, my dear Brother, how, and by whom, Masonry has come to us. You are to endeavor by every just means to regain our rights, and to remember that we are joined by a society of men, whose courage, merit, and good conduct, hold out to us that rank that birth alone gave to our ancestors.

You are now on the same level with them, Avoid every evil by carefully keeping your obligations, and carefully conceal from the vulgar what you are, and wait that happy moment when we all shall be re-united under the same Sovereign in the mansions of eternal bliss.

Let us imitate the example of our Grand Master, Jacques De Molay, who, to the end put his hope in God, and at his last dying moments ended his life saying, SPES MEA IN DEO EST!

§. *Obligation.*

I ——, do of my own free will and accord, in the presence of the Grand Architect of the Universe, and this Consistory of Sovereign Princes of the Royal Secret, or Knights of St. Andrew, faithful guardians of the sacred treasure, most solemnly vow and swear, under all the penalties of my former obligation, that I will never directly or indirectly reveal or make known to any person or persons whatsoever, any or the least part of this royal degree, unless to one duly qualified in the body of a regularly constituted Consistory of the same, or to him or them whom I shall find such after strict and due trial. I furthermore vow and swear, under the above penalties, to always abide and regulate myself agreeably to the statutes and regulations now before me; and when in a Consistory to behave and demean myself as one worthy of being honored with so high a degree, that no part of my conduct may in the least reflect discredit on this Royal Consistory, or disgrace myself. So may God maintain me in equity and justice! Amen! Amen! Amen! Amen! Amen!

BOOK 5th

From the M.S.S. of Bro. Giles F. Yates,
R ⚒ K—H, S.P.R.S. &
Sov. Gnd Ins. Genl of 33:rd—A.L. 5833

31ˢᵗ Degree of the Second Series (1804) of the Southern Jurisdiction of the United States, called

🌸 🌸 🌸
Tribunal of Grand Inquiring Commanders
🌸

§. *Form of the Lodge.*

he Lodge must be hung with blue and strewn with the letters J.E.

There a stand, which supports a chest containing the archives of the Tribunal, covered with a white cloth on which is a great Teutonic Cross.

Upon the table of the president must be a balance, the symbol of Justice.

The Tribunal is presided over the Grand Prince Judge and two Princes Judges.

§. *Form of Reception.*

The Sovereign President acts as Grand Prince Judge; the first Lieutenant as First Prince Judge, the second Lieutenant as second Prince Judge.

The Candidate, decorated as a Knight of the White and Black Eagle, is presented and announced by the Grand Master of Ceremonies.

The Grand Prince Judge sends the Grand Expert to examine the Candidate as a 30° or K—H, or Knight of the White and Black Eagle. He does so, returns and reports. Following this the Grand Judge sends the order to admit his entrance which is done in the ordinary manner.

The Grand Judge says— My Brother, are you prepared to take the necessary obligation of all who aspire to enter within this sacred place?

The Candidate answers—Yes, *when someone places him on his knees before the Altar to receive the following*

§. *Obligation.*

I —— promise and engage on my word of honor and that of a Knight Mason, never to reveal the secrets of the degree of Grand Inquiring Commander and to strictly observe the Statutes and Regulations of the Tribunal.

And I do furthermore promise and swear to render justice to all according to the integrity of my heart. So help me God, and keep me steadfast in the same.

All respond—Amen.

All the Princes then form a circle round the Candidate and hold the points of their swords above his head. The Grand Judge lays his hand upon his head when occurs the

§. *Constitution.*

By virtue of the powers invested in me and by consent of the princes, my Brethren, I receive you a Grand Inquiring Commander and member of this Tribunal.

He then raises him and gives the battery, and the following

§. *Sign, Token & Words.*

Sign of Demand.—Place both hands, crossed, over the navel.

Sign of Response.—Place both hands, crossed, over the head.

Token.—Reciprocally strike with the right hand the right shoulder of the Brother, then join left hands and raise right arms to form a cross. Place foot to foot, knee to knee and in this position each speaks the word in the ear.

The Sacred Word—is JUSTICE.

The Pass Word—is EQUITY.

The Battery—2, 1, 1, 1.

After this they leave the newly admitted, who passes with the Grand Expert into the Sanctuary.

A perfected and ample ritual of the
31st Degree (1827) of the Northern Jurisdiction of
the United States, adopted by
the Southern Jurisdiction, and called

Tribunal of Grand Inquisitors, or Grand Inspectors Inquisitors Commanders, or, the Order of the Five Brethren

§. *Opening and Closing.*

Art thou Kadosh?

    A. Am I in secret?

    Q. Thou art in Secret.

    A. I am Kadosh.

Q. Doest thou know the traitors?

A. I know two of them.

Q. Who are they?

A. Philip the fair, and Clement the 5th.

Q. Thy pass word?

A. Philip De Bologne.

Q. Thy Sacred Word?

A. James De Molay.

Q. Have you any signs?

A. *He makes it and gives word and both embrace.*

The Candidate is introduced into the Chapter of Knights Kadosh by the Master of Ceremonies, by giving the signs and Words, &c.

If the Chapter is already opened, the Master of Ceremonies, or another Brother, rises and says—There is a vacancy in the Tribunal of Grand Inspectors Inquisitors Commanders, and I move that we proceed to fill that vacancy.

The motion is then put and carried.

Master of Ceremonies.—I propose as a suitable Candidate to fill this vacancy, our newly admitted Brother on my right. I believe him to possess all the qualifications necessary to fill that distinguished station.

A Brother Rises and objects saying—I fear that the newly-admitted Brother has not sufficient experience and practice in the rules and duties of our order to be a competent judge of the malefactions of others.

Another Brother may also object thus—The Candidate has been accused of having violated some part of his obligation (*say revelation or signs, &c, specifying it*).

Upon this, the Master of Ceremonies, who acts as the friend of the Candidate, rises and says—Rumors and reports are not proof and inquires are there any to prove these accusations?

A Brother says—A Monk has reported that on threatening him, he gave the Pass Word of a Knight of Kadosh.

Master of Ceremonies says—This accusation can be proved to be false, by a Pilgrim—With your permission I will introduce the Pilgrim who is now in the Neighborhood.

Permission being given, the Master of Ceremonies goes out and returns with a Pilgrim who being called upon to testify speaks as follows—I know this worthy Knight and was witness to the assault made upon him by the Monk of whom you speak. The Monk at first used gentle means and then threats and violence to extort from this Knight some of the secrets of his order, but in vain. The Knight came off victorious having received a few wounds and bruises.

Or, if the charge be that he did not perform acts of corporeal Mercy, the Pilgrim testifies to the contrary, and gives an account of the acts of mercy and charity which the Knight manifested to him.

The Grand Master then says—So far from the Brother proposed as Grand Inspector Inquisitor Commander, being guilty of the violation of the requirements and conditions of our Order, he has proven to be a most worthy and true Knight, and one who has exemplified in practice the duties of a Knight Kadosh.

Brethren, if you approve of him, and believe him to be worthy to belong to our Order of the 5 Brethren, signify it by giving the sign of assent.

The sign of assent being given, the Grand Master orders a certificate of his election to be made out, which he gives to the Candidate, and orders the Master of Ceremonies to conduct the Candidate to the Tribunal of the Five Brethren (which is holden in an adjoining room) for qualification.

The Master of Ceremonies conducts the Candidate to the Tribunal, which is in session.

§. *Decorations of the Tribunal of Grand Inspectors Inquisitors Commanders.*

There are eight golden columns supporting hangings of white. The Assembly is called "Most Illustrious Sovereign Tribunal." The Chief is styled "Most Perfect President." Wardens are called "Inspectors." The Secretary is called "Chancellor."

Garb.—*No apron is worn until after the work is finished. The Apron is wholly white with a Teutonic cross on the flap. The Collar is a broad white ribbon, to* which is suspended a radiant triangle of Gold, hanging in the middle the Arabic figures "31."

The Commanders are decked with Gold Chains, whose links are composed of the interlaced attributes of the different Degrees of Free-Masonry.

Jewel.—A Silver Teutonic Cross.

§. *Reception.*

The Master of Ceremonies conducts the Candidate as ordered to the door of the Sovereign Tribunal, where he knocks 1, 4, 3 and 1. (9)

Answered from within and admission granted Candidate.

The Most Perfect says—What is the desire of our Brethren Knights Kadosh?

Master of Ceremonies replies—Most Perfect, I introduce to you our Illustrious Brother Knight Kadosh, who has been duly chosen a Grand Inspector Inquisitor Commander, and now presents himself to be qualified as such by your most Illustrious Sovereign Tribunal.

The Most Perfect says—Has the Brother a certificate of his election?

Master of Ceremonies.—He has, and he presents it to the Most Perfect who reads it and directs the Secretary of the Tribunal to make a due record thereof.

He then directs the Master of Ceremonies to place in the left hand of the Candidate a pair of scales, and his right hand upon the Book of Statutes. All the Brethren cover his head with their Left hands. In this position he takes his Obligation, as follows:—

§. *Obligation.*

I — — promise and Engage on my word of honor never to reveal the secrets of the grade of Grand Inspector Inquisitor Commander, which are now about to be confided to me, to any one or persons in the world Except to those qualified to receive the same, according to the Statues and constitutions, rules and regulations of Sublime Free and Accepted Masons, or within the walls of a Sovereign Tribunal of this Degree lawfully constituted and empowered to confer this Order of the Five Brethren.

I furthermore promise and engage strictly to observe the statutes, and regulations of this Degree. Under the penalty of expulsion from all the assemblies of Masons. Amen. Amen. Amen. Amen. Amen.

Most Perfect says to Candidate—Attend now my Brother to our instructions.

§. *Lecture.*

Tribunals of Grand Inspectors Inquisitors Commanders were established to try and pass Judgment on all Brethren of the high Degrees, for malefactions against the Order. Each Tribunal consisted of Five Brethren and hence this order was called the Order of the Five Brethren.

While the Pope of Rome was holding his Inquisitional tribunals for the trial of Templars and Free Masons for pretended offenses, We point with pride to our Brethren who like James De Molay and his brave companions, and in later days of John Coustos and other Brethren and Knights, who with unparalleled constancy endured the most dreadful tortures and afflictions, rather than betray the cause of Truth, virtue and Religion.

There were however many weak Brethren who possessed not such fortitude and magnanimity as the Brethren and Knights to whom we have alluded who to Escape bodily sufferings, confessed crimes of which neither they or the Order to which they belonged were Guilty; these were less worthy of blame than other Brethren, who in order to answer some times serving mercenary and selfish Ends, voluntarily violated their obligations and became Traitors to our Orders.

Additional vows and more rigid rules were adopted after the Martyrdom of the Knights of the Temple and Tribunals were Established for the Trial of all Traitors and apostates, the remembrance of which We commemorate in this sacred part of Grade of the order of Kadosh.

We possess the power to reestablish them in form when and if it should become necessary (which God forbid).

As many of these tribunals were established and in such places as was deemed necessary to promote the Ends of their institution; Secret signs, tokens and words of recognition were instituted by the Order of Five Brethren, and statutes and regulations were adopted with which you ought to be acquainted and will be communicated to you for your observance

§. *Sign, Token & Words.*

1st Sign.— Put the two hands on the navel fingers down,

2nd Sign.—in answer carry the two hands, crossed, over the head.

Token.—Foot to foot, knee to knee and take hold of Left hand of the Brother; with your right strike on his right shoulder and say

Pass Word.— JUSTICE.

Answer— EQUITY.

Both together say—SO MOTE IT BE. EL-SHADDAI. (God Almighty)

33rd Degree (1802) of the Southern Jurisdiction of the United States, called
Sovereign Grand Inspector General, or Supreme Council of the 33rd

*T*his Council chamber must be hung with purple, with a number of Skeletons, Skulls, thigh bones and fire brands painted thereon.

The presiding officer, represents, his Most August Majesty, Frederick the 2nd King of Prussia, who was the Sovereign of the whole Masonic order. He must be dressed in robes of Crimson silk, edged with white fur, wear a regal Crown on his head, and have a drawn sword in his hand. His title, "Most Puissant Sovereign." He sits in the East, on a Throne elevated with five steps under a Canopy of Crimson, a triangular pedestal before him, covered with crimson.

The 2nd officer represents his Serene Highness, Louis of Bourbon, Prince of the Blood Royal of France, he wears on his head a Ducal Crown, and has a drawn sword in his hand. His title is "Most Illustrious Inspector General." He sits in the West, on a Throne elevated by 3 steps, and has before him a triangular pedestal, covered with Crimson.

The Treasurer in the North is styled "Illustrious Treasurer General of the Holy Empire." — Table triangular. —

The Secretary in the South is styled "Illustrious Secretary of the Holy Empire" — Table triangular.—

The Master of Ceremonies — "Illustrious Grand Master of Ceremonies."

The Door Keeper must be dressed in the Military Uniform of the order, and is styled "Illustrious Captain of the Life Guards. The Degree must be committed to him, but he is not to be considered as a Member of the Council. The members are styled, "Sovereign Grand Inspectors General."

In the Council or procession, they must always wear Black clothes, a sword, cocked hat, black cockade, and all must wear the attributes of the order.

The Order is worn from the left shoulder to the right hip, and is a white water tabby'd ribbon 4 Inches broad, on the bottom of which is a red and white Rose.—On the part which crosses the breast, must be gilt or embroidered, or cut out of gold, a triangle, surrounded by a Sun, and within the triangle, the figures 33 in Gold. On each side of this figure, must be a dagger thus.[1]

Jewel.—At the bottom of the Order is suspended the Jewel, which is, a large cast black spread eagle, with two heads and gold beaks holding a naked sword in his claws. Gloves — White — No Apron.—

Over the head of the Most Puissant Sovereign is the Great and Awful name of HIM, who gives us Life and Immortality.—Thus: יהוה

In the Center of the Council Chamber, must be a small quadrangular pedestal covered with crimson, on which must be placed Bible open, and a drawn Sword

---

[1] The original manuscript does not have an illustration. The above illustration is taken from Charles T. McClenachan, *The Book of the Ancient and Accepted Scottish Rite of Freemasonry* (New York: Masonic Publishing Co., 1867)

laying thereon. A Human Skeleton on the North side of the pedestal, with a naked dagger in his right hand, in the attitude of striking with it, and in his left, bearing the standard of the order.

The Standard is of white silk 3 1/2 by 2 1/2 feet, edged with Gold fringe and tassels—in the Center a Black spread Eagle with 2 heads, gold beaks, and a naked sword in its Claws, under it, on a blue Scroll, these words in Gold Letters

Deus Meumque Jus

the staff 8 feet in length with a spear on the top.— Thus, over the inside of the Council Chamber door, are these words in Gold Letters

Deus Meumque Jus

In the East must be a Candlestick with 5 branches, in the West one with 3, in the North on with 1, and in the South one with 2.—

§. *To Open.*

S.—Most Illustrious Inspector General, what age are you?

I.—Accomplished 30 Most Puissant Sovereign.

S.—What is your employment?

I.—To Combat for God and my rights, and to inflict Vengeance on Traitors.

S.—What is the hour?

I.— The Watch word is out. The Guards are set, and we remain in perfect security.

S.—Since we are safe from interruption, give notice by the mysterious numbers, that a Supreme Council of the 33rd is going to be opened AD GLORIAM DEI, that we may revolve in our minds, the business of our enterprise, and implore the assistance of the God of Armies, to aid us in our struggle for justice and our rights. —

He then strikes the hilt of his sword 5-3-1-2

The Most Illustrious Inspector General repeats the same, when the Supreme Council is open.

The members of the Council then kneel on both knees, while the Most Puissant Sovereign, also kneeling, humbly and devoutly offer up to God the following prayer:—

LET US PRAY

O thou Great and Eternal Lord God, Father of Light, of Life and of Love, the world's Supreme Architect, who dost from thy Throne in the heavens behold all the people of the Earth, vouchsafe, we beseech thee, to hear and receive the prayers and petitions of thy unworthy servants now prostrate before thee.

Instill into our hearts a knowledge of thy Eternal Word, and grant, that our high Institution may always be governed by the principles of Virtue, religion, and Justice.

Defend us, O Lord, from the machinations of the wicked; frustrate the evil designs of our enemies, and give us strength to overcome all those who may be armed against us, or who may wish to do us evil.

And the honor and the Glory shall be ascribed to thy most Holy and Mighty Name, now and for ever.

The Council answers—Amen.

§. *Form of Reception.*

As this is the most solemn and important of all the degrees of the Royal and Military Art of Free Masonry it is necessary that the utmost precaution should be used, in the selection of persons for admission.

It does not follow that because a Brother may have received the degree of Prince of the Royal Secret, he is then entitled to receive this. None must be admitted whose character is not irreproachable, and whose zeal, virtue, discretion, fidelity, and fortitude are not fully known and approved. Such a person must apply in the following form:

To the Sovereign Grand Inspectors General, in Supreme Council of the 33rd Degree

Most Puissant Brethren,

Ardently attached to the Glorious enterprise established in the degrees of K.H. and Prince of the Royal Secret—and being anxious to arrive at the summit of Masonic Knowledge, and to enjoy its privileges, I most humbly beg leave to offer myself as a Candidate for admission into your Illustrious and Puissant Council and your suffrages in my favour will ever by held in grateful remembrance.

A.B.
K.H.—P.R.S

The Candidate is then Voted for Viva Voce. One nay excludes him for ever, if the reasons which are given shall be deemed sufficient.

The Illustrious Grand Master of Ceremonies goes out to the Candidate, and examines him in all the preceding degrees, as none can be advanced into this Supreme Council, who have not been regularly and lawfully initiated into the Ancient Mysteries, and received every degree, from an Entered Apprentice to the 32nd or Price of the Royal Secret, and produces certificates of the same.

The Candidate must then declare that he believes the Holy Scriptures to be the revealed Word of God, for if he swears on a book which he does not believe, he will deem his obligation of no importance. No one can be admitted, who has not attained 30 years of age. The Candidate then knocks on the door of the Council chamber 5-3-1-2 on which the Most Illustrious Inspector says—

"Most Puissant Sovereign, some person knocks at the door and disturbs the deliberations of the Council. The Most Puissant requests him to go and see who it is. He then goes and knocks 5-3-1-2, and when the door is opened, he demands— "Who is it that knocks and disturbs our deliberations."

The Illustrious Grand Master of Ceremonies answers— "It is a Knight of Kadosh and prince of the Royal Secret, who is sincerely attached to his order, his Country and his God, who feels for the sufferings of humanity in the death of the Master, and humbly solicits admittance into the Supreme Council, that, he may enjoy the privileges which hereunto belong."

The door is then shut, and the Most Illustrious Inspector General reports the answer in the same words to the Most Puissant Sovereign, who desires the Candidate to be admitted if he posses the necessary qualifications.

The Illustrious Grand Master of Ceremonies then introduces the Candidate, who must be dressed in black clothes, and without shoes, hat, apron, sword, his head inclining forwards and downwards, his arms crossed on his breast, his fingers touching his shoulders, a black cord, round his neck, which is held by the Grand Master of Ceremonies in his left hand, and a fire brand in his right.—

In this situation he is led round the Council, and when he passes in front of the Most Puissant Sovereign, he bows before the Sacred and Ineffable name of God, which blazes in the East while the Most Puissant Sovereign says to him—

"Let us with the deepest veneration and piety, humbly adore the fountain of all good, that Glorious and Gracious Being, who with mercy and Beneficence governs the Universe, and all the works of his Creation, Glory be to his Holy Name, now and for ever."

*The Council answers—*Amen.

He is then led round again, and again bows before the Ineffable name; and the Most Puissant Sovereign says:—

"How adorable and wonderful is that Being who irradiates the world with the light of Reason and of Revelation— We adore thee Jehovah Sabaoth for all thy goodness, thy power and thy Glory be to thee for ever and ever."

*The Council answers—*Amen.

He is then led round the 3rd time, and on approaching the East, he again bows before the great Name, and the Most Puissant Sovereign addresses him as follows:—

Most Respectable Knight and Prince, Impressed with the solemn scene through which you are about to pass, in taking an obligation, which of all others is the Most Awful and important that men can subscribe to. And feeling, as I do, a consciousness of the dreadful penalty which the Great Eternal will most assuredly inflict on all those, who violate it—And as temptations may frequently occur, that may put your religion and fortitude to the test— It is necessary we should have some proof of your firmness and resolution of mind. You will therefore my Respectable Brother, advance to that cauldron, and wash your hands in the melted lead which you see therein that your hands may be cleansed from the stains of Vice and immorality; and that you may give us an assurance, that you are capable of enduring any sufferings in the cause of virtue, religion and truth. All of us have gone through the same trial, and have escaped unhurt. Put your trust in God, and resolutely determine to fulfill the Obligation which you are about to take, and the Lead, though melted, will loose its heat, and as you immerse your hands, it will recede from your touch. Brethren attend to see the Mystic Ceremony.

They all advance and see it performed. The Cauldron must be an iron basin, under which must be a furnace or chafing dish, containing a few pieces of lighted Charcoal, and placed in the South, so that in going round the Candidate may pass behind it. Some incense must be thrown on it, composed of Amber, Olibanum, and Mastick, each three parts; Storax, two parts, Labdanum and Benzoine each one part, mixed in a gross powder. This will make it smoke and yield a grateful perfume.

The Cauldron must be half filled with Quicksilver, which has the appearance of melted lead, by cannot be made hot.

After washing his hands in it, the Candidate is led to the Quadrangular Pedestal, at which he knees and takes the Obligation of an Inspector, during which the incense is kept burning, and every Member kneels, inclining his head downwards in humble adoration, with their right hands upon their hearts. The Candidate places both his hands on the Holy Bible, and takes the following

§. *Obligation.*

I —— Knight of Kadosh and Prince of the Royal Secret, do most solemnly pledge my sacred word of Honor, and do most sincerely swear and promise on the Holy Bible, which I verily believe to be the revealed Word of the Everlasting the God, that I will never reveal, either directly or indirectly, any part or parts of the Secrets or Mysteries of this Inspectors degree, which I am now about to receive, or any degrees which I have heretofore received, to any person or persons in the world, except it be to a true and lawful Grand Inspector General of the 33rd who has received it, in as lawful a manner, as I have or unto those to whom the same shall justly and lawfully belong. And I do furthermore swear, that I will strictly and religiously adhere to all the Statutes, Constitutions, Orders, and regulations, of this degree. That I will diligently and faithfully, and without partiality, favor or affection, discharge the duty of Grand Inspector General. That I will never receive or acknowledge any higher degree in Masonry that this. That I will worship the only true and living God in the manner and form, which I conscientiously believe revealed in the holy Scriptures, and regulate my conduct, by the unerring guide of his divine commands. That I will bear true allegiance and fidelity to the Country in which I live, and be obedient to all the orders and laws of the Government. That I will to the utmost of my powers, endeavor inculcate to all around me both by my language and behavior, the duty we owe to out God and our Neighbor, that it is Virtue alone that can make us respectable and religion bless us with happiness.— All this I swear without any equivocation, mental reservation, or self evasion of mind, or in the hope of any future dispensation from any power whatever, under the penalty which I hereby implore upon myself, of being dishonored among men, of having my name exposed in large red letters in all the Councils and Lodges in the World— and I hereby most solemnly Invoke the Great and Eternal God, to pour his curses upon this execrable head, [*here the Candidate places his right hand upon his head*] and to let me languish in misery and wretchedness, should I violate this my Inspectors Obligation.

So may God Almighty bless me with sufficient strength, and resolution to fulfill it in all its points, to the Glory of His Most Holy and Almighty Name— Amen—Amen—Amen.

He kisses the Bible three times, and the blade of the sword three times.

N.B.—If a Jew takes this obligation, he must wear his Tephelin and have the Hebrew Bible on his breast, with his arms crossed thereon.
The Most Puissant Illustrious Sovereign then delivers the sword into the Candidate's right hand, and says to him—

"Respectable Knight and Prince, we place into your hands a weapon of death, which we solemnly enjoin you never to use against the life of a fellow creature, except on the following occasions (vizt), in your own defense, against the common enemies of your Country or your order, when lawfully called so to do."

He then places upon the wedding finger of his left hand, a plain gold ring of this breadth, on the inside of which is engraved the following Motto, vizt.—

DEUS MEUMQUE JUS

and the name of the owner, and says to him:—

"With this ring I wed you to the order, your Country, and your God, and receive you and acknowledge you as a Sovereign Grand Inspector General. Let it always put you in remembrance of the solemn obligations you have taken. Swear to me, never to part with it, but when you believe yourself to be near your death, and then to give it to your wife, oldest son, daughter, or dearest friend as a sacred deposit—under a solemn promise never to part with it but in the like manner."

*The Candidate answers—*To which I swear, and pledge my sacred Honor.

The Most Illustrious Inspector General, then raises him and invests him with the order and Jewel, and gives him the following Signs, Token and Words.—

§. *Signs, Token and Words.*

1st Sign.—Go on both knees, cross your arms over your breast, your fingers touching your shoulders, your head and body bent downwards.

2nd Sign.—Draw your sword, fall on your left knee, and place your left hand upon your heart.

Token.—Kiss the blade of your sword three times.

1st Pass Words.—are DE MOLAY, when the other answers HIRAM ABIFF.

2nd Pass Words.—are FREDERICK, when the other answers OF PRUSSIA.

Grand Words.—are the same as in Kadosh, MI CHAMOCHA BAELIM—ADONAI.— (i.e.) Who is like unto thee in Strength! O God!

The Candidate then puts on his shoes, and takes his seat among the Inspectors.

§. History.

The Most Puissant Grand Sovereign, Grand Master Commander in Chief, Sovereign of Sovereigns of the degree of Prince of the Royal Secret, was our Illustrious Brother, Frederick the 2nd King of Prussia. He established this degree, in connection with our Brother, his Serene Highness, Louis of Bourbon, Prince of the Blood Royal of France, and other Illustrious characters, who had received the degrees of K.H. and Prince of the Royal Secret.

The degree of K.H. or Knight of Kadosh, is a most awful and important degree. In it we have without restriction, solemnly obligated ourselves to destroy an order of men, for crimes committed many Centuries ago, without regard to the common principles of Humanity, or the Laws of the Country. And notwithstanding the utmost precaution, in the selection of Candidates, some unworthy persons may be received into that degree, who through a mistaken zeal for the order, or a religious enthusiasm for the literal observance of Obligations, might be induced to commit acts, which never were contemplated. The King on the first of May 5786, formed and established the 33rd Degree to give some elucidations of the K.H.—

The King was conscious, that agreeably to the common course of human nature, he could not live many years; and he conceived and executed the glorious design if investing the Sovereign Masonic power which he held, as Sovereign Grand Commander of the order of Prince of the Royal Secret—in a Council of Grand Inspectors General—that they might, after his decease, regulate, agreeably to the Constitution and Statutes which he then formed, the government of the Craft in every degree, from the 17th or Knights and West inclusive, leaving the control over the Symbolic Lodge; the Grand, Ineffable and Sublime Lodge of Perfect Masons, and the Knights of the East or Sword, to the Grand Council of Princes of Jerusalem, whom he conceived to be justly entitled to that Honor and power.—

This new Degree he called "Sovereign Grand Inspectors General, or Supreme Council of the 33rd.

The Princes of Kadosh or K.H. are Deputy Grand Inspectors General, acting under special patents, granted for that purpose, but to this degree, the Sovereign power is committed. The Council when formed can take cognizance of every circumstance appertaining to Masonry, from the 17th Degree upwards. Grant patents to deputy Inspectors General, or warrants for Councils hear all appeals from Councils or Individuals, above the Grand Council of Princes of Jerusalem, &c &c as is more fully explained in the Constitution accompanying this degree.

No Inspector General possesses any Individual power in a Country, where a Supreme Council of Inspectors is established, as a Majority of their Votes is necessary to give legality to any of their proceedings. —

In consequence of the power with which the Inspectors of this degree are invested, it is necessary to limit their number. Therefore, a Council cannot consist of a greater number than Nine; at least five of whom must profess the Christian Religion. No business can be transacted or the Degree given, but when three are present, except on its first establishment, as pointed out in the Constitution. There must be one Council of this Degree in each nation or Kingdom of Europe, two in the United States of America, as remote from each other as possible, One in the British West India Islands and one in the French. None of the Inspectors can be possessed of the Manuscript of this Degree, but those two, who first formed each Council. When an Inspector goes to another Country to establish this degree, it shall then be given to him, under an Obligation, never to give it, except in the like manner. The Signs Words and Token are to be given to all the Inspectors.

The unjust and unprovoked cruelties, insults and injuries, inflicted on the Knights Templars, in which, the Knights of the order of St. John of Jerusalem, or Knights of Malta, assisted, which gave rise to the degree of K.H. and feelingly described in that degree, and in Vertot's history of the Knights of Malta. — The Knights Templars, otherwise called Knights of the Temple, were a Masonic order of Knighthood, instituted in the Reign of Pope Gelasius, about the year of Masonry 5117 and so called, because they dwelt in a part of the Temple at Jerusalem, not far from the Sepulcher of Jesus Christ. They entertained Christian strangers and pilgrims charitably, and in their armor led them through the Holy Land, to view the sacred monuments of Christianity, without fear of the Infidels.

This Order continued to increase in numbers, power and wealth, and in about 200 years, was spread over all Europe.— The principal part of their Commanderies were along the Mediterranean Sea. As their influence was extensive, and their possessions great, Philip the Fair, King of France became jealous of them, which soon was increased into hatred, because they espoused the cause of Boniface 8th in that Pontiff's difference with King Philip, an insult which the King had never forgiven.—

On the 13th of October, Anno Lucis 5307 he arrested all the Knights Templars he could find in his kingdom, and brought them to the Stake.

In the year 5312, the whole order was suppressed by Pope Clemens Quintus. And at the request of the King of France and the Pope, the Kings of England, Castile, Arragon and Sicily, the Count of Provence, and all the sovereigns in Europe, arrested the Knights Templars, seized their possessions, and placed Garrisons into their Commanderies.

On the first of October of the same year, the Council of Vienna banished their whole order, in with the Pope, and gave the greatest part of their possessions to the Knights Hospitallers of the Order of St. John of Jerusalem, Knights of Rhodes, now called Knights of Malta, who were established about the year of Masonry 5120 when Honorius was Pope.

The Knights of Kadosh or K.H. were originally called Knights Templars, but after the Massacre, by King Philip, the few who escaped, found it necessary, to change the title and appearance of their order, that they might the better avoid the persecution of their enemies. They then laid aside the Black order and red cross, and substituted in its place—a broad fiery blood colored riband from the left shoulder to the right hip, to which is suspended a Black spread Eagle with 2 heads, with a naked sword in its Claws—.

About the year of Masonry 5767 an Inquiry was instituted at Paris, to prove that those Masons who styled themselves Knights of Kadosh, were in reality Knights Templar. Had the Inquiry succeeded, the whole order, probably would a second time, have been cut off. In consequence of this circumstance it was determined, in the Grand Communications of Berlin and Paris, that they should, in future, be styled, "Knights of the White and Black Eagle."

The Knights of Malta, that they may retain the possessions which they have unlawfully received, are solemnly obligated to exterminate the order of Knights Templars, who are actually they, who have received the degree of K.H. For this reason the Knights of Kadosh, or of the White and Black Eagle, have solemnly pledged to each other, their sacred honors, and have sworn in the name, and in the presence of God, to hold them in enmity, and to exterminate them, whenever it is in their power.—

Although it is a duty we owe to ourselves, to endeavor to destroy that power, which attempts to destroy us—yet it is necessary that the extent of our enmity and hostilities to the Knights of Malta, should be well defined lest we should expose ourselves to ridicule and contempt if not to punishment by the civil Law, it is not intended, that if a Knight of K.H. should go up the Mediterranean on business, and accidentally meet with some of the Knights of that Order, that he should immediately draw the poniard, and stab them to the heart. This would be deemed murder by the Laws of every Country, and would justly be punished with Death. But if any Sovereign power should declare war, against the Knights of Malta, or against any power with whom they have treaties of Offense, and they are actually in the field, then we are bound, by the solemn and awful obligations which we have taken, if the situation of our affairs will admit, of it to join immediately the Army of their Enemies, and to use our utmost exertions both in the Cabinet and the field, to exterminate their order, that we may once more obtain those possessions, which are the indisputable right of the Knights Templars.—

When the whole Masonic body of the different degrees, (as they are all obligated to obey the order of their superiors) are sufficiently powerful, they will be led out against their enemies by the Sovereign of the 33rd. And should success attend our arms—the Knight of Kadosh will then openly declare themselves, and take possession of the Countries, of which they are now illegally deprived and will peaceably rest themselves under the banners and protection of the Sovereign of this degree, from whom they will receive a system of Government, founded on the rights of the Knights and on their zeal, services and virtuous sufferings for so many Centuries.

When we take the field, against our enemies, our forces are to be governed by the orders given in the degree of Prince of the Royal Secret—

But as the Most Illustrious Sovereign of Sovereigns has been most graciously pleased to invest this degree with the Supreme Executive power the Command in Chief of the Troops, after his death, devolves upon us. Therefore His Majesty the King of Prussia, has ordained, that the 1st and 2nd Officers of the Supreme Council of the 33rd shall be the 1st and 2nd in command over the Masonic Troops, District, Nation or Kingdom; over which they have Masonic Jurisdiction.

On the arrival of the Land forces at their Rendezvous at Jerusalem—A Supreme Council General, of all those who have received the 33rd Degree, shall be immediately convened, where each Inspector, must produce his Letter of Credence of this degree, and the possessor of the oldest Letter of Credence, shall be declared and proclaimed to the Troops as Generallissimo, and shall be styled Most Puissant Sovereign, Grand Commander. All the other Military Grades shall be held agreeably to the dates of the several Letters of Credence. Letters of the same date shall be determined by ballot.

Henceforward, all Rank, Honors, Dignities, Titles, possessions &c shall be hereditary. The government of the order always resting in the family of the Sovereign Grand Commander. On the reduction of the Knights of Malta, the Sovereign Grand Commander shall immediately assemble a Supreme Council

General of the 33rd in which shall be formed a Constitution and system of Government for the order, which shall always be military.

At which time the order will assume its real title. The Uniform of the order in the field is, Blue, faced and lined with white, full trimmed, white buttons, on which is the Jewel of the 33rd. On the small buttons, 33.

§. *Address to the New Inspector.*

My Brother, As we have powerful enemies to contend with, we must endeavor so to regulate our conduct, that we may not give just cause of offense to any one; that our wisdom may preserve us from the machinations of the wicked, and our virtue and urbanity subdue the Malice and envy of the Ignorant.

To effect these purposes, you must constantly wear upon your Lips, the guard of Secrecy and cherish in your heart the principles of virtue and honor.

Let us respect the whole human race, and even your enemies, for they are Men, and the same God created us all, and the same Providence provides for them as for us. If your duty should call you into the field, bravely and honorably contend with them, and should you prove victorious, wither not the victors laurels, by meanly insulting a fallen foes. Prove to them by the magnanimity of your conduct, that justice requires not the cowardly aid of an assassins hands, but that Virtue will be its own reward. Convince them of the Villainy of their Conduct, by the uprightness of yours, and of their Injustice, by your mercy. In whatever Country Capricious fortune may throw you, be faithful and obedient to its government and laws, for a Mason who is capable of sacrificing the interests of the Country in which he lives is equally as capable of sacrificing the interests of his order—. Venerate the beings who brought you into existence, be a tender husband to the partner of your bosom, and an affectionate parent, to the offspring of your Loins; rear them up in the paths of Religion and Virtue and teach them to love their Country and to obey its Laws and set them the example of industry and care, and bring up your sons into the Masonic Order. Be true to your friend and your Brethren bear patiently with their failings, and make allowances for the frailties of human nature. Be a living example virtue and benevolence to all around you. Aid the poor and the distressed, whether they are Masons or not, with such assistance as they may want and you can conveniently spare and above all, offer up unceasingly prayers and Thanksgivings to that Great and Eternal God, for the many signal instances of his Divine Mercy, which you have unworthily received at his hands, and ardently seek for the attainment of Bliss, in the Mansions not made with hands, Eternal in the Heavens. Amen.

End of History and Address

§. *Lecture.*

S.—Are you a Sovereign Grand Inspector General?

I.—Most Puissant Sovereign, my Virtue my Courage and my zeal procured me that distinguished honor.

S.—How am I to know that you are a Sovereign Grand Inspector General?

I.—By Giving you the pass Words.

S.—Begin.

I.—DE MOLAY.

S.—HIRAM ABIFF.

I.—FREDERICK OF PRUSSIA

S.—What did you see, when you first entered the Council Chamber?

I.— The Grand Ineffable Name of Almighty God.

S.—Why does it appear in our council?

I.—As our Order and authority are founded on Justice and Equity, we fear not the searching eye of the Supreme Being, and it is likewise to remind us that we are acting in his immediate presence.— It also teaches us, to look up to that source for protection and support, and to worship the only true and living God.

S.—What is the meaning of the Skeletons, Sculls, Bones and firebrands in our Council?—

I.—To put us in mind of the Massacre of our Ancestors by the King of France, who brought thousands of our Knights to the Stake.

S.—Why do you appear in mourning armed with a Sword?

I.—To mourn for their loss, and to be prepared to revenge their death.

S.—Who established this degree?

I.—Our Illustrious Brother, Frederick of Brunswick, King of Prussia.

S.—For what purpose?

I.—To regulate our hatred and opposition to the of Malta, to guide our zeal and exertions through appropriate channels, and to point out the mode of our Enterprise.

S.—What is the Cause of your hatred and opposition to the Knights of Malta?

I.—After the destruction of the greatest part of the order of Knights Templars, by the King of France, in concert with Pope Clemens the 5th their rich possessions were given to the Knights of St. John of Jerusalem, now called Knights of Malta, from the Island of that name, which is a part of our possessions, and also many other places in the Mediterranean, which they hold; And as they have refused to surrender those possessions which were wrested from us by cruelties and injustice, we have bound ourselves, on the increase of our order, to conquer them and regain our possessions, or nobly perish in the attempt.—

S.—Is this the only reason the King had in establishing this degree?

I.—Most Puissant Sovereign, he had others. He knew according to the common course of human events that his dissolution was not very distant, and he determined to establish a Supreme Executive Council of Grand Inspectors General, to whom he might commit the great Masonic power which he possessed, and who, after his decease, might rule the great body of Masons, agreeably to certain Statutes which he framed for that purpose, that when they should become sufficiently strong, to lead them to battle against our enemies. He justly conceived that as every nation is Independent in their Civil government, it was most equitable, they should each possess, a high Masonic Court, from which there could be no appeal. As this would be agreeable to every Government, no jealousies could exist against the order; the Craft would increase, and the great end of the Institution be obtained.

S.—What else did you see on entering the Council Chamber?

I.—I saw in the East a Candlestick with five branches, in the West, one of three, in the North one of one, and in the South on of two.

S.—What do they signify?

I.—Arranging the number of Lights in figures, gives 5312, the year of Masonry, when our order was cut off, which circumstance is likewise alluded to in opening and closing the Council, and in a reception, by the knocks on the door.

S.—What is the meaning of the order you wear?

I.—The White represents the purity and innocence of those who were brought to the stake, and the red represents the blood of those who were murdered. As the Sun gives Light and Life to all the regions of the World, so the Sun on our breasts indicates that, the Supreme and Illustrious Order to which we belong, gives Light and Life to the great Masonic body over the Universe.

S.—What is the reason of the Skeleton's holding the Standard of the Order in his hand?

I.—To indicate the punishment of death which all those will receive who are traitors to the order and who forfeit the Obligations they have taken, It also points out to those, who fight under our banners, that they must conquer, or nobly perish in the glorious attempt.

End of Lecture

§. *To Close.*

S.—Most Illustrious Inspector General, What age are you?

I.—Accomplished thirty, Most Puissant Sovereign.

S.—What is you employment?

I.—To combat for God and my rights, and to inflict Vengeance on traitors.

S.—What is the hour?

I.—The Effulgence of the morning's Sun illumines our Council.

S.—As the Sun has risen to illumine the World, let us my Brethren, rise [*they all rise*] to diffuse into the minds of those who are in darkness, the effulgence of Masonic Light, and to be an example of virtue to an admiring world. Give notice by the Mysterious numbers that I am going to close this Supreme Council.

He then strikes with the hilt of his Sword 5-3-1-2-
The Most Illustrious Inspector General repeats the same.
The Most Puissant Sovereign, then holds up both his hands and says:—

O thou Great and Eternal Lord God Father of Light of Life, and of Love, Most Merciful and Supreme Ruler of Heaven and Earth. Guide us in the paths of Virtue and of Justice. Teach us those Great and vital principles of thy true and Holy Religion, which will make us worship thee in spirit and truth, and to love our neighbors as ourselves, so that we may be prepared to become Members of the Supreme Council above, where all honor, and glory and joy await the righteous and the good, forever and ever.

*They all answer—*Amen, God grant it so may be.—
The Illustrious Inspector General, then holding up his hands says—

May the Holy ONE of Israel, and the Most High and Mighty God of Abraham, of Isaac, and of Jacob, enrich us with his blessings now and forever.

Ordinances &c.

A Sovereign Grand Inspector General, shall wear his hat in all Councils and Lodges, except in the Supreme Council of the 33rd and shall have the privilege of speaking without rising from his seat.

When a Sovereign Grand Inspector General is announced at the door of any Council above the 16th Degree he shall be received under the Arch of Steel. The President, if he is not an Inspector, shall resign his seat to the Visiting Inspector, with whom it is optional whether he receives it. In the Grand Council of Princes of Jerusalem and the Sublime and Ineffable Lodge of Perfect Masons, he shall be placed at the right hand of the Thrice Puissant and the same in the Symbolic Lodge.

The other Ordinances are the same as in the Princes of Jerusalem.

A Sovereign Grand Inspector General shall in every Lodge or Council wear the attributes of his degree.

Every Inspector General must have a Letter of Credence agreeably to the following form written either in Latin, French or English, to which all the Inspectors shall sign their names. When an Inspector signs a Masonic paper, he shall affix to his name these titles and no other: K—H., P.R.S. & Sovereign Grand Inspector General 33rd.

The Letter shall be countersigned by the Secretary General in this manner—

A.B.

K.H.—P.R.S.—Sov.^{n} G.^{d} Insp.^{r} Genl & Sec.^{y} Genl of the H. Empire.

The Letter of Credence shall be headed with the following words in German Text, in a scroll — vizt "Universi Terrarum Orbis Architectonis per Gloriam ab Ingentis" and in the lower part of the plate shall be these words "Ordo ab Chao." The figure shall be the Jewel of the Order, vizt— A black spread Eagle and gold beaks, in the attitude of flying, with a drawn sword in its claws. Immediately under its feet, in a scroll, these words "Deus Meumque Jus." On

413

the right side of the Eagle, the standard of the Order, and on the left, the Colors of the Country, in which the Council is held, to shew that we would arrange ourselves under the banners of our Country, with the same willingness that we would under the standard of our Order.

Letter of Credence.

Universi Terrarum Orbis Architectonis per Gloriam Ingentis

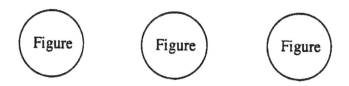

Deus Meumque Jus

Ordo ab Chao

From the East of the Grand, of the Supreme Council of the Most Puissant Sovereigns, Grand Inspectors General, under the celestial Canopy of the Zenith which answers to — — Degrees — — Minutes — — Latitude.

To our Most Illustrious, Most Valiant, and Sublime Princes of the Royal Secret, Knights of K.H.

Illustrious Princes and Knights, Grand Ineffable and Sublime Free and Accepted Masons of all degrees, Ancient and Modern, over the surface of the two Hemispheres.

To all those to whom these Letters of Credence shall come

HEALTH, STABILITY AND POWER.

KNOW YE that we, the undersigned, SOVEREIGN GRAND INSPECTORS GENERAL, duly and lawfully established and Congregated, in SUPREME COUNCIL of the 33rd degree have carefully and duly examined our Illustrious — — Brother — — in the several degrees which he has lawfully received, and at his special request, WE DO HEREBY CERTIFY, ACKNOWLEDGE and PROCLAIM, our Illustrious Brother — — (*add civil or Military titles*) — (*Citizen or Subject of*) residing in — — to be an Expert Master and Past Master of the Symbolic Lodge, and also a Secret Master, Perfect Master, Intimate Secretary, Provost and Judge, Intendant of the Building or Master in Israel, Master Elected of 9, Illustrious, Elected of 15—Sublime Knight Elected—Grand Master Architect, Royal Arch, and Grand Elect Perfect and Sublime Mason. WE DO ALSO CERTIFY him to be a Knight of the East or Sword, Prince of Jerusalem, Knight of the East and West, Knight of the Eagle and Prince of Rose Croix de Heroden, Grand Pontiff, Master Advitam, Patriarch Noachite and Prince of Lebanus, &c., &c., Sovereign Knight of the Sun, K—H Prince of the White and Black Eagle, Prince of the Royal Secret and Sovereign grand Inspector General and member of the Supreme Council of the 33rd Degree.

WE THEREFORE COMMAND, all and Every of our aforesaid KNIGHTS, PRINCES AND SUBLIME MASONS, to receive and acknowledge our said Illustrious Brother — — in his several qualities to the highest degree in Masonry, and we shall reciprocate the attentions shewn to him to those Brethren, who may present themselves to our Supreme Council, furnished with Lawful Certificates or Letters of Credence.

To which LETTER OF CREDENCE, WE the undersigned, SOVEREIGN GRAND INSPECTORS GENERAL, Members of the Supreme Council of the 33rd degree in — — have hereunto subscribed our names and affixed thereto the Grand Seals of the said Illustrious Order, in the Grand Council Chamber near the B∴B∴ under the C∴C∴ this — day of the — month called — of the restoration — Anno Lucis — and of the Christian Æra this — day of — —.

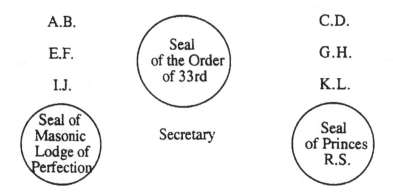

When this Letter of Credence is given to a Brother, who has not received the 33d Degree, the recapitulation of degrees must only be continued to the highest degree he has received inclusively: & instead of the words "highest degree" must be inserted the highest degree he has received. And when given to an Inspector General of the 33rd between the word "Degree" and "we therefore command" must be added "and we hereby authorize & empower our said Illustrious Brother —— to establish; congregate superintend and Inspect all Lodges, Chapters, Councils, Colleges & Consistories of the Royal and Military Order of Ancient and Modern Free Masonry over the surface of the two Hemispheres, agreeable to the Grand Constitutions."

Constitution, Statutes and Regulations

For the Government of the Supreme Council of Inspectors General of the 33rd and for the Government of all Councils, under their Jurisdiction Made and approved in the Supreme Council of the 33rd duly and lawfully established and Congregated in the Grand East of Berlin on the 1st of May Anno Lucis 5786 and of the Christian Æra 1786. At which Council was present in person. His Most August Majesty, Frederick 2nd King of Prussia, Sovereign Grand Commander.

In the Name of the Most Holy, Grand Architect of the Universe

Ordo Ab Chao

The Sovereign Grand Inspectors General, in Supreme Council assembled, do ordain, and declare the following Constitution and Regulations for the Government of Masonic Councils under their Jurisdiction.

ARTICLE 1ST

The Constitution and Regulations made by the nine Commissaries, nominated by the Grand Council of Princes of the Royal Secret in the year 5762 shall be strictly adhered to in all its parts, except in those which militate against the articles of the present Constitution, And which are hereby repealed.

2ND

The 33rd Degree called, Sovereign Grand Inspector General, or Supreme Council of the 33rd is formed and organized in the following manner, vizt —

The Inspector to whom the degree is first given, is authorized and empowered to give it to another Brother, who is duly qualified, both by character and degrees, and to receive from him his obligation. These two give it in like manner to a 3rd when they admit the rest by voting Viva Voce, beginning with the youngest Inspector. One Nay, excludes an applicant for ever, if the reasons which are given for such negation are deemed sufficient.—

3RD

The first two who receive the degree in any Country, shall be the two presiding Officers. In case of the Death, resignation or absence from the Country (not to return) of the first Officer, the second takes his place, and appoints nominates an Inspector, to succeed in his own Office.— If the 2nd Officer should die, resign or leave the Country, the 1st Officer appoints another to succeed him. The Most Puissant Sovereign appoints in like manner, the Illustrious Treasurer and Secretary General of the Holy Empire, the Illustrious Grand Master of Ceremonies, and the Illustrious Captain of the Life Guards— and fills up all vacancies as they may happen.

4TH

Every Inspector who is initiated into this High degree shall, previously thereto, pay into the hands of the Illustrious Treasurer General of the Holy Empire, the sum of Ten Guineas; the like fee shall be demanded from those who receive the degree of K.H. and Prince of the Royal Secret, which sums shall be for the use of the Supreme Council.

5TH

Each Supreme Council is to be composed of Nine Inspectors General, at least five of whom, must profess the Christian Religion — 3 of whom, if the

Most Puissant Sovereign or Illustrious Inspector General are present, form a Council and can proceed to business.

There shall be but one Council of this Degree, in each Nation or Kingdom in Europe; Two in the United States of America, as remote from each other as possible; One in the British West Indies and one in the French West India Islands. —

6TH

The power of the Supreme Council does not interfere with any degree below the 17th or Knights of the East and West. But every Council and Lodge of Perfect Masons are hereby required and directed, to acknowledge them in quality of Inspectors General, and to receive them with the high honors to which they are entitled.

7TH

Any Council or Individual above the Grand Council of Princes of Jerusalem, can appeal to the Supreme Council, in which case, they can be heard in the Council in person.

8TH

The Grand Consistory of Princes of the Royal Secret shall Elect a president from among themselves; but none of their proceedings shall be valid, until they have received the Sanction and approbation of the Supreme Council of the 33rd who (after the decease of his majesty the King of Prussia) are Sovereigns of Masonry—

9TH

The Deputy Inspector can use his patent, in any Country, where a Supreme Council of Inspectors General is established, unless it shall be signed by the said Council.

10TH

The Deputy Inspector heretofore appointed, or who may hereafter be appointed, by virtue of this Constitution, shall have power to grant patents nor to give the degree of K.H. or the higher degrees.

11TH

The Degree of K.H. and the Degrees of Prince of the Royal Secret are never to be given but in the presence of three Sovereign Grand Inspectors General.

12TH

The Supreme Council shall exercise all the sovereign Masonic power of which his August Majesty Frederick the 2nd King of Prussia was possessed— in recalling the patents of Deputy Inspectors for improper, illegal un-Masonic conduct; In which case, information shall be sent to all the Supreme Councils in the World. —

13TH

The Supreme Council of the 33RD is authorized to depute a Brother who is well qualified and the Sovereign Grand Commander may, during their reap, authorize under his Supreme Council, a Brother a Brother who is well qualified to establish a Council of the said Degree, in any Country, in which it is directed to be established by this Constitution who shall conduct himself as in the 2ND Article. —

They also have power to grant patents to Deputy Inspectors general, who must have received the degree of K.H. to establish Lodges and Councils of the Superior degrees, up to the Knights of the Sun inclusive in a Country, where there is no such sublime Lodge or Council already established. The manuscript of this Degree shall not be given to any Inspector but the first two officers of the Council, or to a Brother going to a distant Country to establish the degree.

14TH

In all processions of the Sublime Degrees, the Supreme Council shall walk last, and the last of them, shall be the two Senior Officers, the Grand Standard bearer, appointed for the occasion, dressed in uniform, with the Standard of the Order, immediately preceding them.

15TH

The meetings of the Council shall be held every third New Moon; but they shall meet oftener if occasion requires for the dispatch of business.

There are two Festivals in the Year— One on first of October, when our property was sequestered and given to the Knights of Malta, and the other on the 27TH December, the common Masonic Festival. —

16TH

Every Inspector General of the 33RD shall have Letters of Credence agreeably to the form expressed in the Degree, for which he shall pay to the Secretary General One Guinea for his trouble in affixing the Seals — And one Guinea to the Council for defraying the expense of the plate. —

The Grand Seal of the Supreme Council, is a Large Black Eagle with two heads in the attitude of flying, with a naked sword in its claws in a scroll underneath, these words "Deus Meumque Jus." Over his head in scroll these words "Supreme Council 33ʳᵈ"

17ᵀᴴ

No Inspector General possesses any Individual power in a Country where a Supreme Council is established, as a Majority of their Votes is necessary to give legality to their proceedings. Except by Virtue of a patent granted for special purposes by the Council; and except the Sovⁿ Grand Comʳ as is provided by in Art. 13.

18ᵀᴴ

All moneys arising from initiations into the Councils above the Princes of Jerusalem, shall go to the funds of the Supreme Council.—

FINIS

CPSIA information can be obtained
at www.ICGtesting.com
Printed in the USA
BVHW011457040620
580858BV00014B/898